MCS

M000267564

Windows Server 2012 R2

Configuring Advanced Services
Study Guide

Exam 70-412

MCSA
Windows Server® 2012 R2
Configuring Advanced Services
Study Guide
Exam 70-412

William Panek

SYBEX®
A Wiley Brand

Senior Acquisitions Editor: Jeff Kellum
Development Editor: Gary Schwartz
Technical Editors: Rodney Fournier and Michael Rice
Production Editor: Eric Charbonneau
Copy Editor: Kim Wimpsett
Editorial Manager: Pete Gaughan
Production Manager: Kathleen Wisor
Professional Technology and Strategy Director: Barry Pruett
Associate Publisher: Jim Minatel
Media Project Manager 1: Laura Moss-Hollister
Media Associate Producer: Marilyn Hummel
Media Quality Assurance: Josh Frank
Book Designer: Judy Fung
Proofreader: Josh Chase, Word One New York
Indexer: Ted Laux
Project Coordinator, Cover: Patrick Redmond
Cover Designer: Wiley

This book is dedicated to the three ladies of my life: Crystal, Alexandria, and Paige.

Acknowledgments

I would like to thank my wife and best friend, Crystal. She is always the light at the end of my tunnel. I want to thank my two daughters, Alexandria and Paige, for all of their love and support during the writing of all my books. They make it all worthwhile.

I want to thank my family, especially my brothers, Rick, Gary, and Rob. They have always been there for me. I want to thank my father, Richard, who helped me become the man I am today, and my mother, Maggie, for all of her love and support.

I would like to thank all of my friends and co-workers, especially Vic, Catherine, Jeff, Stephanie, Don, Jason, Doug, Dave, Steve, Pat, Mike (all of them), Tommy, George, Greg, Becca, Deb, Jeri, Lisa, Scotty, and all of the field guys. I want to also thank my team and everyone who works with my group including Moe, Jimmy, Paul, Dana, Dean, Reanna, Todd, and Will F. Because of all of your hard work, you make me look good every day and make it a pleasure to go to work. Thanks to all of you for everything that you do.

I want to thank everyone on my Sybex team, especially my development editor, Gary Schwartz, who helped me make this the best book possible, and Rodney R. Fournier, who is the technical editor of many of my books. It's always good to have the very best technical guy backing you up.

I want to thank three excellent Microsoft engineers who helped me finish the third part of this book; Mike Rice, Winston McMiller, and Jeff Stokes. Thanks for your help and dedication to make this a great book.

I want to thank Eric Charbonneau, who was my production editor, and Jeff Kellum, my acquisitions editor, who served as lead for the entire book. He has always been there for me, and it is always great to write for him.

Finally, I want to thank everyone else behind the scenes who helped make this book possible. It's truly an amazing thing to have so many people work on my books to help make them the very best. I can't thank you all enough for your hard work.

About the Authors

 William Panek holds the following certifications: MCP, MCP+I, MCSA, MCSA+ Security and Messaging, MCSE-NT (3.51 and 4.0), MCSE 2000, 2003, 2012/2012 R2, MCSE+Security and Messaging, MCDBA, MCT, MCTS, MCITP, CCNA, CCDA, and CHFI. Will is also a Microsoft MVP.

After many successful years in the computer industry and a degree in computer programming, Will decided that he could better use his talents and his personality as an instructor. He began teaching for schools such as Boston University and the University of Maryland, just to name a few. He has done consulting and training work for some of the biggest government and corporate companies in the world including the U.S. Secret Service, Cisco, the U.S. Air Force, and the U.S. Army.

In January 2015, Will is now teaching for StormWind (www.stormwind.com). He currently lives in New Hampshire with his wife and two daughters. Will was also a U.S. Representative in the New Hampshire House of Representatives from 2010 to 2012. In his spare time, he likes to golf, ski, shoot, snowmobile, and ride his Harley. Will is also a commercially rated helicopter pilot.

Michael Allen Rice holds these certifications: MCP, MCTS, MCSA, MCSE, MCITP, CompTIA Network+, CompTIA Security+, VMware Certified Professional 5 - DCV, and NetApp Certified Data Management Administrator 7-mode.

Michael currently works as a Data Center Administrator for Intelligent Software Solutions Inc., based in Colorado Springs. He lives there with his wife and two children. He specializes in leading the way for corporate infrastructure in the areas of virtualization, storage, and systems administration. Over the past decade as an IT Professional, Michael has received numerous awards for his outstanding performance and dedication to excellence within the IT Community.

Winston McMiller holds these certifications: MCP, MCP+I, MCSA, MCSE 2000, 2003, 2012/2012 R2, and ITIL. Winston is a Microsoft Premier Field Engineer.

After 18 years in the computer industry and a degree in Information Technology, Winston has done consulting and training for some of the largest companies in the world including the General Electric, HP Enterprise services, Chrysler, and IBM.

He currently lives in the Seattle area. In his spare time, he likes to ski, do photography, and travel. He is an avid audiophile and songwriter.

Jeff Stokes holds these certifications: MCT, MCSA, MCSE 2003, and MCTS: Windows Internals. Jeff Stokes runs @WindowsPerf, a Windows Performance social networking property. He is a frequent guest on RunAsRadio and an avid blogger.

As a previous Premier Field Engineer at Microsoft, Jeff has worked in the Fortune 1000 space for the last eight years. After 21 years in the IT field, Jeff Stokes has established himself as a performance SME and a VDI pioneer in Microsoft technologies, including Windows optimization as a VDI guest. His work appears in VDI optimization guidance papers from Microsoft and other parties.

He currently lives in the Atlanta area. In his spare time, he analyzes performance traces, games, and mentors others in the IT field.

Contents at a Glance

Contents

Table of Exercises

Introduction

This book is drawn from more than 20 years of IT experience. I have taken that experience and translated it into a Windows Server 2012 R2 book that will help you not only prepare for the MCSA: Windows Server 2012 R2 exams but also develop a clear understanding of how to install and configure Windows Server 2012 R2 while avoiding all of the possible configuration pitfalls.

Many Microsoft books just explain the Windows operating system, but with *MCSA: Windows Server 2012 R2 Complete Study Guide*, I go a step further by providing many in-depth, step-by-step procedures to support my explanations of how the operating system performs at its best.

Microsoft Windows Server 2012 R2 is the newest version of Microsoft's server operating system software. Microsoft has taken the best of Windows Server 2003, Windows Server 2008/2008 R2, and Windows Server 2012 and combined them into the latest creation, Windows Server 2012 R2.

Windows Server 2012 R2 eliminates many of the problems that plagued the previous versions of Windows Server, and it includes a much faster boot time and shutdown. It is also easier to install and configure, and it barely stops to ask the user any questions during installation. In this book, I will show you what features are installed during the automated installation and where you can make changes if you need to be more in charge of your operating system and its features.

This book takes you through all the ins and outs of Windows Server 2012 R2, including installation, configuration, Group Policy objects, auditing, backups, and so much more.

Windows Server 2012 R2 has improved on Microsoft's desktop environment, made networking easier, enhanced searching capability, and improved performance—and that's only scratching the surface.

When all is said and done, this is a technical book for IT professionals who want to take Windows Server 2012 R2 to the next step and get certified. With this book, you will not only learn Windows Server 2012 R2 and ideally pass the exams, but you will become a Windows Server 2012 R2 expert.

The Microsoft Certification Program

Since the inception of its certification program, Microsoft has certified more than 2 million people. As the computer network industry continues to increase in both size and complexity, this number is sure to grow—and the need for proven ability will also increase. Certifications can help companies verify the skills of prospective employees and contractors.

The Microsoft certification tracks for Windows Server 2012 R2 include the following:

MCSA: Windows Server 2012 R2   The MCSA is now the lowest-level certification you can achieve with Microsoft in relation to Windows Server 2012 R2. It requires passing three exams: 70-410, 70-411, and 70-412. Or, if you qualify, you can take an Upgrading exam: Exam 70-417. This book assists in your preparation for all four exams.

MCSE: Server Infrastructure or MCSE: Desktop Infrastructure   The MCSE certifications, in relation to Windows Server 2012 R2, require that you become an MCSA first and then pass two additional exams. The additional exams will vary depending on which of the two MCSE tracks you choose. For more information, visit Microsoft's website at www.microsoft.com/learning.

MCSM: Directory Services   The MCSM certification takes things to an entirely new level. It requires passing a knowledge exam (in addition to having the MCSE in Windows Server 2012 R2) and a lab exam. This is now the elite-level certification in Windows Server 2012 R2.

How Do You Become Certified on Windows Server 2012 R2?

Attaining Microsoft certification has always been a challenge. In the past, students have been able to acquire detailed exam information—even most of the exam questions—from online "brain dumps" and third-party "cram" books or software products. For the new generation of exams, this is simply not the case.

Microsoft has taken strong steps to protect the security and integrity of its new certification tracks. Now prospective candidates must complete a course of study that develops detailed knowledge about a wide range of topics. It supplies them with the true skills needed, derived from working with the technology being tested.

The new generations of Microsoft certification programs are heavily weighted toward hands-on skills and experience. It is recommended that candidates have troubleshooting skills acquired through hands-on experience and working knowledge.

Fortunately, if you are willing to dedicate the time and effort to learn Windows Server 2012 R2, you can prepare yourself well for the exam by using the proper tools. By working through this book, you can successfully meet the requirements to pass the Windows Server 2012 R2 exams.

MCITP Exam Requirements

Candidates for MCITP certification on Windows Server 2012 R2 must pass one Windows Server 2012 R2 exams. This book will help you get ready for the 70-412: Configuring Advanced Windows Server 2012 R2 Services exam.

Microsoft provides exam objectives to give you a general overview of possible areas of coverage on the Microsoft exams. Keep in mind, however, that exam objectives are subject to change at any time without prior notice and at Microsoft's sole discretion. Visit the Microsoft Learning website (www.microsoft.com/learning) for the most current listing of exam objectives. The published objectives and how they map to this book are listed later in this introduction.

For a more detailed description of the Microsoft certification programs, including a list of all the exams, visit the Microsoft Learning website at www.microsoft.com/learning.

Tips for Taking the Windows Server 2012 R2 Exams

Here are some general tips for achieving success on your certification exam:

- Arrive early at the exam center so that you can relax and review your study materials. During this final review, you can look over tables and lists of exam-related information.

- Read the questions carefully. Do not be tempted to jump to an early conclusion. Make sure you know *exactly* what the question is asking.

- Answer all questions. If you are unsure about a question, mark it for review and come back to it at a later time.

- On simulations, do not change settings that are not directly related to the question. Also, assume the default settings if the question does not specify or imply which settings are used.

- For questions that you're unsure about, use a process of elimination to get rid of the obviously incorrect answers first. This improves your odds of selecting the correct answer when you need to make an educated guess.

Exam Registration

At the time this book was released, Microsoft exams are given at Prometric testing centers (800-755-EXAM/800-755-3926). As of December 31, 2014, Microsoft will be ending its relationship with Prometric, and all exams will be delivered through the more than 1,000 Authorized VUE Testing Centers around the world. For the location of a testing center near you, go to VUE's website at www.vue.com. If you are outside the United States and Canada, contact your local VUE registration center.

Find out the number of the exam you want to take and then register with the Prometric or VUE registration center nearest to you. At this point, you will be asked for advance payment for the exam. The exams are $150 each, and you must take them within one year of payment. You can schedule exams up to six weeks in advance or as late as one working day prior to the date of the exam. You can cancel or reschedule your exam if you contact the center at least two working days prior to the exam. Same-day registration is available in some locations, subject to space availability. Where same-day registration is available, you must register a minimum of two hours before test time.

When you schedule the exam, you will be provided with instructions regarding appointment and cancellation procedures, ID requirements, and information about the testing center location. In addition, you will receive a registration and payment confirmation letter from Prometric.

Microsoft requires certification candidates to accept the terms of a nondisclosure agreement before taking certification exams.

Who Should Read This Book?

This book is intended for individuals who want to earn their MCITP by taking exam 70-412: Configuring Advanced Windows Server 2012 R2 Services.

Not only will this book help anyone who is looking to pass the Microsoft exams, it will help anyone who wants to learn the real ins and outs of the Windows Server 2012 R2 operating system.

What's Inside?

Here is a glance at what's in each chapter:

Chapter 1: Configure and Manage High Availability   This chapter explains how to set up Windows Server 2012 R2 high availability, including clustering and failover systems.

Chapter 2: Configure File and Storage Solutions   This chapter shows you how to configure file and storage solutions. You will learn how to help your system run faster and give you better response times.

Chapter 3: Implement Business Continuity and Disaster Recovery   This chapter shows you how to protect yourself in the event of a system crash or a catastrophic failure.

Chapter 4: Configure Advanced Network Services   This chapter shows you how to configure the different types of network services and how to configure them properly.

Chapter 5: Configure the Active Directory Infrastructure   This chapter takes you through the different ways to create and manage your Windows Server 2012 R2 Active Directory infrastructure.

Chapter 6: Configure Access and Information Protection Solutions   You will see how to set up your Windows Server 2012 R2 system so that your information stays secure.

What's Included with the Book

This book includes many helpful items intended to prepare you for the 70-412: Configuring Advanced Windows Server 2012 R2 Services exam.

Assessment Test   There is an assessment test at the conclusion of the introduction that can be used to evaluate quickly where you are with Windows Server 2012 R2. This test should be taken prior to beginning your work in this book, and it should help you identify areas in which you are either strong or weak. Note that these questions are purposely more simple than the types of questions you may see on the exams.

Objective Map and Opening List of Objectives   Later in this introduction is a detailed exam objective map showing you where each of the exam objectives is covered. Each chapter also includes a list of the exam objectives covered.

Helpful Exercises   The book includes step-by-step exercises of some of the more important tasks that you should be able to perform. Some of these exercises have corresponding videos that can be downloaded from the book's website. Also, in the following section is a recommended home lab setup that will be helpful in completing these tasks.

Exam Essentials   The end of each chapter also includes a listing of exam essentials. These are essentially repeats of the objectives, but remember that any objective on the exam blueprint could show up on the exam.

Chapter Review Questions   Each chapter includes review questions. These are used to assess your understanding of the chapter and are taken directly from the chapter. These questions are based on the exam objectives, and they are similar in difficulty to items you might actually receive on the 70-412: Configuring Advanced Windows Server 2012 R2 Services exam.

 You can obtain the Sybex Test Engine, flashcards, videos, and glossary at www.sybex.com/go/mcsawin2012r2config

Sybex Test Engine   Readers can access the Sybex Test Engine, which includes the assessment test and chapter review questions in electronic format. In addition, there is a practice exams included with the Sybex test engine for exam 70-412.

Electronic Flashcards   Flashcards are included for quick reference. They are great tools for learning important facts quickly. You may even consider these as additional simple practice questions, which is essentially what they are.

Videos   Some of the exercises include corresponding videos. These videos show you how to do the exercises. There is also a video that shows you how to set up virtualization so that you can complete the exercises within a virtualized environment. This same video also shows you how to install Windows Server 2012 R2 Datacenter on that virtualized machine.

PDF of Glossary of Terms   There is a glossary included that covers the key terms used in this book.

Recommended Home Lab Setup

To get the most out of this book, you will want to make sure you complete the exercises throughout the chapters. To complete the exercises, you will need one of two setups. First, you can set up a machine with Windows Server 2012 R2 and complete the labs using a regular Windows Server 2012 R2 machine.

The second way to set up Windows Server 2012 R2 (the way I set up Server 2012 R2) is by using virtualization. I set up Windows Server 2012 R2 as a virtual hard disk (VHD), and I did all the labs this way. The advantages of using virtualization are that you can always just wipe out the system and start over without losing a real server. Plus, you can set up multiple virtual servers and create a full lab environment on one machine.

I created a video for this book showing you how to set up a virtual machine and how to install Windows Server 2012 R2 onto that virtual machine.

How to Contact the Author/Sybex

Sybex strives to keep you supplied with the latest tools and information you need for your work. Please check the website at www.sybex.com/go/mcsawin2012r2config, where I'll post additional content and updates that supplement this book should the need arise.

You can contact Will Panek by going to www.willpanek.com.

Certification Objectives Maps

In addition to the book chapters, you will find coverage of exam objectives in the flashcards, practice exams, and videos on the book's companion website. www.sybex.com/go/mcsawin2012r2config

Exam objectives are subject to change at any time without prior notice and at Microsoft's sole discretion. Please visit Microsoft's website (www.microsoft.com/learning) for the most current listing of exam objectives.

Objectives

Exam 70-412: Configuring Advanced Windows Server 2012 Services

Configure Network Load Balancing (NLB), Chapter 17

This objective may include, but is not limited to:

Install NLB nodes

Configure NLB prerequisites

Configure affinity

Configure port rules

Configure cluster operation mode

Upgrade an NLB cluster

Configure failover clustering, Chapter 17

This objective may include, but is not limited to:

Configure Quorum

Configure cluster networking

Restore single node or cluster configuration

Configure cluster storage

Implement cluster aware updating

Upgrade a cluster

Manage failover-clustering roles, Chapter 17

This objective may include, but is not limited to:

Configure role-specific settings including continuously available shares

Configure VM monitoring

Configure failover and preference settings

Manage Virtual Machine (VM) Movement, Chapter 17

This objective may include, but is not limited to:

Configure Virtual Machine network health protection

Configure drain on shutdown

Perform quick, live and storage migrations

Import/export/copy of VMS

Configure advanced file services, Chapter 18

    Configure NFS data store

    Configure BranchCache

    Configure File Classification Infrastructure (FCI) using File Server Resource Manager (FSRM)

    Configure file access auditing

Implement Dynamic Access Control (DAC), Chapter 18

    Configure user and device claim types

    Create and configure resource properties and lists

    Create and configure Central Access Rules and Policies

    Configure file classification

    Implement policy changes and staging

    Perform access-denied remediation

Configure and optimize storage, Chapter 18

    Configure iSCSI Target and Initiator

    Configure Internet Storage Name Server (iSNS)

    Implement thin provisioning and trim

    Manage server free space using Features on Demand

    Configure tiered storage

Configure and manage backups, Chapter 19

    Configure Windows Server backups

    Configure Windows Azure backups

    Configure role-specific backups

    Manage VSS settings using VSSAdmin

Recover Servers, Chapter 19

    Restore from backups

    Perform a Bare Metal Restore (BMR)

    Recover servers using Windows Recovery Environment (Win RE) and safe mode

    Configure the Boot Configuration Data (BCD) store

Configure site-level fault tolerance, Chapter 19

    Configure Hyper-V Replica including Hyper-V Replica Broker and VMs

    Configure multi-site clustering including network settings, Quorum, and failover settings

    Configure Hyper-V Replica extended replication

    Configure Global Update Manager

    Recover a multi-site failover cluster

Implement an advanced Dynamic Host Configuration Protocol (DHCP) solution, Chapter 20

>   Create and configure superscopes and multicast scopes

>   Implement DHCPv6

>   Configure high availability for DHCP including DHCP failover and split scopes

>   Configure DHCP Name Protection

>   Configure DNS registration

Implement an advanced DNS solution, Chapter 20

>   Configure security for DNS including DNSSEC, DNS Socket Pool, and cache locking

>   Configure DNS logging

>   Configure delegated administration

>   Configure recursion

>   Configure netmask ordering

>   Configure a GlobalNames zone

>   Analyze zone level statistics

Deploy and manage IPAM, Chapter 20

>   Provision IPAM manually or by using Group Policy

>   Configure server discovery

>   Create and manage IP blocks and ranges

>   Monitor utilization of IP address space

>   Migrate to IPAM

>   Delegate IPAM administration

>   Manage IPAM collections

>   Configure IPAM database storage

Configure a forest or a domain, Chapter 21

>   Implement multi-domain and multi-forest Active Directory environments including interoperability with previous versions of Active Directory

>   Upgrade existing domains and forests including environment preparation and functional levels

>   Configure multiple user principal name (UPN) suffixes

Configure Trusts, Chapter 21

>   Configure external, forest, shortcut, and realm trusts

>   Configure trust authentication

>   Configure SID filtering

>   Configure name suffix routing

Configure Sites, Chapter 21

> Configure sites and subnets
>
> Create and configure site links
>
> Manage site coverage
>
> Manage registration of SRV records
>
> Move domain controllers between sites

Manage Active Directory and SYSVOL replication, Chapter 21

> Configure replication to Read-Only Domain Controllers (RODCs)
>
> Configure Password Replication Policy (PRP) for RODCs
>
> Monitor and manage replication
>
> Upgrade SYSVOL replication to Distributed File System Replication (DFSR)

Install and configure Active Directory Certificate Services (AD CS), Chapter 22

> Describe and explain the new features in Windows Server 2012 Active Directory Certificate Services
>
> Install and configure Active Directory Certificate Services using Server Manager and Windows PowerShell
>
> Manage Active Directory Certificate Services using management consoles and Windows PowerShell
>
> Configure CRL distribution points
>
> Install and configure Online Responder
>
> Implement administrative role separation
>
> Configure CA Disaster recovery
>
> Manage certificates.
>
> Manage certificate templates
>
> Implement and manage certificate deployment, validation, and revocation
>
> Manage certificate renewal
>
> Manage certificate enrollment and renewal to computers and users using Group Policies
>
> Configure and manage key archival and recovery
>
> Manage trust between organizations including Certificate Trust List (CTL)
>
> Managing Cross certifications and bride CAs
>
> Monitoring CA Health

Install and Configure Active Directory Federation Services (AD FS), Chapter 22

> Implement claims-based authentication including Relying Party Trusts
>
> Configure authentication policies
>
> Configure Workplace Join
>
> Configure multi-factor authentication

Install and configure Active Directory Rights Management Services (AD RMS), Chapter 22

    Install a licensing or certificate AD RMS server

    Manage AD RMS Service Connection Point (SCP)

    Manage RMS templates

    Configure Exclusion Policies

    Backup and restore AD RMS

Assessment Test

1. In a secure environment, IPsec encryption should only be disabled for inter-node cluster communication (such as cluster heartbeat) under what circumstances?

   A. Certificates use weak encryption methods such as DES

   B. LowerQuorumPriorityNodeID is set on a node.

   C. DatabaseReadWriteMode is set to 2

   D. Group Policy Updates have a high processing latency

2. In Windows Server 2012 R2, Failover Clustering supports how many nodes?

   A. 8000

   B. 1024

   C. 64

   D. 1000

3. In Windows Server 2012 R2, Dynamic Quorum has a feature to dynamically adjust cluster node votes in order to maintain an odd vote count where no witness is being used. What is the name of this feature?

   A. Witness Dynamic Weighting

   B. Tie Breaker for a 50% Node Split

   C. Lower Quorum Priority Node

   D. Force quorum resiliency

4. What authentication mechanism does Active Directory–detached clusters utilize?

   A. NTLM

   B. MIT Kerberos Realms

   C. AD Kerberos

   D. SSL

5. True or False: Shared virtual hard disks can be utilized by SQL Server and Exchange Server for virtualized workloads?

   A. True

   B. False

6. What is the default TCP port for iSCSI?

   A. 3389

   B. 21

   C. 1433

   D. 3260

7. You are a server administrator, and you are trying to save hard drive space on your Windows Server 2012 R2 machine. Which feature can help you save hard disk space?

   A. ADDS

   B. HDSaver.exe

   C. Features On Demand

   D. WinRM

8. Your company is headquartered in Colorado Springs and has a remote site location in Tampa. The Colorado Spring office has a file server named FS01. FS01 has the BranchCache for Network Files role service installed. Your Tampa Office has a file server named FS02. FS02 has been configured as a BranchCache-hosted cache server. You need to preload the data from the file shares on FS01 to the cache on FS02. You have already generated hashes for the file shares on FS01. Which cmdlet should you run next?

   A. Set-BCCache

   B. Publish-BCFileContent

   C. Export-BCCachePackage

   D. Add-BCDataCacheExtension

9. What command would be used to register an iSCSI initiator manually to an iSNS server?

   A. iscsicli addisnsserver server_name

   B. iscsicli listisnsservers server_name

   C. iscsicli removeisnsserver server_name

   D. iscsicli refreshisnsserver server_name

10. You have a Windows Server 2012 R2 file server named FS01. FS01 has the File Server Resource Manager role service installed. You attempt to delete a classification property, and you receive the error message "The classification property is in use and cannot be deleted." You need to delete the Contains Personal Information classification property. What should you do?

   A. Clear the Contains Personal Information classification property value for all files.

   B. Set files that have a Contains Personal Information classification property value of Yes to No.

   C. Disable the classification rule that is assigned the Contains Personal Information classification property.

   D. Delete the classification rule that is assigned the Contains Personal Information classification property.

11. After you update multiple drivers on your Windows Server 2012 R2 machine, the machine hangs at the logon screen, and you can't log into the machine. You need to get this computer up and running as quickly as possible. Which of the following repair strategies should you try first to correct your problem?

A. Restore your computer's configuration with your last backup.

B. Boot your computer with the Last Known Good Configuration option.

C. Boot your computer with the Safe Mode option.

D. Boot your computer to the Recovery Console and manually copy the old driver back to the computer.

12. You enable the Boot Logging option on the Advanced Boot Options menu. Where can you find the log file that is created?

A. \Windows\ntbtlog.txt

B. \Windows\System32\netlog.txt

C. \Windows\netlog.txt

D. \Windows\System32\netboot.log

13. You need to ensure that you can recover your Windows Server 2012 R2 configuration and data if the computer's hard drive fails. What should you do?

A. Create a system restore point.

B. Create a backup of all file categories.

C. Perform an Automated System Recovery (ASR) backup.

D. Create a complete PC Backup and Restore image.

14. You have a file server named FS01 that is running on a Server Core installation of Windows Server 2012 R2. You need to make sure your users can access previous versions of files that are shared on FS01 using the Previous Versions tab. Which tool should you use?

A. Wbadmin

B. Vssadmin

C. Ntsdutil.exe

D. ADSI Editor

15. You are unable to boot your Windows Server 2012 R2 computer, so you decide to boot the computer to Safe Mode. Which of the following statements regarding Safe Mode is false?

A. When the computer is booted to Safe Mode, there is no network access.

B. Safe Mode loads all of the drivers for the hardware that is installed on the computer.

C. When you run Safe Mode, boot logging is automatically enabled.

D. When you run Safe Mode, the screen resolution is set to 800×600.

16. You are the network administrator for Stellacon Corporation. Stellacon has two trees in its Active Directory forest, stellacon.com and abc.com. Company policy does not allow DNS zone transfers between the two trees. You need to make sure that when anyone in abc.com tries to access the stellacon.com domain, all names are resolved from the stellacon.com DNS server. What should you do?

   A. Create a new secondary zone in abc.com for stellacon.com.

   B. Create a new secondary zone in stellacon.com for abc.com.

   C. Configure conditional forwarding on the abc.com DNS server for stellacon.com.

   D. Configure conditional forwarding on the stellacon.com DNS server for abc.com.

17. Your IT team has been informed by the compliance team that they need copies of the DNS Active Directory Integrated zones for security reasons. You need to give the compliance department a copy of the DNS zone. How should you accomplish this goal?

   A. Run dnscmd /zonecopy.

   B. Run dnscmd /zoneinfo.

   C. Run dnscmd /zonefile.

   D. Run dnscmd /zoneexport.

18. You administer a network that assigns IP addresses via DHCP. You want to make sure that one of the clients always receives the same IP address from the DHCP server. You create an exclusion for that address, but you find that the computer isn't being properly configured at bootup. What's the problem?

   A. You excluded the wrong IP address.

   B. You must configure the client manually. You cannot assign the address via the DHCP server.

   C. You need to create a superscope for the address.

   D. You need to make a reservation for the client that ties the IP address to the computer's MAC address. Delete the exclusion.

19. You are the network administrator for a small company with two DNS servers: DNS1 and DNS2. Both DNS servers reside on domain controllers. DNS1 is set up as a standard primary zone, and DNS2 is set up as a secondary zone. A new security policy was written stating that all DNS zone transfers must be encrypted. How can you implement the new security policy?

   A. Enable the Secure Only setting on DNS1.

   B. Enable the Secure Only setting on DNS2.

   C. Configure Secure Only on the Zone Transfers tab for both servers.

   D. Delete the secondary zone on DNS2. Convert both DNS servers to use Active Directory Integrated zones.

20. You are the network administrator for a midsize computer company. You have a single Active Directory forest, and your DNS servers are configured as Active Directory Integrated zones. When you look at the DNS records in Active Directory, you notice that there are many records for computers that do not exist on your domain. You want to make sure that only domain computers register with your DNS servers. What should you do to resolve this issue?

    A. Set dynamic updates to None.

    B. Set dynamic updates to Nonsecure And Secure.

    C. Set dynamic updates to Secure Only.

    D. Set dynamic updates to Domain Users Only.

21. Which of the following does not need to be created manually when you are setting up a replication scenario involving three domains and three sites?

    A. Sites

    B. Site links

    C. Subnets

    D. Connection objects

22. You need to deactivate the UGMC option on some of your domain controllers. At which level in Active Directory would you deactivate UGMC?

    A. Server

    B. Forest

    C. Domain

    D. Site

23. Your network contains two Active Directory forests named contoso.com and fabrikam .com. Both forests contain multiple domains. All domain controllers run Windows Server 2012 R2. contoso.com has a one-way forest trust to fabrikam.com. A domain named paris.eu.contoso.com hosts several legacy applications that use NTLM authentication. Users in a domain named london.europe.fabrikam.com report that it takes a long time to be authenticated when they attempt to access the legacy applications hosted in paris.eu.contoso.com. You need to reduce how long it takes for the london.europe .fabrikam.com users to be authenticated in paris.eu.contoso.com. What should you do?

    A. Create an external trust.

    B. Create a two-way transitive trust.

    C. Disable SID filtering on the existing trust.

    D. Create a shortcut trust.

24. A system administrator suspects that there is an error in the replication configuration. How can the system administrator look for specific error messages related to replication?

    A. By going to Event Viewer ➤ Directory Service Log

    B. By using the Computer Management tool

C. By going to Event Viewer ➤ System Log

D. By using the Active Directory Sites and Services administrative tool

25. Which of the following services of Active Directory is responsible for maintaining the replication topology?

A. File Replication Service

B. Windows Internet Name Service

C. Knowledge Consistency Checker

D. Domain Name System

26. You are the administrator at Adacom. You need to make sure you have daily backup of the AD CS database, logs, and private key. What command or commands should you run?

A. Run certutil -backup.

B. Run certutil -backupdb.

C. Ntbackup /systemstate.

D. Run certdb.ps1.

27. You are the new administrator at MMG Publishing. The previous administrator made a failed attempt to implement Active Directory. You attempt to implement AD RMS and receive an error that states, "The SCP is registered, but the root cluster cannot be contacted." You must remove the SCP. What tool should you use?

A. Setspn

B. Active Directory sites and services

C. ADSI Edit

D. Remove-SCP

28. ABC Company wants to allow external partners to log into a web application and run reports. What AD FS component does Company ABC need to configure for this access?

A. Certificate exchange

B. Transitive trust

C. One-way trust

D. Relying-party trust

29. Which TCP ports does AD RMS use to access the global catalog server?

A. 445

B. 1433

C. 22

D. 3268

Answers to Assessment Test

1. D. Group Policy Updates have a high processing latency, because IPsec encryption is interrupted until updates to the Group Policies are complete. If the updates to Group Policy do not occur quickly cluster heartbeat can be impacted (eg if the processing delay exceeds the heartbeat threshold).

2. C. In Windows Server 2012 the number of cluster nodes increased to 64. 8000 is the number of VMs/Clustered Roles. 1024 is the maximum amount of VMs or Clustered Roles per cluster node, and 1000 is the maximum amount of VMs or Clustered Roles per cluster node in Windows Server 2008 R2.

3. B. Witness Dynamic Weighting and Lower Quorum Priority Node are options in PowerShell to modify Dynamic Quorum, but they are not a good answer. Force quorum resiliency is completely incorrect.

4. A. NTLM is the only supported authentication mechanism that will utilize local security authorities (non-active directory integrated Windows Servers).

5. A. Prior to Windows Server 2012 R2, shared virtual hard disks did not exist. At release of Windows Server 2012 R2, shared virtual disks were supported for file server roles as well as Exchange Server and SQL Server workloads.

6. D. The iSCSI default port is TCP 3260. Port 3389 is used for RDP, port 1433 is used for Microsoft SQL, and port 21 is used for FTP.

7. C. Windows Server 2012 R2 Features On Demand allows an administrator not only to disable a role or feature but also to remove the role or feature's files completely from the hard drive.

8. C. After generating hashes on the Colorado Springs file server that will be preloading Tampa's file server cache with file share data, the next logical step is to run Export-BCCachePackage to get the data to FS02 from FS01.

9. A. The `iscsicli addisnsserver server_name` command manually registers the host server to an iSNS server. `refreshisnsserver` refreshes the list of available servers. `removeisnsserver` removes the host from the iSNS server. `listisnsservers` lists the available iSNS servers.

10. D. Since there is a classification rule that is currently configured and applied to company resources, you will be unable to delete the Contains Personal Information classification property manually because the classification rule controls the property. In this case, you have to delete the classification rule in order to be able to delete the classification property.

11. B. If you need to get a stalled computer up and running as quickly as possible, you should start with the Last Known Good Configuration option. This option is used when you've made changes to your computer's hardware configuration and are having problems restarting but have not logged into the machine. The Last Known Good Configuration option will revert to the configuration used the last time the computer was successfully booted.

12. A. When you enable boot logging, the file created is \Windows\ntbtlog.txt. This log file is used to troubleshoot the boot process.

13. D. Using images allows you to back up and restore your entire Windows Server 2012 R2 machine instead of just certain parts of data.

14. B. Out of the tools listed, remember that Vssadmin gives you the ability to use Shadow Copies, which in turn provides backups and previous versions of shared data. Wbadmin is used for Windows Server Backups, Ntsdutil.exe is used for Active Directory maintenance, and the ADSI Editor is used for extended Active Directory attribute management.

15. B. When you run your computer in Safe Mode, you simplify your Windows Server 2012 R2 configuration. Only the drivers that are needed to get the computer up and running are loaded.

16. C. Conditional forwarding allows you to send a DNS query to different DNS servers based on the request. Conditional forwarding lets a DNS server on a network forward DNS queries according to the DNS domain name in the query.

17. D. The dnscmd /zoneexport command creates a file using the zone resource records. This file can then be given to the compliance department as a copy.

18. D. An exclusion just marks addresses as excluded; the DHCP server doesn't maintain any information about them. A reservation marks an address as reserved for a particular client.

19. D. Active Directory Integrated zones give you many benefits over using primary and secondary zones including less network traffic, secure dynamic updates, encryption, and reliability in the event of a DNS server going down. The Secure Only option is for dynamic updates to a DNS database.

20. C. The Secure Only option is for DNS servers that have an Active Directory Integrated zone. When a computer tries to register with DNS dynamically, the DNS server checks Active Directory to verify that the computer has an Active Directory account. If the computer that is trying to register has an account, DNS adds the host record. If the computer trying to register does not have an account, the record gets tossed away, and the database is not updated.

21. D. By default, Connection objects are automatically created by the Active Directory replication engine. You can choose to override the default behavior of Active Directory replication topology by manually creating Connection objects, but this step is not required.

22. D. The NTDS settings for the site level are where you would activate and deactivate UGMC.

23. D. Remember that a shortcut trust is used to eliminate multiple hops to and from certain domains within a multiforest, multidomain infrastructure. By configuring a shortcut trust between the two domains, you will reduce the slowness and authentication latency between them.

24. A. The Directory Service event log contains error messages and information related to replication. These details can be useful when you are troubleshooting replication problems.

25. C. The Knowledge Consistency Checker (KCC) is responsible for establishing the replication topology and ensuring that all domain controllers are kept up-to-date.

26. A and B. Certutil -backup backs up the CA certificate including the private key in the backup. Certutil -backupdb backs up only the certificate database and logs.

27. B and C. Under AD Sites and Services, navigate to Services — RightsManagementServices and remove the SCP object. This operation can also be done by using ADSI Edit.

28. D. The relying party is the organization that receives and processes claims from a resource partner. The resource partner issues claims-based security tokens that contain published web-based applications that users in the account partner can access. This accomplished through a relying-party trust.

29. D. AD RMS contacts the global catalog through port 3268.

Chapter

1

Configure and Manage High Availability

THE FOLLOWING 70-412 EXAM OBJECTIVES ARE COVERED IN THIS CHAPTER:

✓ **Configure Network Load Balancing (NLB)**

- This objective may include, but is not limited to:
  - Install NLB nodes
  - Configure NLB prerequisites
  - Configure affinity
  - Configure port rules
  - Configure cluster operation mode
  - Upgrade an NLB cluster

✓ **Configure failover clustering**

- This objective may include, but is not limited to:
  - Configure Quorum
  - Configure cluster networking
  - Restore single node or cluster configuration
  - Configure cluster storage
  - Implement cluster aware updating
  - Upgrade a cluster

✓ **Manage failover-clustering roles**

- This objective may include, but is not limited to:
  - Configure role-specific settings including continuously available shares

- Configure VM monitoring

- Configure failover and preference settings

✓ **Manage Virtual Machine (VM) Movement**

- This objective may include, but is not limited to:

  - Configure Virtual Machine network health protection

  - Configure drain on shutdown

  - Perform quick, live and storage migrations

  - Import/export/copy of VMS

The R2 update to Windows Server 2012 has improved upon the rich high availability capabilities already present in Windows Server 2012. The management, reporting, and ease of use of the feature set are all worth mentioning, but the expansion of features is the greatest benefit of the R2 update with regard to high availability.

The exam will cover the new features at a high level, and it will cover the basic configuration and operational functions for both a failover cluster and a network load balancer. This chapter will introduce how to achieve high availability with hardware and operational changes as well as how to use the high availability features of Windows Server 2012 R2.

Any discussion of high availability, network load balancers, and clustering would not be complete without a discussion of high availability in general. The chapter will first cover what it means, both from a purely technical perspective and from a business perspective.

Components of High Availability

High availability is a buzzword that many application and hardware vendors like to throw around to get you to purchase their products. Many different options are available to achieve high availability, and there also seems to be a number of definitions and variations that help vendors sell their products as high-availability solutions.

When it comes right down to it, however, high availability simply means providing services with maximum uptime by avoiding unplanned downtime. Often, *disaster recovery (DR)* is also closely lumped into discussions of high availability, but DR encompasses the business and technical processes that are used to recover once a disaster has happened.

Defining a high availability plan usually starts with a *service level agreement (SLA)*. At its most basic, an SLA defines the services and metrics that must be met for the availability and performance of an application or service. Often, an SLA is created for an IT department or service provider to deliver a specific level of service. An example of this might be an SLA for a Microsoft Exchange server. The SLA for an Exchange server might have uptime metrics on how much time during the month the mailboxes need to be available to end users, or it might define performance metrics for the amount of time it takes for email messages to be delivered.

When determining what goes into an SLA, two other factors need to be considered. However, you will often see them discussed only in the context of disaster recovery, even though they are important for designing a highly available solution. These factors are the *recovery point objective (RPO)* and the *recovery time objective (RTO)*.

An RTO is the length of time an application can be unavailable before service must be restored to meet the SLA. For example, a single component failure would have an RTO of less than five minutes, and a full-site failure might have an RTO of three hours. An RPO is essentially the amount of data that must be restored in the event of a failure. For example, in a single server or component failure, the RPO would be 0, but in a site failure, the RPO might allow for up to 20 minutes of lost data.

SLAs, on the other hand, are usually expressed in percentages of the time the application is available. These percentages are also often referred to by the number of nines the percentage includes, as shown in Table 1.1.

TABLE 1.1   Availability percentages

Availability rating	Allowed unplanned downtime/year
99 percent	3.7 days
99.9 percent	8.8 hours
99.99 percent	53 minutes
99.999 percent	5.3 minutes

Two important factors that affect an SLA are the *mean time between failure (MTBF)* and the *mean time to recovery (MTTR)*. To be able to reduce the amount of unplanned downtime, the time between failures must be increased, and the time it takes to recover must be reduced. Modifying these two factors will be addressed in the next several sections of this chapter.

Achieving High Availability

Windows Server 2012 R2 is the most secure and reliable Windows version to date. It also is the most stable, mature, and capable of any version of Windows. Although similar claims have been made for previous versions of Windows Server, you can rest assured that Windows Server 2012 R2 is much better than previous versions for a variety of reasons.

An honest look at the feature set and real-world use should prove that this latest version of Windows provides the most suitable foundation for creating a highly available solution. However, more than just good software is needed to be able to offer high availability for applications.

High Availability Foundation

Just as a house needs a good foundation, a highly available Windows server needs a stable and reliable hardware platform on which to run. Although Windows Server 2012 R2 will technically run on desktop-class hardware, high availability is more easily achieved with server-class hardware. What differentiates desktop-class from server-class hardware? *Server-class hardware* has more management and monitoring features built into it so that the health of the hardware is capable of being monitored and maintained.

Another large difference is that server-class hardware has redundancy options. Server-class hardware often has options to protect from drive failures, such as RAID controllers, and to protect against power supply failures, such as multiple power supplies. Enterprise-class servers have even more protection.

More needs to be done than just installing Windows Server 2012 R2 to ensure that the applications remain running with the best availability possible. Just as a house needs maintenance and upkeep to keep the structure in proper repair, so too does a server. In the case of a highly available server, this means *patch management*.

Installing Patches

Microsoft releases monthly updates to fix security problems with its software, both for operating system fixes and for applications. To ensure that your highly available applications are immune to known vulnerabilities, these patches need to be applied in a timely manner during a scheduled maintenance window. Also, to address stability and performance issues, updates and service packs are released regularly for many applications, such as Microsoft SQL Server, Exchange Server, and SharePoint Portal Server. Many companies have a set schedule—daily, weekly, or monthly—to apply these patches and updates after they are tested and approved.

Desired Configuration Manager (DCM), an option in Microsoft System Center Configuration Manager 2012 and newer, is a great tool for helping to validate that your cluster nodes are patched. It can leverage the SCCM client to collect installed patches and help reporting within the enterprise on compliancy with desired system states based on the software installed.

To continue with the house analogy, if you were planning to have the master bath remodeled, would you rather hire a college student on spring break looking to make some extra money to do the job or a seasoned artisan? Of course, you would want someone with experience and a proven record of accomplishment to remodel your master bath.

Likewise, with any work that needs to be done on your highly available applications, it's best to hire only decidedly qualified individuals. This is why obtaining a Microsoft certification is definitely an excellent start to becoming qualified to configure a highly available server properly. There is no substitute for real-life and hands-on experience. Working with highly available configurations in a lab and in production will help you know not only what configurations are available but also how the changes should be made.

For example, it may be possible to use Failover Clustering for a WINS server, but in practice WINS replication may be easier to support and require less expensive hardware in order to provide high availability. This is something you would know only if you had enough experience to make this decision.

As with your house, once you have a firm and stable foundation built by skilled artisans and a maintenance plan has been put into place, you need to ascertain what more is needed. If you can't achieve enough uptime with proper server configuration and mature operational processes, a cluster may be needed.

Windows Server 2012 R2 provides two types of clustering: *Failover Clustering* and *Network Load Balancing (NLB)*. Failover clustering is used for applications and services such as SQL Server and Exchange Server. Network Load Balancing is used for network-based services such as web and FTP servers. The remaining sections of this chapter will cover both of these clustering options in depth.

To Cluster or Not to Cluster

Clustering is often thrown into the mix when someone wants to achieve higher availability. This is a good step toward improved availability, but the return on the investment of a cluster doesn't always add up. Although Windows Server 2012 R2 greatly simplifies both the creation and management of a failover cluster, there is added complexity and cost in terms of hardware, software, and personnel.

How do you determine whether to cluster applications? Sometimes, even though it is possible to cluster applications, they perform worse when clustered. At other times, only a small improvement is made when a cluster is created. You have to balance the slight improvement over the increased hardware cost, complexity, and level of training required for administrators.

Configure Network Load Balancing

Network Load Balancing is a form of clustering where the nodes are highly available for a network-based service. This is typically a port listener configuration where a farm of, say, Microsoft Internet Information Services servers all listen on ports 80 and 443 for incoming web traffic from client endpoints. These nodes, while not fully clustered in a technical sense, are load balanced, where each node handles some of the distributed network traffic.

Network Load Balancing at the software level (as I will discuss here) is generally reserved for light loads or loads in lower-budget environments, such as a test or QA environment, for example. Generally speaking, Network Load Balancing in large production environments relies on hardware-based solutions to front-end network load balancing and distributes it on a session-based load to multiple hosts. This type of configuration, however, is out of scope for this book.

Install NLB Nodes

You can install NLB nodes like any other server build. You want the host patched, provisioned with appropriate resources (typically with multiple network interface cards for capacity and responsiveness), and monitored for health and reliability. In Exercise 1.1, you'll install NLB nodes.

EXERCISE 1.1

Installing NLB Nodes

1. Once you have multiple hosts ready for the installation of NLB, simply run the Add Roles And Features Wizard and select Network Load Balancing in the Features area of the wizard.

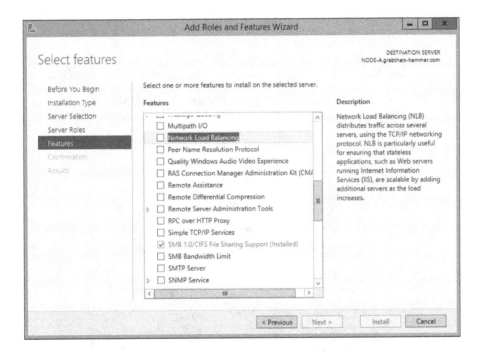

2. This wizard places a new application in your Start menu, the Network Load Balancing Manager (shown here), the execution of which loads the console.

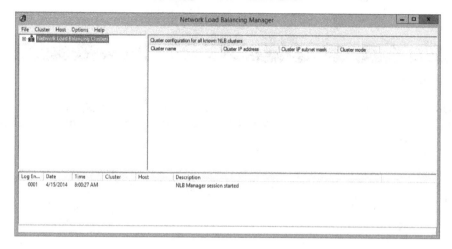

3. Right-click Network Load Balancing Clusters and select New Cluster. You are then presented with the connection wizard where you can specify the name of one of your hosts.

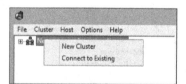

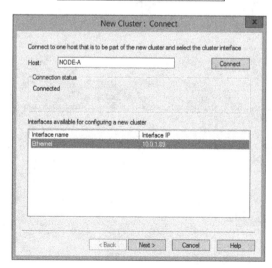

4. The next screen reveals a prompt to add any additional IPs and assign a priority level. You can do all this later, so hit Next.

5. The next wizard screen is where you specify the cluster IP address. This is the address that the endpoints or clients or users of the NLB cluster will contact. Typically the network team will assign a cluster IP address for this use.

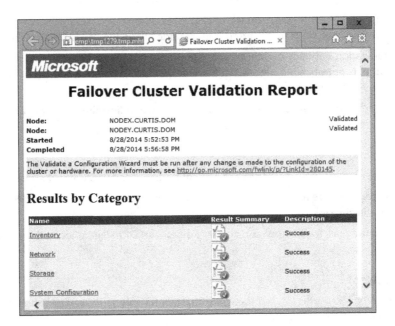

6. On the next screen, you configure the operation mode and specify a name.

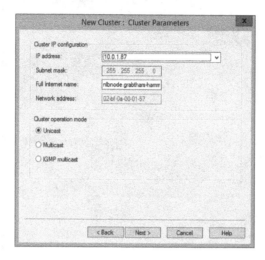

With regard to the cluster operation modes, the differences between them are as follows:

Unicast

The cluster adapters for all nodes are assigned the same MAC address.

The outgoing MAC address for each packet is modified based on priority to prevent upstream switches from discovering that all nodes have the same MAC address.

Communication between cluster nodes (other than heartbeat and other administrative NLB traffic) is not possible unless there are additional adapters (because all nodes have the same MAC address).

Depending on load, this configuration can cause switch flooding since all inbound packets are sent to all ports on the switch.

Multicast

The cluster adapters for all nodes are assigned their own MAC unicast address.

The cluster adapters for all nodes are assigned a multicast MAC address (derived from the IP of the cluster).

Non-NLB network traffic between cluster nodes works fine since they all have their own MAC address.

IGMP Multicast

This is much like multicast, but the MAC traffic goes only to the switch ports of the NLB cluster, preventing switch flooding.

7. After selecting the appropriate settings, the next page is where port rules are configured. By default, it is set up to be wide open. Most implementations will limit NLB ports to just the ports needed for the application. For example, a web server would need port 80 enabled. It is also in this area where you can configure filtering mode.

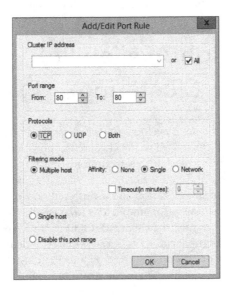

The affinity sets a client's preference to a particular NLB host. It is not recommended to set affinity to None when UDP is an expected traffic type.

8. After clicking OK and finishing the wizard, you can add nodes to the NLB cluster by right-clicking and selecting Add Host To Cluster. Doing so presents a fairly straightforward wizard to add the host, specify a priority value, and then join the cluster. Shortly, your console will look similar to the one shown here.

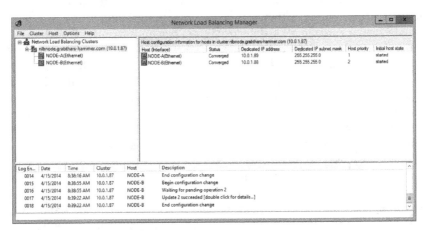

Upgrading an NLB Cluster

Upgrading an NLB cluster is a fairly straightforward process. You execute a drainstop on the NLB cluster node or remove existing connections to the application on the local host, and then you can perform an in-place upgrade in a rolling manner.

Achieving High Availability with Failover Clustering

Taking high availability to the next level for enterprise services often means creating a failover cluster. In a failover cluster, all of the clustered application or service resources are assigned to one node or server in the cluster. Commonly clustered applications are SQL Server and Exchange Server; commonly clustered services are File and Print. Since the differences between a clustered application and a clustered service are primarily related to the number of functions or features, for simplicity's sake I will refer to both as *clustered applications*. Another, more frequently, clustered resource is a Hyper-V virtual machine.

If there is a failure of the primary node or if the primary node is taken offline for maintenance, the clustered application is started on another cluster node. The client requests are then automatically redirected to the new cluster node to minimize the impact of the failure.

How does Failover Clustering improve availability? By increasing the number of server nodes available on which the application or virtual machine can run, you can move the application or virtual machine to a healthy server if there is a problem, if maintenance needs to be completed on the hardware or the operating system, or if patches need to be applied. The clustered application being moved will have to restart on the new server regardless of whether the move was intentional. This is why the term *highly available* is used instead of *fault tolerant*. Virtual machines, however, can be moved from one node to another node using a process known as *live migration*. Live migration is where one or more virtual machines are intentionally moved from one node to another with their current memory state intact through the cluster network with no indicators to the virtual machine consumer that the virtual machine has moved from one server to another. However, in the event of a cluster node or virtual machine failure, the virtual machine will still fail and will then be brought online again on another healthy cluster node.

Figure 1.1 shows an example of SQL Server running on the first node of a Windows Server 2012 R2 failover cluster.

The clustered SQL Server in Figure 1.2 can be failed over to another node in the cluster and still service database requests. However, the database will be restarted.

Failover clustering is notorious for being complicated and expensive. Windows Server 2012 R2 makes strides in removing both of these concerns. Troubleshooting and other advanced concepts are outside of the scope of the Microsoft MCSA exams and thus this book, so I will cover only the basic requirements and concepts needed to configure a failover cluster.

FIGURE 1.1   Using Failover Clustering to cluster SQL Server

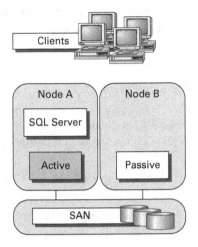

FIGURE 1.2   Failing the SQL Server service to another node

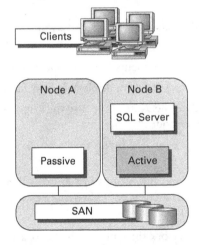

Failover Clustering Requirements

The Failover Clustering feature is available in the Datacenter, Standard, and Hyper-V editions of Windows Server 2012 R2.

To be able to configure a failover cluster, you must have the required components. A single failover cluster can have up to 64 nodes when using Windows Server 2012 R2, however, and the clustered service or application must support that number of nodes.

To create a failover cluster, an administrator must make sure that all the hardware involved meets the cluster requirements. To be supported by Microsoft, all hardware must be certified for Windows Server 2012 R2, and the complete failover cluster solution must pass all tests in the Validate A Configuration Wizard. Although the exact hardware will depend on the clustered application, a few requirements are standard:

- Server components must be marked with the "Certified for Windows Server 2012 R2" logo.
- Although not explicitly required, server hardware should match and contain the same or similar components.
- All of the Validate A Configuration Wizard tests must pass.

The requirements for Failover Clustering storage have changed from previous versions of Windows. For example, Parallel SCSI is no longer a supported storage technology for any of the clustered disks. There are, however, additional requirements that need to be met for the storage components:

- Disks available for the cluster must be Fibre Channel, iSCSI, or Serial Attached SCSI.
- Each cluster node must have a dedicated network interface card for iSCSI connectivity. The network interface card you use for iSCSI should not be used for network communication.
- Multipath software must be based on Microsoft's Multipath I/O (MPIO).
- Storage drivers must be based on storport.sys.
- Drivers and firmware for the storage controllers on each server node in the cluster should be identical.
- Storage components must be marked with the "Certified for Windows Server 2012 R2" logo.

In addition, there are network requirements that must be met for Failover Clustering:

- Cluster nodes should be connected to multiple networks for communication redundancy.
- Network adapters should be the same make, use the same driver, and have the firmware version in each cluster node.
- Network components must be marked with the "Certified for Windows Server 2012 R2" logo.

There are two types of network connections in a failover cluster. These should have adequate redundancy because total failure of either could cause loss of functionality of the cluster. The two types are as follows:

Public Network   This is the network through which clients are able to connect to the clustered service application.

Private Network   This is the network used by the nodes to communicate with each other.

To provide redundancy for these two network types, additional network adapters would need to be added to the node and configured to connect to the networks.

In previous versions of Windows Server, support was given only when the entire cluster configuration was tested and listed on the Hardware Compatibility List. The tested configuration listed the server and storage configuration down to the firmware and driver versions. This proved to be difficult and expensive from both a vendor and a consumer perspective to deploy supported Windows clusters.

When problems did arise and Microsoft support was needed, it caused undue troubleshooting complexity as well. With Windows Server 2012 R2 Failover Clustering and simplified requirements, including the "Certified for Windows Server 2012 R2" logo program and the Validate A Configuration Wizard, it all but eliminates the guesswork of getting the cluster components configured in a way that follows best practices and allows Microsoft support to assist you easily when needed.

Cluster Quorum

When a group of people sets out to accomplish a single task or goal, a method for settling disagreements and for making decisions is required. In the case of a cluster, the goal is to provide a highly available service in spite of failures. When a problem occurs and a cluster node loses communication with the other nodes because of a network error, the functioning nodes are supposed to try to bring the redundant service back online.

How, though, is it determined which node should bring the clustered service back online? If all the nodes are functional despite the network communications issue, each one might try. Just like a group of people with their own ideas, a method must be put in place to determine which idea, or node, to grant control of the cluster. Windows Server 2012 R2 Failover Clustering, like other clustering technologies, requires that a quorum exist between the cluster nodes before a cluster becomes available.

A *quorum* is a consensus of the status of each of the nodes in the cluster. Quorum must be achieved in order for a clustered application to come online by obtaining a majority of the votes available (see Figure 1.3). Windows Server 2012 R2 has four quorum models, or methods, for determining quorum and for adjusting the number and types of votes available:

- Node majority (no witness)
- Node majority with witness (disk or file share)
- Node and file share majority
- No majority (disk witness only)

FIGURE 1.3   Majority needed

When a majority of the nodes are communicating, the cluster is functional.

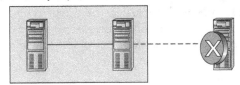

When a majority of the nodes are not communicating, the cluster stops.

Witness Configuration

Most administrators follow some basic rules. For example, when you configure a quorum, the voting components in the cluster should be an odd number. For example, if I set up a quorum for five elements and I lose one element, I continue to work. If I lose two elements, I continue to work. If I lose three elements, the cluster stops—as soon as it hits half plus 1, the cluster stops. This works well with an odd number.

If the cluster contains an even number of voting elements, an administrator should then configure a disk witness or a file share witness. The advantage of using a witness (disk or file share) is that the cluster will continue to run even if half of the cluster nodes simultaneously go down or are disconnected. The ability to configure a disk witness is possible only if the storage vendor supports read-write access from all sites to the replicated storage.

One of the advantages of Windows Server 2012 R2 is the advanced quorum configuration option. This option allows you to assign or remove quorum votes on a per-node basis. Administrators now have the ability to remove votes from nodes in certain configurations. For example, if your organization uses a multisite cluster, you may choose to remove votes from the nodes in the backup site. This way, those backup nodes would not affect your quorum calculations.

Dynamic Quorum Management

Another advantage in Windows Server 2012 R2 is dynamic quorum management. *Dynamic quorum management* automatically manages the vote assignment to nodes. With this feature enabled, votes are automatically added or removed from nodes when that node either joins or leaves a cluster. In Windows Server 2012 R2, dynamic quorum management is enabled by default.

Validating a Cluster Configuration

Configuring a failover cluster in Windows Server 2012 R2 is much simpler than in previous versions of Windows Server. Before a cluster can be configured, the Validate A Configuration Wizard should be run to verify that the hardware is configured in a fashion that is supportable. Before you can run the Validate A Configuration Wizard, however, the Failover Clustering feature needs to be installed using Server Manager. The account that is used to create a cluster must have administrative rights on each of the cluster nodes and have permissions to create a cluster name object in Active Directory. Follow these steps:

1. Prepare the hardware and software perquisites.

2. Install the Failover Clustering feature on each server.

3. Log in with the appropriate user ID and run the Validate A Configuration Wizard.

4. Create a cluster.

5. Install and cluster applications and services.

To install the Failover Clustering feature on a cluster node, follow the steps outlined in Exercise 1.2.

EXERCISE 1.2

Installing the Failover Cluster Feature

1. Press the Windows key and select Administrative Tools ➢ Server Manager.

2. Select number 2, Add Roles And Features.

3. At the Select Installation Type screen, choose a role-based or feature-based installation.

4. At the Select Destination Server screen, choose Select A Server From The Server Pool and click Next.

5. At the Select Server Roles screen, click Next.

6. At the Select Features screen, click the Failover Clustering check box. If the Add Features dialog box appears, click the Add Features button. Click Next.

7. At the Confirmation screen, click the Install button.

8. Once the installation is complete, click the Close button.

9. Close Server Manager.

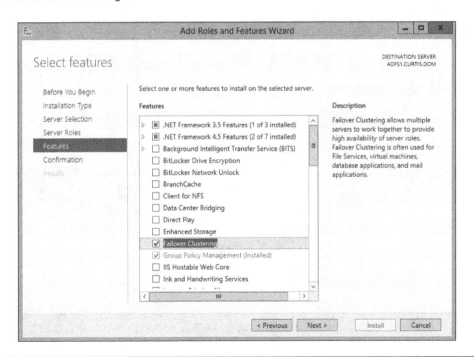

Using the Validate A Configuration Wizard before creating a cluster is highly recommended. This wizard validates that the hardware configuration and the software configuration for the potential cluster nodes are in a supported configuration. Even if the configuration passes the tests, take care to review all warnings and informational messages so that they can be addressed or documented before the cluster is created.

Running the Validate A Configuration Wizard does the following:

- Conducts four types of tests (software and hardware inventory, network, storage, and system configuration)
- Confirms that the hardware and software settings are supportable by Microsoft support staff

You should run the Validate A Configuration Wizard before creating a cluster or after making any major hardware or software changes to the cluster. Doing this will help you identify any misconfigurations that could cause problems with the failover cluster.

Running the Validate a Configuration Wizard

The Validate A Configuration Wizard, shown in Figure 1.4, is simple and straightforward to use, as its "wizard" name would suggest. It should be run after the Failover Clustering feature has been installed on each of the cluster nodes, and it can be run as many times as required.

FIGURE 1.4   The Validate A Configuration Wizard

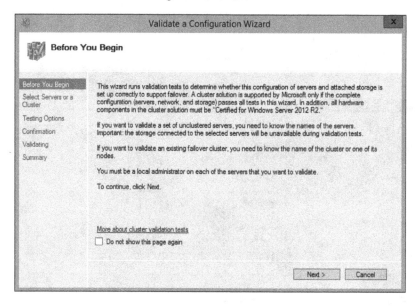

When you are troubleshooting cluster problems or have changed the configuration of the cluster hardware, it is a good idea to run the Validate A Configuration Wizard again to help pinpoint potential cluster configuration problems.

If you already have a cluster configured and want to run the Validate A Configuration Wizard, you can do so; however, you will not be able to run all of the storage tests without taking the clustered resources offline. You will be prompted either to skip the disruptive tests or to take the clustered resources offline so that the tests can complete.

Exercise 1.3 shows the exact steps to follow to run the Validate A Configuration Wizard successfully on clusters named NODEA and NODEB, which are not yet clustered.

I am using NODEA and NODEB in the exercises. You need to replace these two nodes with your own two servers to complete these exercises.

EXERCISE 1.3

Running the Validate A Configuration Wizard

1. Press the Windows key and select Administrative Tools ➢ Failover Cluster Management.

2. In the Actions pane (right side of screen), click Validate Configuration.

3. At the Before You Begin screen, click Next.

4. Type **NODEA** in the Enter Name field and click Add.

5. Type **NODEB** in the Enter Name field and click Add.

6. Click Next.

7. Leave Run All Tests (Recommended) selected and click Next.

8. Click Next at the Confirmation screen.

9. Let the test complete, review the report in the Summary window, and then click Finish.

Addressing Problems Reported by the Validate A Configuration Wizard

After the Validate A Configuration Wizard has been run, it will show the results, as shown in Figure 1.5. This report can also be viewed in detail later using a web browser. The report is named with the date and time the wizard was run, and it is stored in %windir%\cluster\ Reports.

FIGURE 1.5 Validate A Configuration Wizard results

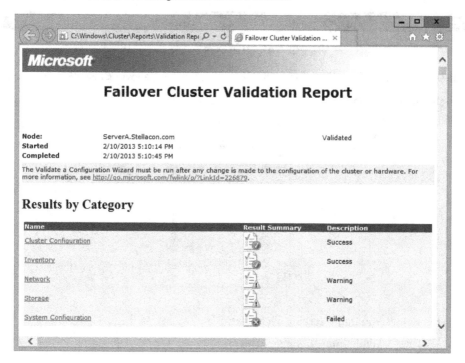

How should errors listed in the report be addressed? Often, the errors reported by the Validate A Configuration Wizard are self-explanatory; however, sometimes additional help is required. The following three guidelines should help troubleshoot the errors:

- Read all of the errors because multiple errors may be related.

- Use the checklists available in the Windows Server help files to ensure that all the steps have been completed.

- Contact the hardware vendor for updated drivers, firmware, and guidance for using the hardware in a cluster.

Multisite, Stretched, or Geographically Dispersed Clusters (Geoclustering)

One issue you may face is if you have multiple sites or if the cluster is geographically dispersed. If the failover cluster does not have a shared common disk, data replication between nodes might not pass the cluster validation "storage" tests.

Setting up a cluster in a multisite, stretched, or geocluster (these terms can be used interchangeably) configuration is a common practice. As long as the cluster solution does not require external storage to fail over, it will not need to pass the storage test to function properly.

Creating a Cluster

After you have successfully validated a configuration and the cluster hardware is in a supportable state, you can create a cluster. The process for creating a cluster is straightforward and similar to the process of running the Validate A Configuration Wizard. To create a cluster with two servers, follow the instructions in Exercise 1.4.

EXERCISE 1.4

Creating a Cluster

1. Open the Failover Cluster Management MMC.

2. In the Management section of the center pane, select Create A Cluster.

3. Read the Before You Begin information and click Next.

4. In the Enter Server Name box, type **NODEA** and then click Add.

5. Again, in the Enter Server Name box, type **NODEB** and then click Add. Click Next.

6. At the Validation screen, choose No for this exercise and then click Next.

7. In the Access Point For Administering The Cluster section, enter **Cluster1** for the cluster name.

8. Type an IP address and then click Next. This IP address will be the IP address of the cluster.

EXERCISE 1.4 *(continued)*

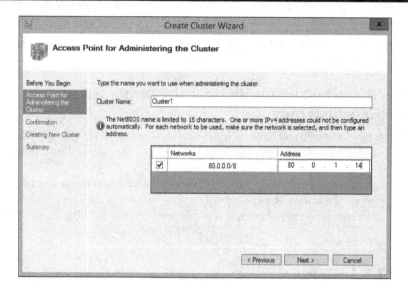

9. In the Confirmation dialog box, verify the information and then click Next.

10. On the Summary page, click Finish.

Working with Cluster Nodes

Once a cluster is created, a couple of actions are available. First you can add another node to the cluster by using the Add Node Wizard from the Failover Cluster Management Actions pane.

At this point, you also have the option to pause a node, which prevents resources from being failed over or moved to the node. You typically would pause a node when the node is involved in maintenance or troubleshooting. After a node is paused, it must be resumed to allow resources to be run on it again.

Another action available to perform on a node at this time is *evict*. Eviction is an irreversible process. Once you evict the node, it must be re-added to the cluster. You would evict a node when it is damaged beyond repair or is no longer needed in the cluster. If you evict a damaged node, you can repair or rebuild it and then add it back to the cluster using the Add Node Wizard.

Clustering Roles, Services, and Applications

Once the cluster is created, applications, services, and roles can be clustered. Windows Server 2012 R2 includes a number of built-in roles and features that can be clustered.

The following roles and features can be clustered in Windows Server 2012 R2 (see Figure 1.6):

FIGURE 1.6   High availability roles

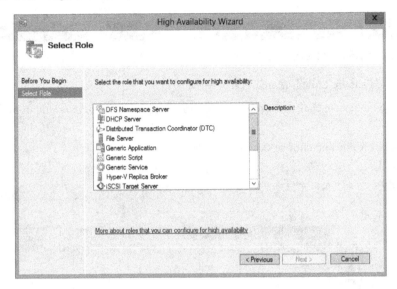

- DFS Namespace Server
- DHCP Server
- Distributed Transaction Coordinator (DTC)
- File Server
- Generic Application
- Generic Script
- Generic Service
- Hyper-V Replica Broker
- iSCSI Target Server
- iSNS Server
- Message Queuing
- Other Server
- Virtual Machine
- WINS Server

In addition, other common services and applications can be clustered on Windows Server 2012 R2 clusters:

- Enterprise database services, such as Microsoft SQL Server
- Enterprise messaging services, such as Microsoft Exchange Server

To cluster a role or feature such as Print Services, the first step is to install the role or feature on each node of the cluster. The next step is to use the Configure A Service Or Application Wizard in the Failover Cluster Management tool. Exercise 1.5 shows you how to cluster the Print Services role once an appropriate disk has been presented to the cluster.

EXERCISE 1.5

Clustering the Print Services Role

1. Open the Failover Cluster Management MMC.

2. In the console tree, click the arrow next to the cluster name to expand the items underneath it.

3. Right-click Roles and choose Configure Role.

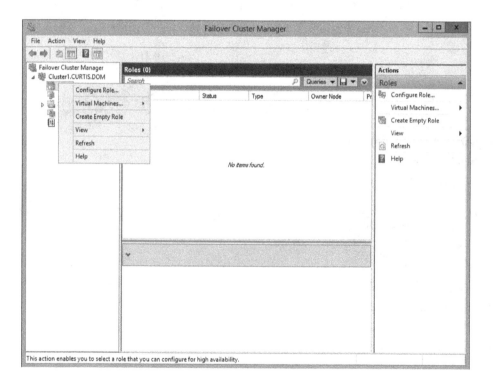

4. Click Next on the Before You Begin page.

5. Click Other Server on the Select Role screen and then click Next.

6. Type the name of the print server, such as **Print1**, and type in the IP address that will be used to access the print service, such as **80.0.0.34**. Then click Next.

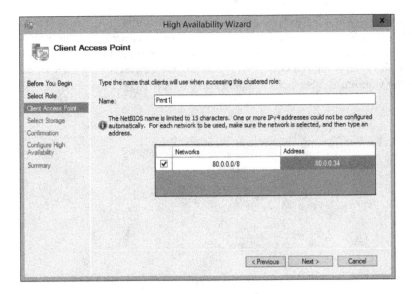

7. At the Select Storage page, just click Next.

8. Click Next at the Confirmation page.

9. After the wizard runs and the Summary page appears, you can view a report of the tasks the wizard performed by clicking View Report.

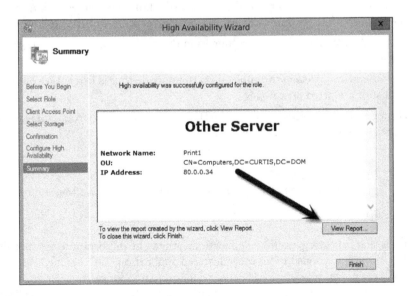

10. Close the report and click Finish.

The built-in roles and features all are configured in a similar fashion. Other applications, such as Microsoft Exchange Server 2013, have specialized cluster configuration routines that are outside the scope of this exam. Applications that are not developed to be clustered can also be clustered using the Generic Application, Generic Script, or Generic Service option in the Configure A Service Or Application Wizard, as shown in Figure 1.7.

FIGURE 1.7   Configuring a generic application

Clustered Application Settings

Windows Server 2012 R2 has options that allow an administrator to fine-tune the failover process to meet the needs of their business. These options will be covered in the next few sections.

Failover occurs when a clustered application or service moves from one node to another. The process can be triggered automatically because of a failure or server maintenance or can be done manually by an administrator. The failover process works as follows:

1. The cluster service takes all of the resources in the application offline in the order set in the dependency hierarchy.

2. The cluster service transfers the application to the node that is listed next on the application's list of preferred host nodes.

3. The cluster service attempts to bring all of the application's resources online, starting at the bottom of the dependency hierarchy.

These steps can change depending on the use of Live Migration.

In a cluster that is hosting multiple applications, it may be important to set specific nodes to be primarily responsible for each clustered application. This can be helpful from a troubleshooting perspective since a specific node is targeted for hosting service. To set a preferred node and an order of preference for failover, use the General tab in the Properties dialog box of the clustered application.

Also, the order of failover is set in this same dialog box by moving the order in which the nodes are listed. If NODEA should be the primary node and NODEC should be the server that the application fails to first, NODEA should be listed first and selected as the preferred owner. NODEC should be listed second, and the remaining cluster nodes should be listed after NODEC.

As shown in Figure 1.8, a number of failover settings can be configured for the clustered service. The failover settings control the number of times a clustered application can fail in a period of time before the cluster stops trying to restart it. Typically, if a clustered application fails a number of times, some sort of manual intervention will be required to return the application to a stable state.

FIGURE 1.8   Clustered application failover settings

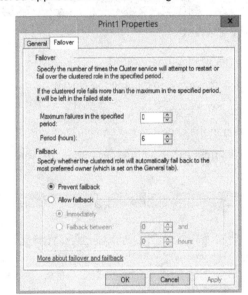

Specifying the maximum number of failures will keep the application from trying to restart until it is manually brought back online after the problem has been resolved. This is beneficial because if the application continues to be brought online and then fails, it may show as being functional to the monitoring system, even though it continues to fail. After the application is put in a failed state, the monitoring system will not be able to contact the application and should report it as being offline.

Figure 1.8 also shows the failback settings for Print1. Failback settings control whether and when a clustered application would fail back to the preferred cluster node once it becomes available. The default setting is Prevent Failback. If failback is allowed, two additional options are available, either to fail back immediately after the preferred node is available or to fail back within a specified time.

The time is specified in the 24-hour format. If you want to allow failback between 10 p.m. and 11 p.m., you would set the failback time to be between 22 and 23. Setting a failback time to off-hours is an excellent way to ensure that your clustered applications are running on the designated nodes and automatically scheduling the failover process for a time when it will impact the fewest users.

One tool that is valuable in determining how resources affect other resources is the dependency viewer. The *dependency viewer* visualizes the dependency hierarchy created for an application or service. Using this tool can help when troubleshooting why specific resources are causing failures and allow an administrator to visualize the current configuration better and adjust it to meet business needs. Exercise 1.6 will show you how to run the dependency viewer.

EXERCISE 1.6

Using the Dependency Viewer

1. Open the Failover Cluster Management MMC.

2. In the console tree, click the arrow to expand the cluster.

3. Click Roles.

4. Under the Roles section in the center of the screen, click one of the roles (such as Print1).

5. Right-click the role and under More Actions click Show Dependency Report.

6. Review the dependency report.

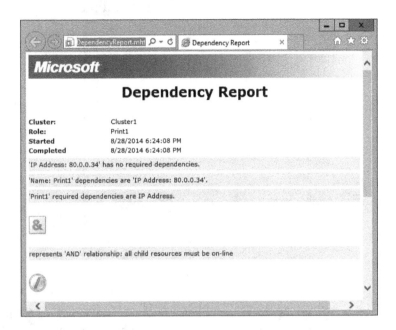

7. Close the Dependency Report and close the Failover Cluster Manager.

Exercise 1.6 generated a dependency report that shows how the print service is dependent on a network name and a clustered disk resource. The network name is then dependent on an IP address.

Resource Properties

Resources are physical or logical objects, such as a file share or IP address, which the failover cluster manages. They may be a service or application available to clients, or they may be part of the cluster. Resources include physical hardware devices such as disks and logical items such as network names. They are the smallest configurable unit in a cluster and can run on only a single node in a cluster at a time.

Like clustered applications, resources have a number of properties available for meeting business requirements for high availability. This section covers resource dependencies and policies.

Dependencies can be set on individual resources and control how resources are brought online and offline. Simply put, a dependent resource is brought online after the resources that it depends on, and it is taken offline before those resources. As shown in Figure 1.9, dependencies can be set on a specific resource, such as the print spooler.

FIGURE 1.9   Resource dependencies

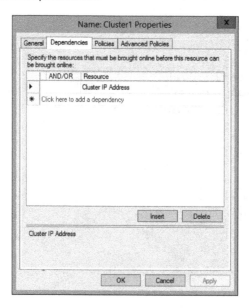

Resource policies are settings that control how resources respond when a failure occurs and how resources are monitored for failures. Figure 1.10 shows the Policies tab of a resource's Properties dialog box.

FIGURE 1.10   Resource policies

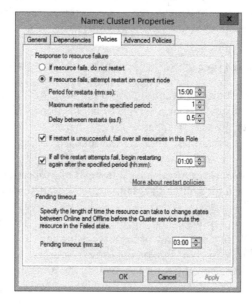

The Policies tab sets configuration options for how a resource should respond in the event of a failure. The options available are as follows:

If Resource Fails, Do Not Restart   This option, as it would lead you to believe, leaves the failed resource offline.

If Resource Fails, Attempt Restart On Current Node   With this option set, the resource tries to restart if it fails on the node on which it is currently running. There are two additional options if this is selected so that the number of restarts can be limited. They set the number of times the resource should restart on the current node in a specified length of time. For example, if you specify 5 for Maximum Restarts In The Specified Period and 10:00 (mm:ss) for Period For Restarts, the cluster service will try to restart the resource five times during that 10-minute period. After the fifth restart, the cluster service will no longer attempt to restart the service on the active node.

If Restart Is Unsuccessful, Fail Over All Resources In This Service Or Application   If this option is selected, when the cluster service is no longer trying to restart the resource on the active node, it will fail the entire service or application to another cluster node. If you wanted to leave the application or service with a failed resource on the current node, you would clear this check box.

If All The Restart Attempts Fail, Begin Restarting Again After The Specified Period (hh:mm)   If this option is selected, the cluster service will restart the resource at a specified interval if all previous attempts have failed.

Pending Timeout   This option is used to set the amount of time in minutes and seconds that the cluster service should wait for this resource to respond to a change in states. If a resource takes longer than the cluster expects to change states, the cluster will mark it as having failed. If a resource consistently takes longer than this and the problem cannot be resolved, you may need to increase this value. Figure 1.11 shows the Advanced Policies tab.

FIGURE 1.11   Resource Advanced Policies

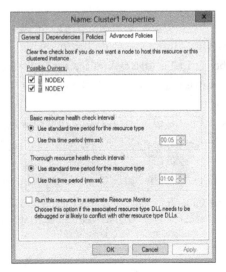

The options available on the Advanced Policies tab are as follows:

Possible Owners   This option allows an administrator to remove specific cluster nodes from running this resource. Using this option is valuable when there are issues with a resource on a particular node and the administrator wants to keep the applications from failing over to that node until the problem can be repaired.

Basic Resource Health Check Interval   This option allows an administrator to customize the health check interval for this resource.

Thorough Resource Health Check Interval   This option allows an administrator to customize the thorough health check interval for this resource.

Run This Resource In A Separate Resource Monitor   If the resource needs to be debugged by a support engineer or if the resource conflicts with other resources, this option may need to be used.

Windows Server 2012 R2 Clustering Features

Many new features are included in the Windows Server 2012 R2 release for clustering. It is a rich feature set of high availability with greatly improved flexibility based on the needs of IT organizations. The new features relate to quorum behavior, virtual machine hosting, Active Directory–detached clusters, and a new dashboard.

Windows PowerShell Cmdlets for Failover Clusters   As I have explained throughout this book, Windows PowerShell is a command-line shell and scripting tool. Windows Server 2012 R2 clustering has new cmdlets that provide powerful ways to script cluster configuration and management tasks. Windows PowerShell cmdlets have now replaced the Cluster.exe command-line interface.

Cluster Shared Volumes   *Cluster Shared Volumes (CSV)* allows for the configuration of clustered virtual machines. CSV allows you to do the following:

- Reduce the number of LUNs (disks) required for your virtual machines.
- Make better use of disk space. Any VHD file on that LUN can use the free space on a CSV volume.
- More easily track the paths to VHD files and other files used by virtual machines.
- Use a few CSV volumes to create a configuration that supports many clustered virtual machines.

CSV volumes also are utilized for the Scale-Out-File-Server cluster role.

Management of Large-Scale Clusters   One new advantage of Windows Server 2012 R2 clusters is the ability for Server Manager to discover and manage the nodes in a cluster. By starting the Failover Cluster Manager from Server Manager, you can do remote multiserver management and role and feature installation. Administrators now have the ability to manage a cluster from one convenient location.

Management and Mobility of Clustered Virtual Machines   Microsoft has built Windows Server 2012 R2 "from the cloud up." Microsoft, as well as the industry as a whole, is moving toward the cloud and virtualization. With that in mind, administrators can now configure settings such as prioritizing the starting or placement of virtual machines in the clustered workloads. This allows administrators to allocate resources efficiently to your cluster.

Cluster-Aware Updating   One issue that every administrator has dealt with is updating a system or application while it is running. For example, if you are running Microsoft Exchange and you want to do an Exchange update, when do you take the server offline to do the update? It always seems that someone is on the system 24 hours a day. Well, Windows Server 2012 R2 clustering has a solution. *Cluster-Aware Updating (CAU)* is a new automated feature that allows system updates to be applied automatically while the cluster remains available during the entire update process.

Scale-Out File Server for Application Data   By utilizing *Microsoft Storage Spaces*, you can create a highly available clustered file share that utilizes SMB 3.0 and CSV to provide scalable access to data.

Scale-out file servers are useful for storing the following application data:

- Hyper-V virtual machine storage
- SQL Server database files

Be aware that scale-out file servers are not useful at all for typical file share data because they benefit only from applications that require a persistent connection to their storage.

Shared Virtual Hard Disks   In the previous versions of Windows, Failover Cluster nodes running as virtual machines had to use iSCSI or virtual HBAs to connect directly to SAN-based storage. With Windows Server 2012 R2, you can set your Hyper-V virtualized cluster to use a shared VHDX virtual disk. Shared virtual hard disks can reside on the following:

- A scale-out file server failover cluster
- Cluster CSV volumes

Shared virtual hard disks are extremely useful in providing highly available shared storage for the following virtualized workloads:

- SQL Server
- Virtual Machine Manager
- Exchange Server

Virtual Machine Drain on Shutdown   When needing to perform maintenance on a Hyper-V failover cluster, you may have a lot of virtual machines on one node of a cluster. Inevitably, you will need to restart a cluster node for updates or shut it down for maintenance.

In previous versions of Windows, virtual machines running on the cluster would save their state, and then the cluster node would shut down. Windows Server 2012 R2 helps alleviate this issue by automatically draining the virtual machines running on a node before it shuts down or restarts. Windows does this by attempting to live migrate all virtual machines on the cluster node to other nodes in the cluster when at all possible.

This feature is turned on by default, but it can be disabled through PowerShell.

Active Directory–Detached Clusters   Previous versions of Windows Failover Clustering have depended on Active Directory to provide computer objects for the cluster name object as well as virtual computer objects. With Active Directory–detached failover clusters, communication to the cluster-form clients will use NTLM authentication rather than the normal Kerberos authentication. This is useful in maintaining high availability should a person accidently delete a virtual computer object in Active Directory that a clustered resource depends on for Kerberos authentication.

Dynamic Witness   Earlier in this chapter, I mentioned the Dynamic Quorum model and how votes were dynamically adjusted based on the number of nodes in a cluster. In Windows Server 2012 R2, there is a new feature called *dynamic witness* that is enabled by default when the cluster is configured to use a dynamic quorum. Since it is preferred to have an odd number of votes at any one time in a cluster, the dynamic witness will turn on or off the witness vote in order to ensure that there are an odd number of votes in the cluster.

Tie Breaker For 50% Node Split   Like the *dynamic witness* feature just described, the Tie Breaker For 50% Node Split option in Windows Server 2012 R2 dynamically adjusts cluster node votes in order to maintain an odd number of votes in a cluster where no witness is being used.

This is useful for a cluster in a multisite, stretched, or geocluster configuration.

Global Update Manager Mode   Since the first release of Microsoft Cluster Services appearing in Windows NT 4.0 Enterprise, all nodes in a cluster maintain a local database that keeps a copy of the cluster configuration. The *Global Update Manager (GUM)* is a component of the cluster that ensures that before a change is marked as being committed for the entire cluster, all nodes have received and committed that change to their local cluster database. If one or more nodes do not report back or commit a change, the cluster node is kicked out of being a member of the cluster. Another issue that can occur is that for various clustered applications, such as SQL and Exchange, their performance can be negatively impacted by the time it takes the GUM to coordinate with all the nodes of a cluster for any changes. The GUM is only as fast as the slowest node in the cluster.

With Windows Server 2012 R2, a new feature was added to Failover Clustering called *Global Update Manager mode*. This feature allows you to configure the GUM read-write modes manually in order to greatly speed up the processing of changes by the GUM and to improve the performance of certain clustered resources.

Turn Off IPsec Encryption For Inter-node Cluster Communications   In network environments where IPsec is used, slow Group Policy updates and other issues can cause

Active Directory Domain Services to be temporarily unavailable to cluster nodes. If the cluster intracluster communications protocol uses IPsec encryption, then these delays could cause cluster nodes to drop out of the cluster for failure to communicate in a timely manner with the rest of the nodes in the cluster. Windows Server 2012 R2 now provides a way to turn off IPsec encryption on the cluster communication network.

Cluster Dashboard   Starting with Windows Server 2012, Failover Clustering supports up to 64 nodes in a cluster. Keeping track of the status and resources on all of these nodes can be an administrative headache! Managing more than one failover cluster and determining what a certain cluster hosts can be painful as well. Fortunately, in Windows Server 2012 R2, the *Failover Cluster Manager*'s main dashboard has been updated to make it easier to see the status and health of multiple clusters.

Hyper-V Replica Broker   Starting with Windows Server 2012, Hyper-V supported continuous replication of virtual machines to another server or cluster for disaster recovery purposes. The Hyper-V Recovery Broker allows for virtual machines in a cluster to be replicated. The Hyper-V Recovery Broker keeps track of which cluster nodes virtual machines are residing on and ensures that replication is maintained.

Hyper-V Manager Integration into Failover Cluster Manager   In Windows Server 2012 R2, the Hyper-V Management Console is integrated with Failover Cluster Manager for managing virtual machines that are clustered. Normal Hyper-V operations such as configuring, exporting, importing, configuring replication, stopping, starting, and live migrating virtual machines are supported directly through Failover Cluster Manager.

Virtual Machine Monitoring   Starting with Windows Server 2012, Failover Clustering now supports Virtual Machine Monitoring for Windows Server 2012/2012 R2 virtual machines. Virtual Machine Monitoring monitors administrator-selected Windows services running within a virtual machine and will automatically restart a service if it should fail. If the service does not start for the configured number of restart attempts, the virtual machine will fail over to another node and then restart. For example, you can configure Failover Clustering to monitor the Print Spooler service on a Windows Server 2012 R2 virtual machine. If the Print Spooler service goes offline, then the cluster will attempt to restart the Print Spooler service within the virtual machine. If the service still fails, Failover Clustering will move the virtual machine to another node.

Summary

High availability is more than just clustering. It is achieved through improved hardware, software, and processes. This chapter focused on how to configure Failover Clustering and Network Load Balancing in order to achieve high availability and scalability.

High availability should be approached through proper hardware configuration, training, and operational discipline. Failover clustering provides a highly available base for many applications, such as databases and mail servers.

Network load-balanced clusters are used to provide high availability and scalability for network-based applications, such as VPNs and web servers. Network load balanced clusters can be configured with any edition of Windows Server 2012 R2 except for the Windows Server 2012 R2 Hyper-V Edition.

Exam Essentials

Know how to modify failover and failback settings.   These settings are set on the clustered service or application, but they can be modified by settings on the resources.

Know the hardware requirements for Failover Clustering and Network Load Balancing.   Failover clustering and Network Load Balancing have distinct hardware requirements. Know the differences.

Review Questions

1. Which of the following editions of Windows Server 2012 R2 can be configured in a failover cluster? (Choose all that apply.)

    A. Windows Server 2012 R2 Hyper-V edition

    B. Windows Server 2012 R2 Standard edition

    C. Windows Server 2012 R2 Foundation edition

    D. Windows Server 2012 R2 Datacenter edition

2. Which of the following editions of Windows Server 2012 can be configured in a Network Load Balancing cluster? (Choose all that apply.)

    A. Windows Server 2012 R2 Essentials edition

    B. Windows Server 2012 R2 Standard edition

    C. Windows Server 2012 R2 Hyper-V edition

    D. Windows Server 2012 R2 Datacenter edition

3. What is the maximum number of nodes that can participate in a Windows Server 2012 failover cluster?

    A. 2

    B. 4

    C. 16

    D. 64

4. Which of the following actions should be performed against an NLB cluster node if maintenance needs to be performed while not terminating current connections?

    A. Evict

    B. Drainstop

    C. Pause

    D. Stop

5. What is the maximum number of nodes that can participate in a Windows Server 2012 R2 NLB cluster?

    A. 4

    B. 8

    C. 16

    D. 32

6. Which of the following applications would be better suited on a failover cluster instead of a network load-balanced cluster? (Choose all that apply.)

   A. SQL Server

   B. Website

   C. Exchange Mailbox Server

   D. VPN services

7. Which of the following applications would be better suited on a Network Load Balancing cluster instead of a failover cluster? (Choose all that apply.)

   A. SQL Server

   B. Website

   C. Database servers

   D. Terminal Services

8. To configure an NLB cluster with unicast, what is the minimum number of network adapters required in each node?

   A. One

   B. Two

   C. Three

   D. Six

9. In a four-node cluster set to a Node And File Share Majority quorum model, how many votes can be lost before quorum is lost?

   A. One

   B. Two

   C. Three

   D. Four

10. In a three-node cluster set to a Node Majority quorum model, how many cluster nodes can be offline before quorum is lost?

   A. Zero

   B. One

   C. Two

   D. Three

Chapter

2

Configure File and Storage Solutions

THE FOLLOWING 70-412 EXAM OBJECTIVES ARE COVERED IN THIS CHAPTER:

✓ **Configure advanced file services**

- Configure NFS data store
- Configure BranchCache
- Configure File Classification Infrastructure (FCI) using File Server Resource Manager (FSRM)
- Configure file access auditing

✓ **Implement Dynamic Access Control (DAC)**

- Configure user and device claim types
- Create and configure resource properties and lists
- Create and configure Central Access Rules and Policies
- Configure file classification
- Implement policy changes and staging
- Perform access-denied remediation

✓ **Configure and optimize storage**

- Configure iSCSI Target and Initiator
- Configure Internet Storage Name Server (iSNS)
- Implement thin provisioning and trim
- Manage server free space using Features on Demand
- Configure tiered storage

Taking the time to understand and configure file and storage solutions fully is essential to managing an IT infrastructure efficiently. Companies will rely heavily on your ability as an administrator to properly manage their users and data. In this chapter, you will learn about some of the tools that will help to make you successful in controlling how data is accessed and stored, as well as how users will interact with that data throughout their environment.

Configure Advanced File Services

Windows Server has come a long way in terms of its file and storage capabilities. I have talked quite a bit about the new features and functionality provided in Windows Server 2012 R2. In this section, you will take a closer look at some of the advanced configuration options available in the Network File System (NFS), BranchCache, and the File Server Resource Manager (FSRM).

Configure the NFS Data Store

The NFS role service and feature set gives IT administrators the ability to integrate a Windows Server–based environment with Unix-based operating systems. Most corporate environments today consist of a mixed operating system infrastructure to some extent. Using a Windows NFS file server, you can configure file shares for use by multiple operating systems throughout the environment.

Windows Server 2012 R2 takes those capabilities even further by enabling you to integrate with platforms such as ESXi. ESXi is VMware's exclusive operating system–independent hypervisor. ESXi is referred to as a *bare-metal* operating system because once it is installed on server virtualization hardware, guest virtual machines can be installed without requiring the use of any other underlying operating system. With Windows Server 2012 R2, you can use an NFS share efficiently as an ESXi data store to house all of your guest virtual machines. Let's take a look at configuring an NFS data store in Exercise 2.1.

For this exercise, you will need the following:

- A Windows Server 2012 R2 server
- A VMware ESXi 5 server

Configure the NFS Data Store

1. Open Server Manager on your Windows Server 2012 R2 machine.

2. Launch the Add Roles And Features Wizard from the dashboard.

3. Install the Server for NFS role on the server. A reboot is not required.

4. Create a new folder on your server named NFS_Datastore, right-click and select Properties, and then navigate to the NFS Sharing tab, as shown here.

5. Click the Manage NFS Sharing button to open the NFS Advanced Sharing page and then check the Share This Folder box, as shown here. Notice how enabling the share also enables the share's default settings. The share settings let you configure share authentication and user access further if the need arises. The default settings will work just fine for this exercise.

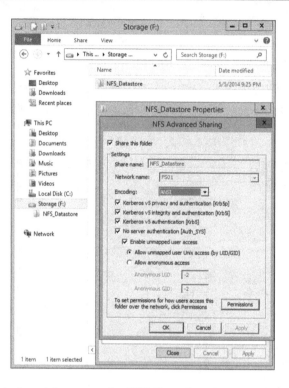

6. Click the Permissions tab to open the NFS Share Permissions page. This is where you will configure the type of access that will be allowed by machines accessing this NFS data store. By default, the NFS share permissions are set to Read-Only and do not include root access. For this exercise, you will need to change the type of access to Read-Write and check the box to allow root access, as shown here.

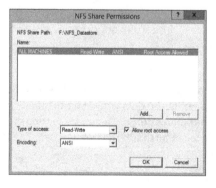

7. Click OK to close the NFS Share Permissions page and then click Apply and OK on the NFS Advanced Sharing page. Your new NFS share is now built, ready to be presented as an NFS data store to a VMware ESXi host. Be sure to record the network path displayed on the NFS Sharing tab of the share's Properties page. You will need that information to perform a proper mount on the ESXi host.

8. Switch to your ESXi host and launch the Add Storage Wizard from the Configuration tab.

9. On the Select Storage Type page of the wizard, select the Network File System storage type; click Next to continue to the Locate Network File System page.

10. On this page of the wizard, you will fill in the server and folder information for the NFS share that you will be using as a vSphere data store. Using the information recorded from step 7, properly fill out the server and folder fields and then name your new data store as shown here.

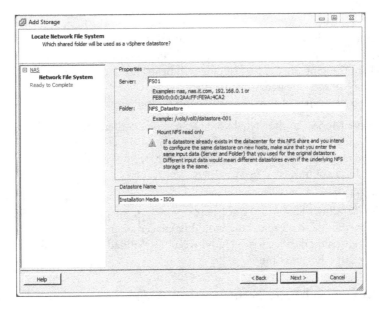

11. Click Next to continue to the Ready To Complete page of the wizard. Review the information and click Finish. Once the Create NAS data store task completes on the ESXi host, you are ready to use your Windows Server 2012 R2 shared folder as a vSphere ESXi data store. The graphic shown here confirms that the NFS share is mounted and available from the ESXi host.

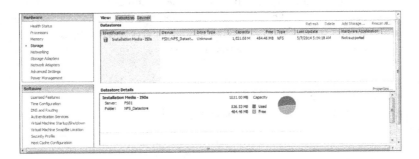

The previous exercise shows how versatile Windows Server 2012 R2 shares can be. The same principals can be applied to making Windows Server shares available to other Unix-based operating systems such as ESXi. Now that you have configured a NFS data store, let's take a look at what BranchCache has to offer.

Configure BranchCache

BranchCache is a technology that was introduced with Windows Server 2008 R2 and Windows 7. BranchCache allows an organization with slower links between offices to cache data so that downloads between offices do not have to occur each time a file is accessed.

For example, John comes into work and logs into the network. John accesses the corporate website and downloads a media file that takes four minutes to download. With BranchCache enabled, when Judy comes into work, connects to the corporate website, and tries to download the same media file, the file will be cached from the previous download and Judy will have immediate access to the file.

You can set up two types of BranchCache configurations:

Distributed Cache Mode   In the distributed cache mode configuration, all Windows 7 and Windows 8 client machines cache the files locally on the client machines. Thus, in the previous example, after John downloaded the media file, Judy would receive the cached media file from John's Windows 7 or Windows 8 machine.

Hosted Mode   In the hosted mode configuration, the cache files are cached on a local (within the site) Windows Server 2012 R2 machine. So, in the previous example, after John downloads the media file, the cached file would be placed on a Windows Server 2012 R2 machine by default, and all other users (Judy) would download the media file from the Windows Server 2012 R2 machine.

Distributed Cache Mode Requirements

If you decide to install BranchCache in the distributed cache mode configuration, a hosted cache server running Windows Server 2012 R2 is not required at the branch office. To set up distributed cache mode, the client machines must be running Windows 7 Enterprise, Windows 7 Ultimate, Windows 8 Pro, or Windows 8 Enterprise.

The Windows 7 or Windows 8 machines would download the data files from the content servers at the main branch office, and then these machines become the local cache servers. To set up distributed cache mode, you must install a Windows Server 2012 R2 content server at the main office first. After the content server is installed, physical connections (WAN or VPN connections) between the sites and branch offices must be established.

Client computers running Windows 7 and Windows 8 have BranchCache installed by default. However, you must enable and configure BranchCache and configure firewall exceptions. Complete Exercise 2.2 to configure BranchCache firewall rule exceptions.

EXERCISE 2.2

Configuring BranchCache Firewall Exceptions

1. On a domain controller, open the Group Policy Management Console.

2. In the Group Policy Management Console, expand the following path: Forest ➤ Domains ➤ Group Policy Objects. Make sure the domain you choose contains the BranchCache Windows 7/Windows 8 client computer accounts that you want to configure.

3. In the Group Policy Management Console, right-click Group Policy Objects and select New. Name the policy **BranchCache Client** and click OK. Right-click BranchCache Client and click Edit. The Group Policy Management Editor console opens.

4. In the Group Policy Management Editor console, expand the following path: Computer Configuration ➤ Policies ➤ Windows Settings ➤ Security Settings ➤ Windows Firewall With Advanced Security ➤ Windows Firewall With Advanced Security – LDAP ➤ Inbound Rules.

5. Right-click Inbound Rules and then click New Rule. The New Inbound Rule Wizard opens.

6. On the Rule Type screen, click Predefined, expand the list of choices, and then click BranchCache – Content Retrieval (Uses HTTP). Click Next.

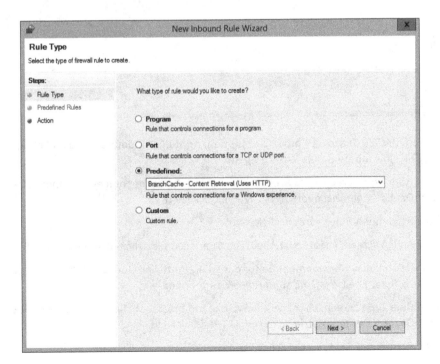

7. On the Predefined Rules screen, click Next.

8. On the Action screen, ensure that Allow The Connection is selected and then click Finish. You must select Allow The Connection for the BranchCache client to be able to receive traffic on this port.

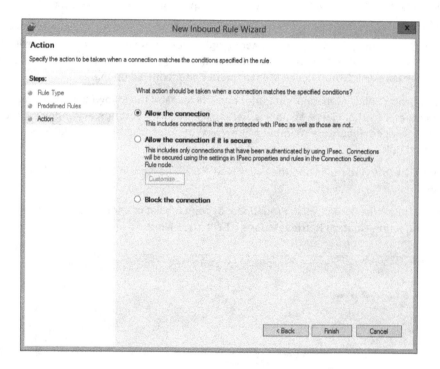

9. To create the WS-Discovery firewall exception, right-click Inbound Rules and click New Rule. The New Inbound Rule Wizard opens.

10. On the Rule Type screen, click Predefined, expand the list of choices, and then click BranchCache – Peer Discovery (Uses WSD). Click Next.

11. On the Predefined Rules screen, click Next.

12. On the Action screen, ensure that Allow The Connection is selected and then click Finish.

13. In the Group Policy Management Editor console, right-click Outbound Rules and then click New Rule. The New Outbound Rule Wizard opens.

14. On the Rule Type screen, click Predefined, expand the list of choices, and then click BranchCache – Content Retrieval (Uses HTTP). Click Next.

15. On the Predefined Rules screen, click Next.

16. On the Action screen, make sure that Allow The Connection is selected and then click Finish.

17. Create the WS-Discovery firewall exception by right-clicking Outbound Rules and then click New Rule. The New Outbound Rule Wizard opens.

18. On the Rule Type screen, click Predefined, expand the list of choices, and then click BranchCache – Peer Discovery (Uses WSD). Click Next.

19. On the Predefined Rules screen, click Next.

20. On the Action screen, make sure that Allow The Connection is selected and then click Finish.

Now that you have looked at the distributed cache mode configuration, let's take a look at the hosted mode configuration.

Hosted Mode Requirements

To set up a hosted mode BranchCache configuration, you must first set up a Windows Server 2012 R2 hosted cache server at the main and branch offices. You also need Windows 7 Enterprise, Windows 7 Ultimate, Windows 8 Pro, or Windows 8 Enterprise computers at the branch offices.

The Windows 7 or Windows 8 machines download the data from the main cache server, and then the hosted cache servers at the branch offices obtain a copy of the downloaded data for other users to access.

Your network infrastructure must also allow for physical connections between the main office and the branch offices. These connections can be VPNs or some type of WAN links. After these requirements are met, your cache server must obtain a server certificate so that the client computers in the branch offices can positively identify the cache servers.

Exercise 2.3 walks you through the process of installing the BranchCache feature on a Windows Server 2012 R2 machine. To begin this exercise, you must be logged into the Windows Server 2012 R2 machine as an administrator.

EXERCISE 2.3

Installing BranchCache on Windows Server 2012 R2

1. Open Server Manager by selecting the Server Manager icon or by running `servermanager.exe`.

2. Select Add Roles And Features.

3. Select Next at the Before You Begin pane (if shown).

4. Select Role-Based Or Feature-Based Installation and select Next to continue.

5. Select the Select A Server From The Server Pool option and click Next.

6. At the Select Server Roles screen, click Next.

7.   At the Select Features screen, click the check box for BranchCache. Then click Next.

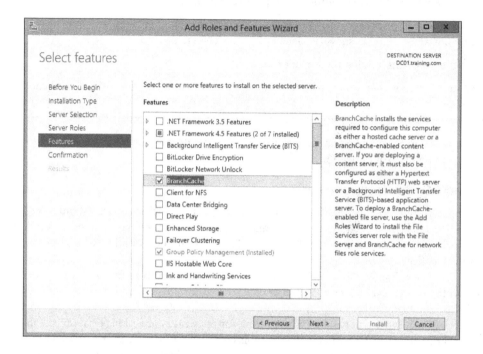

8.   Check the Restart The Destination Server If Required box and then click the Install button. If a dialog box appears about restarting, click the Yes button. The system should restart.

9.   After the system restarts, log in as the administrator.

Make sure to repeat this exercise on all branch office cache servers. One of the requirements for BranchCache is a physical connection between the main office and the branch offices.

BranchCache and PowerShell

As stated throughout this book, PowerShell is a command-line shell and scripting tool. BranchCache has many different PowerShell cmdlets that allow you to configure and maintain the BranchCache feature. Table 2.1 shows just some of the different PowerShell cmdlets for BranchCache.

TABLE 2.1   PowerShell cmdlets for BranchCache

Cmdlet	Description
Add-BCDataCache Extension	Increases the amount of cache storage space that is available on a hosted cache server by adding a new cache file
Clear-BCCache	Deletes all data in all data and hash files
Disable-BC	Disables the BranchCache service
Disable-BCDowngrading	Disables downgrading so that client computers that are running Windows 8 Consumer Preview do not request Windows 7–specific versions of content information from content servers
Enable-BCDistributed	Enables BranchCache and configures a computer to operate in distributed cache mode
Enable-BCHostedClient	Configures BranchCache to operate in hosted cache client mode
Enable-BCHostedServer	Configures BranchCache to operate in hosted cache server mode
Enable-BCLocal	Enables the BranchCache service in local caching mode
Export-BCCachePackage	Exports a cache package
Export-BCSecretKey	Exports a secret key to a file
Get-BCClient Configuration	Gets the current BranchCache client computer settings
Get-BCContent ServerConfiguration	Gets the current BranchCache content server settings
Get-BCDataCache	Gets the BranchCache data cache
Get-BCStatus	Gets a set of objects that provide BranchCache status and configuration information
Import-BCCachePackage	Imports a cache package into BranchCache
Import-BCSecretKey	Imports the cryptographic key that BranchCache uses for generating segment secrets
Set-BCAuthentication	Specifies the BranchCache computer authentication mode
Set-BCCache	Modifies the cache file configuration
Set-BCSecretKey	Sets the cryptographic key used in the generation of segment secrets

Enhanced Features in Windows Server 2012 R2 BranchCache

Microsoft continues to improve on many of the features of Windows Server, and BranchCache is no different. Microsoft has improved BranchCache in Windows Server 2012 R2 and Windows 8. The following list includes some of the enhanced features:

Office sizes and the number of branch offices are not limited. Windows Server 2012 R2 BranchCache allows any number of offices along with any number of users once an administrator deploys hosted cache mode with multiple hosted cache servers.

There are no requirements for a Group Policy object (GPO) for each office location, streamlining deployment. All that is required to deploy BranchCache is a single GPO that contains a small number of settings.

Client computer configuration is automatic. Administrators have the ability to configure their clients through the use of a Group Policy object. If this is done, client configuration will automatically be configured through the GPO, and if a client can't find a hosted cache server, the client will automatically self-configure as a hosted cache mode client.

BranchCache is deeply integrated with the Windows file server. BranchCache is automatically integrated with Windows file server technology. Because of this, the process of finding duplicate pieces in independent files is greatly improved.

Duplicate content is stored and downloaded only once. BranchCache stores only one instance of the content on a hosted cache server or content server, and because of this, you get greater disk storage savings. Since client computers at the remote offices download only one instance of any content, your network saves on additional WAN bandwidth.

Small changes to large files produce bandwidth savings. One advantage of BranchCache is the file server chunking system that helps divide files and web pages into smaller parts. Now when a file is changed, only the part of that file that has been changed gets replicated. This allows BranchCache to use lower bandwidth requirements.

Offline content creation improves performace. When BranchCache is deployed as content or file servers, the data is calculated offline before a client even has the chance to request it. Because of this, the systems get faster performance and bandwidth.

Cache encryption is enabled automatically. BranchCache stores its cached data as encrypted data. This guarantees data security without the need to encrypt the entire drive.

You can deploy multiple hosted cache servers. In Windows 7 and Windows Server 2008 R2, BranchCache was able to deploy only one hosted cache server per office location. Windows Server 2012 R2 allows you to deploy as many hosted cache servers as are needed at a location.

Configure File Classification Infrastructure Using File Server Resource Manager

The *File Server Resource Manager (FSRM)* is a suite of tools that allows an administrator to place quotas on folders or volumes, filter file types, and create detailed storage reports. These tools allow an administrator to plan and implement policies on data properly and as needed.

One of the advantages of using FSRM is all of the included features that allow administrators to manage the data that is stored on their file servers. Some of the features included with FSRM are as follows:

File Management Tasks FSRM allows an administrator to apply a policy or action to data files. Some of the actions that can be performed are encrypting files and running custom commands.

Quota Management Quotas give an administrator the ability to limit how much disk space a user can use on a file server. Administrators have the ability to limit space to an entire volume or to specific folders.

File Classification Infrastructure This feature uses rules to assign specific properties to files automatically and then performs tasks on those files based on the classification. A few examples of file classification properties are Country, Department, Birthday, and Social Security Number. The tasks performed using these classifications include restricting file access, implementing file encryption, and setting file expiration policies.

File Screening Management Administrators can set up file screening on the server and limit what types of files can be stored on that server. For example, an administrator can set a file screen on the server so that any file ending in ·bmp gets rejected.

Storage Reports Administrators can create reports that show them how data is classified and accessed. You also have the ability to see what users are trying to save unauthorized file extensions.

Installing FSRM is easy when using either Server Manager or PowerShell. To install using Server Manager, you go into Add Features and choose File And Storage Services ➢ File Services ➢ File Server Resource Manager. To install FSRM using PowerShell, use the following command:

```
Install-WindowsFeature -Name FS-Resource-Manager -IncludeManagementTools
```

Configuring FSRM using the Windows GUI version is straightforward, but setting up FSRM using PowerShell is a bit more challenging. Table 2.2 describes some of the PowerShell commands for FSRM.

TABLE 2.2 PowerShell commands for FSRM

PowerShell cmdlet	Description
Get-FsrmAutoQuota	Gets auto-apply quotas on a server
Get-FsrmClassification	Gets the status of the running file classification
Get-FsrmClassificationRule	Gets classification rules
Get-FsrmFileGroup	Gets file groups

TABLE 2.2 PowerShell commands for FSRM *(continued)*

PowerShell cmdlet	Description
Get-FsrmFileScreen	Gets file screens
Get-FsrmFileScreenException	Gets file screen exceptions
Get-FsrmQuota	Gets quotas on the server
Get-FsrmSetting	Gets the current FSRM settings
Get-FsrmStorageReport	Gets storage reports
New-FsrmAutoQuota	Creates an auto-apply quota
New-FsrmFileGroup	Creates a file group
New-FsrmFileScreen	Creates a file screen
New-FsrmQuota	Creates an FSRM quota
New-FsrmQuotaTemplate	Creates a quota template
Remove-FsrmClassificationRule	Removes classification rules
Remove-FsrmFileScreen	Removes a file screen
Remove-FsrmQuota	Removes an FSRM quota from the server
Set-FsrmFileScreen	Changes configuration settings of a file screen
Set-FsrmQuota	Changes configuration settings for an FSRM quota

Configure File Access Auditing

One of the most important aspects of controlling security in networked environments is ensuring that only authorized users are able to access specific resources. Although system administrators often spend much time managing security permissions, it is almost always possible for a security problem to occur.

Sometimes the best way to find possible security breaches is actually to record the actions that specific users take. Then, in the case of a security breach (the unauthorized shutdown of a server, for example), system administrators can examine the log to find the cause of the problem.

The Windows Server 2012 R2 operating system and Active Directory offer you the ability to audit a wide range of actions. In the following sections, you'll see how to implement auditing for Active Directory.

Overview of Auditing

The act of *auditing* relates to recording specific actions. From a security standpoint, auditing is used to detect any possible misuse of network resources. Although auditing does not necessarily prevent resources from being misused, it does help determine when security violations have occurred (or were attempted). Furthermore, just the fact that others know that you have implemented auditing may prevent them from attempting to circumvent security.

You need to complete several steps in order to implement auditing using Windows Server 2012 R2:

1. Configure the size and storage settings for the audit logs.

2. Enable categories of events to audit.

3. Specify which objects and actions should be recorded in the audit log.

Note that there are trade-offs to implementing auditing. First, recording auditing information can consume system resources. This can decrease overall system performance and use up valuable disk space. Second, auditing many events can make the audit log impractical to view. If too much detail is provided, system administrators are unlikely to scrutinize all of the recorded events. For these reasons, you should always be sure to find a balance between the level of auditing details provided and the performance-management implications of these settings.

Implementing Auditing

Auditing is not an all-or-none type of process. As is the case with security in general, system administrators must choose specifically which objects and actions they want to audit.

The main categories for auditing include the following:

Audit account logon events

Audit account management

Audit directory service access

Audit logon events

Audit object access

Audit policy change

Audit privilege use

Audit process tracking

Audit system events

In this list of categories, four of the categories are related to Active Directory. Let's discuss these auditing categories in a bit more detail.

Audit Account Logon Events   You enable this auditing event if you want to audit when a user authenticates with a domain controller and logs onto the domain. This event is logged in the security log on the domain controller.

Audit Account Management   This auditing event is used when you want to watch what changes are being made to Active Directory accounts. For example, when another administrator creates or deletes a user account, it would be an audited event.

Audit Directory Service Access   This auditing event occurs whenever a user or administrator accesses Active Directory objects. Let's say that an administrator opens Active Directory and clicks a user account; even if nothing is changed on that account, an event is logged.

Audit Logon Events   Account logon events are created for domain account activity. For example, you have a user who logs onto a server so that they can access files; the act of logging onto the server creates this audit event.

Audit Object Access   Audit object access allows you to audit objects within your network, such as folders, files, and printers. If you suspect that someone is trying to hack into an object (for example, the finance folder), this is the type of auditing you should use. You still would need to enable auditing on the actual object (the finance folder in this case).

Audit Policy Change   Audit policy change allows you to audit changes to user rights assignment policies, audit policies, or trust policies. This auditing allows you to see whether anyone changes any of the other audit policies.

Audit Privilege Use   Setting the audit privilege use allows an administrator to audit each instance of a user exercising a user right. For example, if a user changes the system time on a machine, this is a user right. Logging on locally is another common user right.

To audit access to objects stored within Active Directory, you must enable the Audit Directory Service Access option. Then you must specify which objects and actions should be tracked.

Exercise 2.4 walks you through the steps you must take to implement the auditing of Active Directory objects on domain controllers.

EXERCISE 2.4

Enabling Auditing of Active Directory Objects

1.   Open the Local Security Policy tool (located in the Administrative Tools program group).

2.   Expand Local Policies ➤ Audit Policy.

3.   Double-click the Audit Directory Service Access setting.

4.   In the Audit Directory Service Access Properties dialog box, place check marks next to Success and Failure. Click OK to save the settings.

5.   Close the Local Security Policy tool.

Viewing Auditing Information

One of the most important aspects of auditing is regularly monitoring the audit logs. If this step is ignored, as it often is in poorly managed environments, the act of auditing is useless. Fortunately, Windows Server 2012 R2 includes the *Event Viewer* tool, which allows system administrators to view audited events quickly and easily. Using the filtering capabilities of Event Viewer, you can find specific events of interest.

Exercise 2.5 walks you through the steps that you must take in order to generate some auditing events and to examine the data collected for these actions. In this exercise, you will perform some actions that will be audited, and then you will view the information recorded within the audit logs.

EXERCISE 2.5

Generating and Viewing Audit Logs

1. Open the Active Directory Users and Computers tool.

2. Within an OU that has auditing enabled, right-click a user account and select Properties.

3. In the user's account Properties dialog box, add the middle initial **A** for this user account and enter **Software Developer** in the Description box. Click OK to save the changes.

4. Close the Active Directory Users and Computers tool.

5. Open the Event Viewer tool from the Administrative Tools program group. Select the Security item under Windows Logs. You will see a list of audited events categorized under Directory Service Access. Note that you can obtain more details about a specific item by double-clicking it.

6. When you have finished viewing the security log, close the Event Viewer tool.

Using the *Auditpol.exe* Command

There may be a time when you need to look at the auditing policies set on a user or system. This is where an administrator can use the Auditpol.exe command. Auditpol not only gives administrators the ability to view an audit policy but also lets them set, configure, modify, restore, and even remove an audit policy. Auditpol is a command-line utility, and there are multiple switches that can be used with Auditpol. The following is the syntax used with Auditpol, and Table 2.3 describes some of the switches.

```
Auditpol command [<sub-command><options>]
```

Here's an example:

```
Auditpol /get /user:mrice /category:"Detailed Tracking" /r
```

TABLE 2.3   Auditpol commands

Command	Description
/backup	Allows an administrator to save the audit policy to a file
/clear	Allows an administrator to clear an audit policy
/get	Gives administrators the ability to view the current audit policy
/list	Allows you to view selectable policy elements
/remove	Removes all per-user audit policy settings and disables all system audit policy settings
/restore	Allows an administrator to restore an audit policy from a file that was previously created by using auditpol /backup
/set	Gives an administrator the ability to set an audit policy
/?	Displays help

Enhanced Features in Windows Server 2012 R2 Auditing

Auditing in Windows Server 2012 R2 and Windows 8 has been enhanced in many ways. Microsoft has increased the level of detail in the security auditing logs. Microsoft has also simplified the deployment and management of auditing policies. The following list includes some of the major enhancements:

Global Object Access Auditing   Administrators using Windows Server 2012 R2 and Windows 8 have the ability to define computer-wide system access control lists (SACLs). Administrators can define SACLs either for the file system or for the registry. After the specified SACL is defined, the SACL is then applied automatically to every object of that type. This can be helpful to administrators for verifying that all critical files, folders, and registry settings on a computer are protected. This is also helpful for identifying when an issue occurs with a system resource.

"Reason For Access" Reporting   When an administrator is performing auditing in Windows Server 2012 R2 and Windows 8, they can now see the reason why an operation was successful or unsuccessful. Previously, they lacked the ability to see the reason why an operation succeeded or failed.

Advanced Audit Policy Settings   In Windows Server 2012 R2, there are 53 advanced audit policy settings that can be used in place of the 9 basic auditing settings. These advanced audit settings also help eliminate the unnecessary auditing activities that can make audit logs difficult to manage and decipher.

Expression-Based Audit Policies   Administrators have the ability, because of Dynamic Access Control, to create targeted audit policies by using expressions based on user, computer, and resource claims. For example, an administrator has the ability to create an audit policy that tracks all Read and Write operations for files that are considered high-business impact. Expression-based audit policies can be directly created on a file or folder or created through the use of a Group Policy.

Removable Storage Device Auditing   Administrators have the ability to monitor attempts to use a removable storage device on your network. If an administrator decides to implement this policy, an audit event is created every time one of your users attempts to copy, move, or save a network resource onto a removable storage device.

Implement Dynamic Access Control

One of the advantages of Windows Server 2012 R2 is the ability to apply data governance to your file server. This will help control who has access to information and auditing. You get these advantages through the use of *Dynamic Access Control (DAC)*. Dynamic Access Control allows you to identify data by using data classifications (both automatic and manual) and then control access to these files based on these classifications.

DAC also gives administrators the ability to control file access by using a central access policy. This central access policy will also allow an administrator to set up audit access to files for reporting and forensic investigation.

DAC allows an administrator to set up Active Directory Rights Management Service (AD RMS) encryption for Microsoft Office documents. For example, you can set up encryption for any documents that contain financial information.

Dynamic Access Control gives an administrator the flexibility to configure file access and auditing to domain-based file servers. To do this, DAC controls claims in the authentication token, resource properties, and conditional expressions within permission and auditing entries.

Administrators have the ability to give users access to files and folders based on Active Directory attributes. For example, a user named Dana is given access to the file server share because in the user's Active Directory (department attribute) properties, the value contains the value Sales. Over the next few sections, you will take a deep dive into implementing Dynamic Access Control.

For DAC to function properly, an administrator must enable Windows 8 computers and Windows Server 2012 R2 file servers to support claims and compound authentication.

Configure User and Device Claim Types

Dynamic Access Control is a must-have for any corporate environment. DAC takes folder and file permissions to a whole new level by enabling more granular methods of access and authentication within Active Directory. In this section, you will focus on configuring user and device claim types. Let's start off by enabling DAC (see Exercise 2.6).

EXERCISE 2.6

Enable Dynamic Access Control

1. On a domain controller, launch Server Manager and then navigate to the Group Policy Management Console under Tools.

2. Launch Group Policy Management and navigate to Default Domain Controllers Policy.

3. Right-click Default Domain Controllers Policy and select Edit to launch the Group Policy Management Editor.

4. Within the Group Policy Management Editor, navigate to Computer Configuration ➢ Policies ➢ Administrative Templates ➢ System ➢ KDC, as shown here.

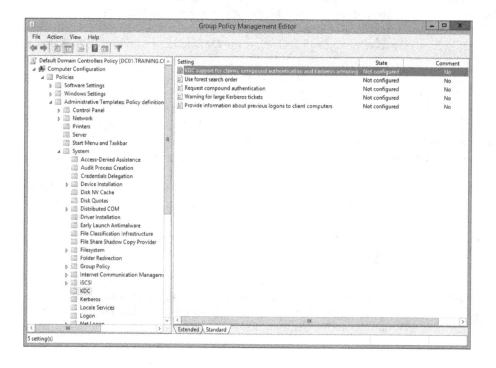

5. Double-click the KDC Support For Claims, Compound Authentication, And Kerberos Armoring policy, and select the Enabled radio button, as shown here.

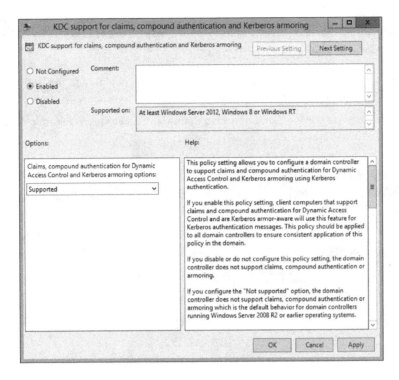

6. Click Apply and OK to save the new policy setting.

That's all there is to it. Now you are ready to take a look at user and device claims. For the next exercise, you will need to have a functional Active Directory environment populated with multiple users across multiple departments. A simple lab environment consisting of a domain controller and a domain-joined file server will be sufficient.

Now that you have successfully enabled DAC within the environment, everything is managed from the Active Directory Administrative Center on a domain controller. You can now set what's referred to as *conditions* on your environment's folder and file server hierarchy. Conditions are user or device claims that you can set. For example, you could set a condition on a folder or file that limits user access to a specific department, or you could set a condition that allows a user to view folders and files from only a specific workstation. Setting these types of conditions will make managing your environment easier, and it will do so with enhanced security. Allowing file and folder access from only domain-joined machines bars users from connecting with an unsecured personal device. Also, setting conditions based upon the Active Directory department attribute makes user access available to those files and folders based on them being in that specific department. Let's put this into practice (see Exercise 2.7).

EXERCISE 2.7

Configure User and Device Claim Types

1. On a domain controller, launch Server Manager and then navigate to the Active
   Directory Administrative Center under Tools.

2. Launch the Active Directory Administrative Center and navigate to Dynamic Access
   Control, as shown here.

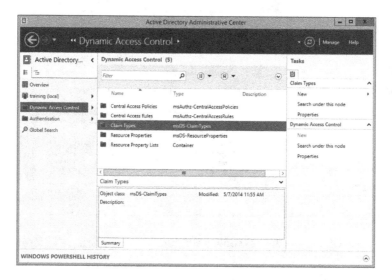

3. Select New ➢ Claim Type to open the Create Claim Type dialog box.

4. This is where you will choose what claims will be used to define permissions. You can
   filter claim types with the search field. Search for and select the Department claim type,
   as shown here. Notice how the Display Name, Description, User Claim Type, and Protect
   From Accidental Deletion fields are enabled by default.

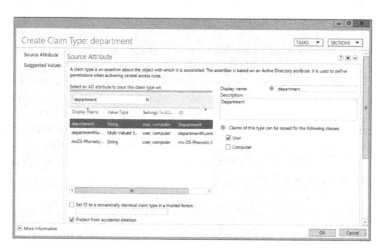

5. Click OK to finish creating the new claim type. You can now use the Active Directory department attribute as a condition for allowing access on file shares.

6. Navigate to a shared folder within the environment and open the Advanced Security Settings properties on that share.

7. Click the Add button to create a new permission entry.

8. Select a principal. A principal can be any Active Directory user or group. You must select a principal before the option Add A Condition becomes available.

9. Click Add A Condition to bring up the condition's parameters, as shown here. For this exercise, I have selected a user who belongs to the IT department. As long as that user remains in the IT department, the user will have full control over this file share.

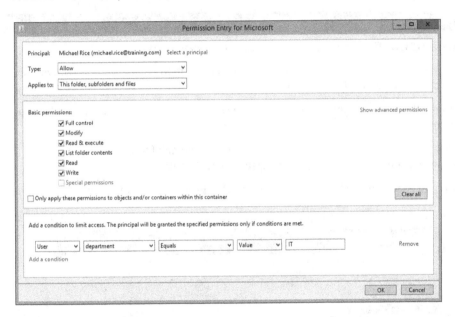

10. Click OK to save this new conditional permission entry.

That was just one example of how Dynamic Access Control can be used to control folder and file access. Spend some time configuring different user and device claims types. It is really handy to be able to change a user's department, country, or office location in Active Directory and have that change automatically affect what folders and files that user can access throughout the environment.

Create and Configure Resource Properties and Lists

Now that you have a practical understanding of configuring user and device claims, the next logical Dynamic Access Control configuration is to configure resource properties and lists. *Resource properties* are used to define additional properties that will appear on files and folders. These additional properties can be used for file access based on file classifications such as country or department. There are quite a few default resource properties already configured in DAC, and you can also create your custom resource properties as needed.

Once you have selected or created resource properties, they are added to the Global Resource Property List within DAC. The default resource properties have already been added for you. Note that any custom resource properties you create will also be added automatically to the Global Resource Property List. The list is then automatically pushed out via Group Policy and downloaded to all of the file servers within the environment. In Exercise 2.8, you will create and configure Resource Properties and Lists.

EXERCISE 2.8

Create and Configure Resource Properties and Lists

1. On a domain controller, launch Server Manager and then navigate to the Active Directory Administrative Center under Tools.

2. Launch the Active Directory Administrative Center and navigate to Dynamic Access Control.

3. Click and open Resource Properties. You will see that all of the default resource properties are listed, but they are all disabled by default.

4. Right-click and enable the Department resource property, as shown here.

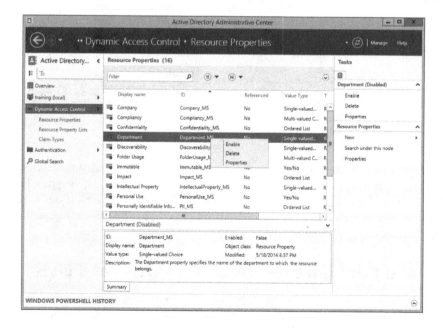

5. You'll also create a custom resource property. On the same page that you enabled the Department resource property, click New ➤ Resource Property.

6. Name the resource property **Country** and then click Add to list all of the countries that will be values of this resource property, as shown here.

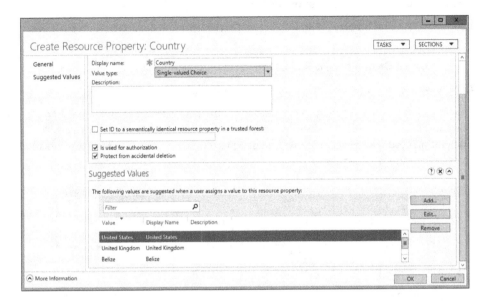

7. Click OK to create this new resource property.

8. Navigate to and open the global resource property list within the DAC management GUI to verify that both the Country and Department resource properties are enabled and ready to be downloaded to your file servers.

Now that you have defined resource properties, you can use those properties to create and configure central access rules and policies.

Create and Configure Central Access Rules and Policies

Central access rules are used to govern file and folder access based on the resource properties that have been previously defined, such as those you configured in the previous exercise. Let's say you wanted to limit access to a corporate software share to only corporate IT personnel. DAC uses central access rules and policies to accomplish this task. Once the rule has been created, Group Policy will be used to keep all of the environment's file servers up-to-date with all of your dynamic access control central access rules. Exercise 2.9 will demonstrate the configuration of Central Access Rules and Policies.

EXERCISE 2.9

Create and Configure Central Access Rules and Policies

1. On a domain controller, launch Server Manager and then navigate to the Active Directory Administrative Center under Tools.

2. Launch the Active Directory Administrative Center and navigate to Dynamic Access Control.

3. Click and open Central Access Rules. The list should be empty.

4. Click New ➢ Central Access Rule.

5. Provide a name and set proper permissions for the resource, as shown here. For this exercise, I have created a central access rule named Corporate IT Software & Installation Media Access, which will be used to limit user access to IT resources to only members of the IT department.

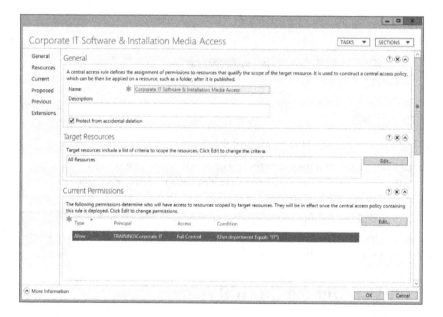

6. Click OK to create the new central access rule.

7. Navigate to and open Central Access Policies within the DAC management GUI.

8. Click New ➢ Central Access Policy. Note that a central access policy can contain multiple central access rules.

9. Name the central access policy and add the central access rule created in step 6 of this exercise. Your screen should look similar to what's shown here.

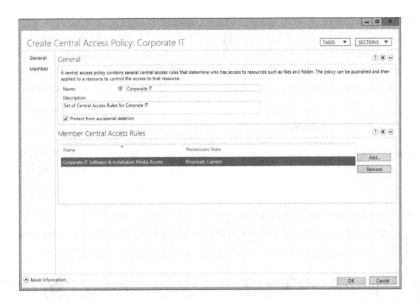

10. Now you can configure Group Policy in Active Directory to push out the new central access policy. Launch the Group Policy Manager on your domain controller and edit the default Domain Controllers Policy.

11. Drill down to Computer Configuration ➤ Policies ➤ Windows Settings ➤ Security Settings ➤ File System ➤ Central Access Policy and then right-click and select Manage Central Access Policies.

12. Add the central access policy, as shown here.

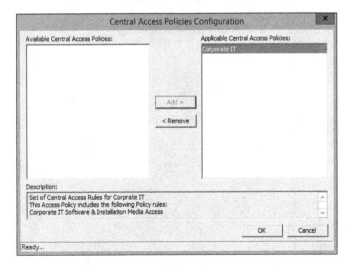

13. Click OK to save the new central access policy configuration.

By now, I'm sure you can see the power you have with Dynamic Access Control. By taking the time to configure central access rules and policies for your company's users and devices fully, you will enhance environmental security and ease of management significantly. Now that the new central access policy is applied to your environment, all you have to do to finish completely enabling DAC on your file shares is to configure file classification.

Configure File Classification

Administrators can set file classifications and then manage the data more effectively by using these classifications. By classifying files and then setting policies to those classifications, an administrator can set policies on those classifications that assist with managing environmental resources. These policies include restricting file access, file encryption, and file expirations. In Exercise 2.10, you will configure file classification through Dynamic Access Control and then test your work by using the Effective Access tab in the Advanced Security Settings of a file share.

EXERCISE 2.10

Configure File Classification

1. On a DAC-enabled file share, right-click and open Properties.

2. Select the Classification tab and enable values for both the Country and Department file classification properties, as shown here.

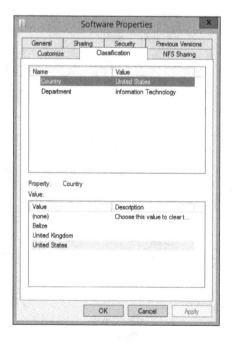

3. Click Apply to save the file classification.

4. Select the Security tab and click Advanced.

5. Select the Central Policy tab, making sure the central policy is set to the appropriate central access policy, as shown here. If you change the central access policy, make sure to click Apply before changing tabs.

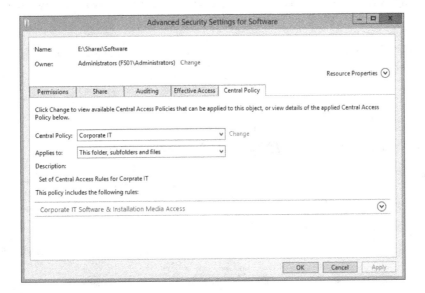

6. Select the Effective Access tab and test the effective access of a user to test your work.

Implement Policy Changes and Staging

One of the nice features of DAC is its ability to stage and test the effects of a new central access policy before actually implementing it. In Exercise 2.11, you will stage a central access policy and then test the effects of that policy on a file share.

EXERCISE 2.11

Implement Policy Stages and Staging

1. On a domain controller, launch Server Manager and then navigate to the Active Directory Administrative Center under Tools.

2. Launch the Active Directory Administrative Center and navigate to Dynamic Access Control.

3. Click Central Access Rules.

EXERCISE 2.11 *(continued)*

4. Right-click and open the properties of a central access policy.

5. Click the Proposed Permissions section, as shown here, to edit and stage the newly proposed permissions. For demonstration purposes, I have staged a policy change that would allow authenticated users to view the contents of the software library under the conditions that the user is a domain user who is logged into a domain computer.

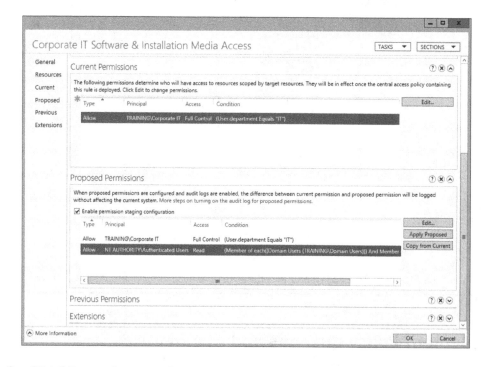

6. Click OK to set the new policy staging.

7. Switch to your file server and log in as an authenticated user.

8. Run a gpupdate /force from the command line to update the Group Policy settings on the file server.

9. As just an authenticated user, browse the share on which you staged your policy change. Notice how you have access as that authenticated user.

10. Now check the Event Viewer on the file server. Expand Windows Logs and then select Security. Under the Central Access Policy Staging task category, open the entries with Event ID 4818. You will notice how the authenticated user was allowed access to this share because of the staging policy.

11. Applying the staged policy is relatively straightforward. Switch to your domain controller and open the properties of the central access rule that was used in step 4 of this exercise. In the Proposed Permissions section, click Apply Proposed to save and enable the staged policy change, as shown here.

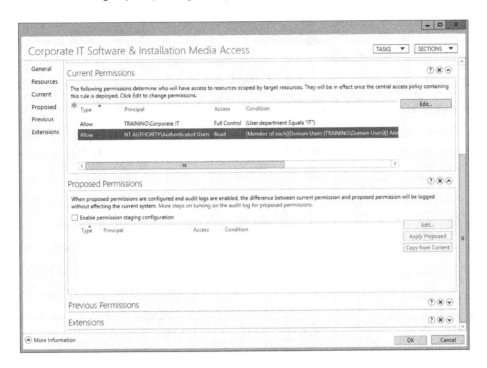

12. Verify that the current permissions reflect the applied proposed permissions and then click OK to close the Central Access Rules Properties dialog box.

Perform Access-Denied Remediation

One of the best features of Windows Server 2012 R2 is the ability to configure Access-Denied Assistance. With Access-Denied Assistance, you can set a preconfigured Windows error message to be displayed to users when they try to access resources to which they don't have proper permissions to access. The best part is that users can "request assistance" via the displayed error message. When a user requests assistance, an email notification can notify the administrator who is either on duty or on call that one of their users needs help accessing a resource. When the user requests assistance, they are provided with a dialog box that will be attached to the email sent to the administrator. Within the dialog box, the user can explain why they need access to the desired resource. In Exercise 2.12, you will configure and test Access-Denied Assistance using Group Policy.

EXERCISE 2.12

Configure Access-Denied Assistance

1. On a domain controller, launch Server Manager and then navigate to Group Policy Management under Tools.

2. Launch the Group Policy Management Tool and create a new GPO that targets both your file servers and domain-joined client machines.

3. Within the Group Policy Object Editor, navigate to Computer Configuration ➤ Policies ➤ Administrative Templates ➤ System ➤ Access-Denied Assistance and double-click Customize Message For Access Denied Errors.

4. Enable the policy, configure an access-denied message that will be displayed to users who are denied access, and check the box to enable users to request assistance, as shown here.

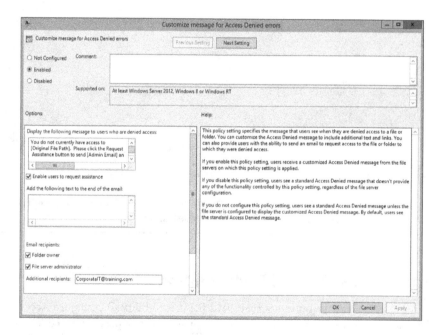

One of the great things about this policy is that it comes with preconfigured macros you can use to automate the access-denied message that will be displayed to users. Here are the four macros available within the access-denied message:

[Original File Path]: The original file path that was accessed by the user

[Original File Path Folder]: The parent folder of the original file path that was accessed by the user

[Admin Email]: The administrator email recipient list

[Data Owner Email]: The data owner email recipient list

For this exercise, I have configured the following access-denied message: "You do not currently have access to [*Original File Path*]. Please click the Request Assistance button to send [*Admin Email*] an email requesting assistance."

5. Click OK to save and close the policy.

6. Invoke the Enable Access-Denied Assistance On Client For All File Types policy here as well.

7. Launch the File Server Resource Manager on one of your file servers to configure the email notification settings for the access-denied assistance email service.

8. Within the File Server Resource Manager, click Configure Options to configure the SMTP server and email addresses that will be used for access-denied assistance email notifications, as shown here.

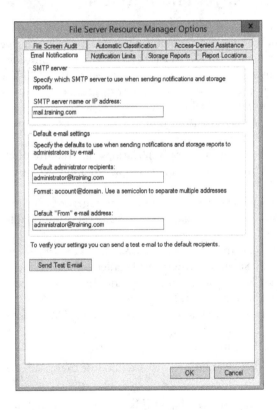

9. Click the Send Test Email button to verify your settings.

10. Click OK to save the configuration.

11. Test your work by trying to access a resource as a user who does not have permission for that resource and then use the Request Assistance feature to ask for help.

Configure and Optimize Storage

Disk storage is a requirement for just about every computer and application used in any corporate environment. Administrators have some familiarity with storage, whether it is internal storage, a locally attached set of disks, or network attached storage (NAS). In this section, you will examine the various aspects of Windows Server 2012 R2 file and storage solutions. Though I'll discuss the various types of file and storage technologies, this section will primarily focus on iSCSI because of the native features in Windows Server 2012 R2. You will also look at some of the advanced configuration options of implementing thin provisioning and trim, managing server free space, and configuring tiered storage.

Configure iSCSI Target and Initiator

Internet Small Computer System Interface (iSCSI) is an Internet protocol used to establish and manage a connection between a computer (initiator) and a storage device (target). It does this by using a connection through TCP port 3260, which allows it to be used over a LAN, a WAN, or the Internet. Each initiator is identified by its iSCSI Qualified Name (iqn), and it is used to establish its connection to an iSCSI target.

iSCSI was developed to allow block-level access to a storage device over a network. This is different from using a NAS device that connects through the use of Common Internet File System (CIFS) or NFS.

Block-level access is important to many applications that require direct access to storage. Microsoft Exchange and Microsoft SQL are examples of applications that require direct access to storage.

By being able to leverage the existing network infrastructure, iSCSI was also developed as an alternative to Fibre Channel storage by alleviating the additional hardware costs associated with a Fibre Channel storage solution.

iSCSI also has another advantage over Fibre Channel in that it can provide security for the storage devices. iSCSI can use Microsoft Challenge Handshake Authentication Protocol (CHAP or MS-CHAP) for authentication and Internet Protocol Security (IPsec) for encryption. Windows Server 2012 R2 is able to connect an iSCSI storage device out of the box with no additional software needing to be installed. This is because the Microsoft iSCSI initiator is built into the operating system.

Windows Server 2012 R2 supports two different ways to initiate an iSCSI session:

- Through the native Microsoft iSCSI software initiator that resides on Windows Server 2012 R2
- Using a hardware iSCSI host bus adapter (HBA) that is installed in the computer

Both the Microsoft iSCSI software initiator and iSCSI HBA present an iSCSI qualified name that identifies the host initiator. When the Microsoft iSCSI software initiator is used, the CPU utilization may be as much as 30 percent higher than on a computer with a hardware iSCSI HBA. This is because all of the iSCSI process requests are handled within the operating system. Using a hardware iSCSI HBA, process requests can be offloaded to the adapter, thus freeing the CPU overhead associated with the Microsoft iSCSI software initiator. However, iSCSI HBAs can be expensive, whereas the Microsoft iSCSI software initiator is free.

It is worthwhile installing the Microsoft iSCSI software initiator and performing load testing to see how much overhead the computer will have prior to purchasing an iSCSI HBA or HBAs, depending on the redundancy level. Exercise 2.13 explains how to install and configure an iSCSI connection.

EXERCISE 2.13

Configuring iSCSI Storage Connection

1. Press the Windows key or the Start button in the lower-left corner and select Administrative Tools ➤ iSCSI Initiator.

2. If a dialog box appears, click Yes to start the service.

3. Click the Discovery tab.

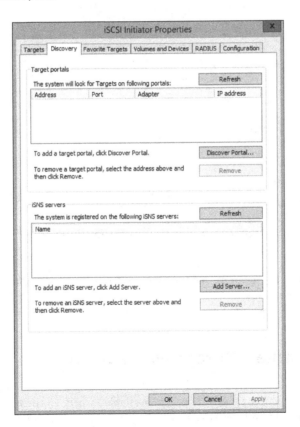

4. In the Target Portals portion of the page, click Discover Portal.

EXERCISE 2.13 *(continued)*

5.   Enter the IP address of the target portal and click OK.

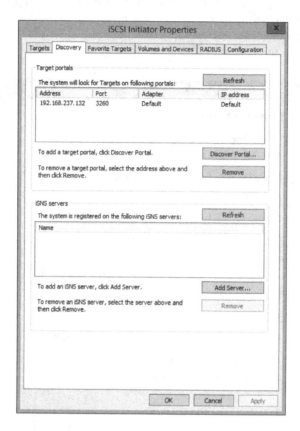

6.   The IP address of the target portal appears in the Target Portals box.

7.   Click OK.

To use the storage that has now been presented to the server, you must create a volume on it and format the space.

Configure Internet Storage Name Server

Internet Storage Name Service (iSNS) allows for the central registration of an iSCSI environment because it automatically discovers available targets on the network. The purpose of iSNS is to help find available targets on a large iSCSI network.

The Microsoft iSCSI initiator includes an iSNS client that is used to register with the iSNS. The iSNS feature maintains a database of clients that it has registered either through DCHP discovery or through manual registration. iSNS DHCP is available after the installation of the service, and it is used to allow iSNS clients to discover the location of the iSNS. However, if iSNS DHCP is not configured, iSNS clients must be registered manually with the `iscsicli` command.

To execute the command, launch a command prompt on a computer hosting the Microsoft iSCSI and type **`iscsicli addisnsserver server_name`**, where `server_name` is the name of the computer hosting iSNS. Exercise 2.14 walks you through the steps required to install the iSNS feature on Windows Server 2012 R2, and then it explains the different tabs in iSNS.

EXERCISE 2.14

Installing the iSNS Feature on Windows Server 2012 R2

1. Open Server Manager.

2. Launch the Add Roles And Features Wizard.

3. Choose role-based or featured-based installation and click Next.

4. Choose your server and click Next.

5. Click Next at the Roles screen.

6. At the Select Features screen, choose the iSNS Server Service check box. Click Next.

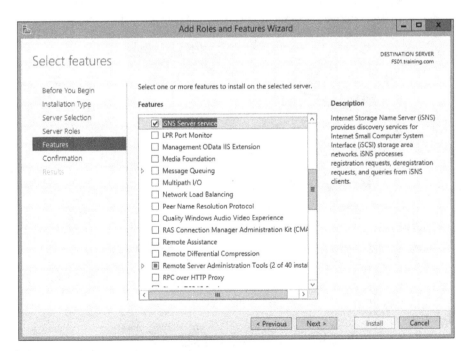

EXERCISE 2.14 *(continued)*

7. At the Confirmation screen, click the Install button.

8. Click the Close button. Close Server Manager and reboot.

9. Log in and open the iSNS server under Administrative Tools.

10. Click the General tab. This tab displays the list of registered initiators and targets. In addition to their iSCSI qualified names, it lists storage node type (Target or Initiator), alias string, and entity identifier (the fully qualified domain name [FQDN] of the machine hosting the iSNS client).

11. Click the Discovery Domains tab. The purpose of discovery domains is to provide a way to separate and group nodes. This is similar to zoning in Fibre Channel.

    The following options are available on the Discovery Domains tab:

    Create creates a new discovery domain.

    Refresh repopulates the Discovery Domain drop-down list.

    Delete deletes the currently selected discovery domain.

    Add adds nodes that are already registered in iSNS to the currently selected discovery domain.

    Add New adds nodes by entering the iSCSI qualified name of the node. These nodes do not have to be currently registered.

    Remove Used removes selected nodes from the discovery domain.

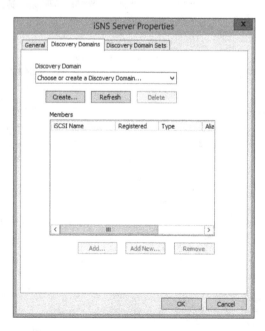

12. Click the Discovery Domain Sets tab. The purpose of discovery domain sets is to separate further discovery domains. Discovery domains can be enabled or disabled, giving administrators the ability to restrict further the visibility of all initiators and targets.

The options on the Discovery Domain Sets tab are as follows:

The *Enable* check box indicates the status of the discovery domain sets and turns them off and on.

Create creates new discovery domain sets.

Refresh repopulates the Discovery Domain Sets drop-down list.

Delete deletes the currently selected discovery domain set.

Add adds discovery domains to the currently selected discovery domain set.

Remove removes selected nodes from the discovery domain sets.

13. Close the iSNS server.

Implement Thin Provisioning and Trim

Thin provisioning and trim can be useful features that allow organizations to get the most out of their storage arrays. These solutions apply directly to a virtualized environment using virtual disks that are thin provisioned.

Thin provisioning is a way of providing what is known as just-in-time allocations. Blocks of data are written to disk only as they are used instead of zeroing out all of the blocks of data that have been allocated to the virtual disk configuration. Thin provisioning is tricky to manage properly because you could easily find yourself in a position where you have an over-provisioned environment because of over-allocation.

For example, you have 100 VMs that are all provisioned with 40GB thin-provisioned virtual disks. Each VM is currently utilizing only 20GB of the total 40GB that has been allocated. The problem is that you have only 2TB worth of storage. Without realizing it, you've over-provisioned your environment by 200 percent because of thin provisioning.

This is where trim comes in to help us manage thin provisioning. *Trim* automatically reclaims free space that is not being used. In addition to trim, Windows Server 2012 R2 provides standardized notifications that will alert administrators when certain storage thresholds are crossed.

Manage Server Free Space Using Features on Demand

Features on Demand was first introduced in Windows Server 2012. This feature lets you conserve disk space within the environment by installing only basic operating system components with every new installation of a Windows Server 2012 R2 or Windows 8 machine. Instead of loading unnecessary payload files, those files are stored in a central repository and used as needed to install roles and features. When I talk about *payload files*, I am talking about the binaries for all permissions, settings, and components of a feature. Features on Demand gives you the ability not only to disable Windows Server features but also to remove all of the payloads. This lets administrators keep a tighter security footprint at the operating system level, which is similar to a Server Core installation but without the limitation of not being able to control which source files are loaded during operating system installation.

Configure Tiered Storage

Tiered storage is an excellent new feature in Windows Server 2012 R2 that gives administrators the ability to use solid-state drives (SSDs) and conventional hard-disk drives (HDDs) within the same storage pool. You can configure virtual disks that span SSD and HDD tiers, which are presented as a single LUN. One of the really nice things about this feature is that with Windows Server 2012 R2, data is automatically saved to either an SSD or an HDD based on actual usage within the environment. Most frequently accessed data is stored on an SSD, and the less frequently accessed data is stored on an HDD.

Quite a few organizations these days use some sort of charge-back or show-back application to track and even charge for hosted solutions and services. Having the capability to tier storage gives users more options in selecting a plan that works for them. It also makes it possible for administrators to keep high I/O servers and applications on faster and better-performing drives without having to move data manually across multiple tiers of storage.

Summary

In this chapter, I discussed how configuring file and storage solutions can be highly effective within your organization. You now have a better understanding of how Windows Server 2012 R2 can provide you with extended functionality for effectively controlling corporate data. Quite a few of these solutions are essential to managing a Windows Server environment to the best of your ability. Take the time to complete each exercise thoroughly until you are comfortable with performing the majority of these tasks without documentation.

You learned how to configure and test some of the great features provided by Dynamic Access Control. Many of the exam questions will involve using both DAC and FSRM to manage and control shared resources. You will also want to focus heavily on auditing capabilities and the storage solutions talked about throughout the chapter. Configure and test the full extent of all of these applications and solutions to prepare appropriately for the exam.

Exam Essentials

Understand the purpose and function of auditing.   Auditing helps determine the cause of security violations and helps troubleshoot permissions-related problems. Configure and test the effects of auditing within a file share hierarchy in a lab environment.

Know storage technologies.   Understand how to use the Fibre Channel, iSCSI, and NAS storage technologies. Know how to configure an iSCSI initiator and how to establish a connection to a target. Practice configuring tiered storage and using thin provisioning and trim.

Understand the features and functionality of BranchCache.   BranchCache helps eliminate the problems of slow access and bandwidth issues when sharing data across multiple, geographically disparate locations. By syncing and caching data between sites, users can use company-wide shared resources more efficiently when slower site links exist between site locations.

Know how to configure Dynamic Access Control.   DAC has a wide array of features and functionality that will make an administrator's job of controlling file and folder access much easier. It will also provide tighter data security and data classification throughout the environment.

Understand file classification.   File classification is used when an administrator needs to manage and control both the type and the amount of data that is stored on their servers. You can use both Dynamic Access Control and the File Sever Resource Manager to implement file classification.

Review Questions

1. LaDonna is a system administrator for an Active Directory environment that is running in Native mode. Recently, several managers have reported suspicions about user activities and have asked her to increase security in the environment. Specifically, the requirements are as follows:

   - The accessing of certain sensitive files must be logged.

   - Modifications to certain sensitive files must be logged.

   - System administrators must be able to provide information about which users accessed sensitive files and when they were accessed.

   - All logon attempts for specific shared machines must be recorded.

   Which of the following steps should LaDonna take to meet these requirements? (Choose all that apply.)

   A. Enable auditing with the Computer Management tool.

   B. Enable auditing using the Group Policy Management Console.

   C. Enable auditing with the Active Directory Domains and Trusts tool.

   D. Enable auditing with the Event Viewer tool.

   E. View the audit log using the Event Viewer tool.

   F. View auditing information using the Computer Management tool.

   G. Enable failure and success auditing settings for specific files stored on NTFS volumes.

   H. Enable failure and success auditing settings for logon events on specific computer accounts.

2. What is the default TCP port for iSCSI?

   A. 3260

   B. 1433

   C. 21

   D. 3389

3. You create a GPO and link it to the Engineering OU. You want to monitor users in the Engineering OU who connect to the file server. What type of auditing do you enable?

   A. Audit object access

   B. Audit system events

   C. Audit logon events

   D. Audit process tracking

4. You have been hired by a small company to implement new Windows Server 2012 R2 systems. The company wants you to set up a server for users' home folder locations. What type of server would you be setting up?

A. File server

B. Web server

C. Exchange server

D. PDC server

5. Your company has decided to implement a Windows 2012 R2 server. The company IT manager before you always used FAT32 as the system partition. Your company wants to know whether it should move to NTFS. Which of the following are some advantages of NTFS? (Choose all that apply.)

A. Security

B. Quotas

C. Compression

D. Encryption

6. What command would be used to register an iSCSI initiator manually to an iSNS server?

A. `iscsicli refreshisnsserver server_name`

B. `iscsicli listisnsservers server_name`

C. `iscsicli removeisnsserver server_name`

D. `iscsicli addisnsserver server_name`

7. You are a server administrator, and you are trying to save hard drive space on your Windows Server 2012 R2 machine. Which feature can help you save hard disk space?

A. Features On Demand

B. `HDSaver.exe`

C. WinRM

D. ADDS

8. You are an IT administrator who manages an environment that runs multiple Windows Server 2012 R2 servers from multiple site locations across the United States. Your Windows Server 2012 R2 machines use iSCSI storage. Other administrators report it is difficult to locate available iSCSI resources on the network. You need to make sure other administrators can easily access iSCSI resources using a centralized repository. What feature should you deploy?

A. The iSCSI Target Storage Provider feature

B. The Windows Standards-Based Storage Management feature

C. The iSCSI Target Server role feature

D. The iSNS Server service feature

9. Your company is headquartered in Colorado Springs and has a remote site location in Tampa. The Colorado Spring office has a file server named FS01. FS01 has the BranchCache for Network Files role service installed. Your Tampa Office has a file server named FS02. FS02 has been configured as a BranchCache hosted cache server. You need to preload the data from the file shares on FS01 to the cache on FS02. You have already generated hashes for the file shares on FS01. Which cmdlet should you run next?

    A. Export-BCCachePackage

    B. Publish-BCFileContent

    C. Set-BCCache

    D. Add-BCDataCacheExtension

10. You have a Windows Server 2012 R2 file server named FS01. FS01 has the File Server Resource Manager role service installed. You attempt to delete a classification property, and you receive the error message "The classification property is in use and cannot be deleted." You need to delete the Contains Personal Information classification property. What should you do?

    A. Clear the Contains Personal Information classification property value for all files.

    B. Delete the classification rule that is assigned the Contains Personal Information classification property.

    C. Disable the classification rule that is assigned the Contains Personal Information classification property.

    D. Set files that have a Contains Personal Information classification property value of Yes to No.

Chapter

3

Implement Business Continuity and Disaster Recovery

THE FOLLOWING 70-412 EXAM OBJECTIVES ARE COVERED IN THIS CHAPTER:

✓ **Configure and manage backups**

- Configure Windows Server backups
- Configure Windows Azure backups
- Configure role-specific backups
- Manage VSS settings using VSSAdmin

✓ **Recover Servers**

- Restore from backups
- Perform a Bare Metal Restore (BMR)
- Recover servers using Windows Recovery Environment (Win RE) and safe mode
- Configure the Boot Configuration Data (BCD) store

✓ **Configure site-level fault tolerance**

- Configure Hyper-V Replica including Hyper-V Replica Broker and VMs
- Configure multi-site clustering including network settings, Quorum, and failover settings
- Configure Hyper-V Replica extended replication
- Configure Global Update Manager
- Recover a multi-site failover cluster

Throughout this book, I have stressed the importance of setting up your network properly. Once your network is set up and running properly, your users will get the most functionality out of the network. Your users will also become dependent on the network. Try taking a network offline for even 10 minutes, and your users will scream and complain.

Now that you have your users hooked, you must protect the network and the data. If your company loses their data, can they survive? Probably not. Most companies would go bankrupt if they lost all of their data and had no way to recover it. Data protection and recoverability is one of the most critical jobs you have as an administrator.

It is important to have multiple servers available to provide backup in case of a problem. The same goes for Active Directory itself—it too should be backed up. This way, if there is a massive disaster after which you need to restore your directory services, you will have that option available to you.

The process of reformatting a computer from scratch after a catastrophic system failure is a bare-metal restore and usually involves reinstalling the operating system and all of the system software.

In this chapter, you will learn about all the different ways to protect and recover your system.

Protecting the System

One of the worst events you will experience is a computer that won't boot. But far worse is discovering that there is no recent backup for that computer.

The first step in preparing for disaster recovery is to expect that a disaster will happen at some point and to take proactive measures to plan for recovery before the failure occurs. Here are some of the preparations you can make:

- Keep your computer up-to-date with Windows Update.

- Perform regular system backups.

- Use current software to scan for malware (such as viruses, spyware, and adware) and make sure you have the most recent updates.

- Perform regular administrative functions, such as monitoring the logs in the Event Viewer utility.

If you can't start Windows Server 2012 R2, you can use several options and utilities to identify and resolve Windows errors. The following is a broad list of troubleshooting options:

- If you have recently made a change to your computer's configuration by installing a new device driver or application and Windows Server 2012 R2 will not load properly, you can use the Last Known Good Configuration, roll back the driver, or use System Restore to restore a previous system configuration.

- If you can boot your computer to Safe Mode and you suspect you have a system conflict, you can temporarily disable an application or processes, troubleshoot services, or uninstall software.

- If your computer will not boot to Safe Mode, you can use the Startup Repair tool to replace corrupted system files.

- If necessary, you can use the Windows Server Backup utility to restore files from backup media and to restore a complete image of your computer.

To safeguard your server, one of the most important functions is to protect Active Directory. Active Directory is the heart and soul of a Microsoft network, and losing your data would be a catastrophic event. So, let's start by discussing how to protect Active Directory.

Backup and Recovery of Active Directory

If you have deployed Active Directory in your network environment, your users now depend on it to function properly in order to do their jobs. From network authentications to file access to print and web services, Active Directory has become a mission-critical component of your business. Therefore, the importance of backing up the Active Directory data store should be evident.

As I discussed in earlier chapters, it is important to have multiple domain controllers available to provide backup in case of a problem. The same goes for Active Directory itself—it too should be backed up by being saved. This way, if a massive disaster occurs in which you need to restore your directory services, you will have that option available to you.

Backups are just good common sense, but here are several specific reasons to back up data:

Protect Against Hardware Failures   Computer hardware devices have finite lifetimes, and all hardware eventually fails. I discussed this when I mentioned MTBF earlier in the book. *Mean Time Between Failures (MTBF)* is the average time a device will function before it actually fails. There is also a rating derived from benchmark testing of hard disk devices that tells you when you may be at risk for an unavoidable disaster. Some types of failures, such as corrupted hard disk drives, can result in significant data loss.

Protect Against Accidental Deletion or Modification of Data   Although the threat of hardware failures is real, in most environments mistakes in modifying or deleting data are much more common. For example, suppose a system administrator accidentally deletes all of the objects within a specific OU. Clearly, it's important to be able to retrieve this information from a backup.

Keep Historical Information   Users and system administrators sometimes modify files and then later find out that they require access to an older version of the file. Or a file is accidentally deleted, and a user does not discover that fact until much later. By keeping multiple backups over time, you can recover information from prior backups when necessary.

Protect Against Malicious Deletion or Modification of Data   Even in the most secure environments, it is conceivable that unauthorized users (or authorized ones with malicious intent!) could delete or modify information. In such cases, the loss of data might require valid backups from which to restore critical information.

Windows Server 2012 R2 includes a Backup utility that is designed to back up operating system files and the Active Directory data store. It allows for basic backup functionality, such as scheduling backup jobs and selecting which files to back up. Figure 3.1 shows the main screen of the Windows Server 2012 R2 Backup utility.

FIGURE 3.1   The main screen of the Windows Server 2012 R2 Backup utility

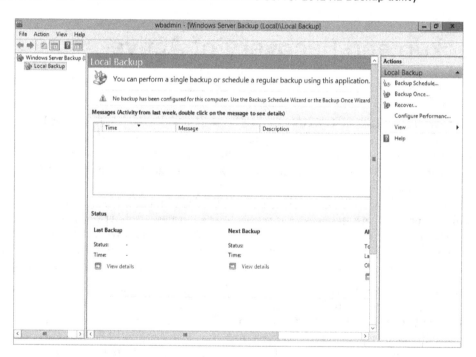

In the following sections, you'll learn about the details of using the Windows Server 2012 R2 Backup utility and how you can restore Active Directory when problems do occur.

Overview of the Windows Server 2012 R2 Backup Utility

Although the general purpose behind performing backup operations—protecting information—is straightforward, system administrators must consider many options when determining the optimal backup-and-recovery scenario for their environment. Factors include what to back up, how often to back up, and when the backups should be performed.

In this section, you'll see how the Windows Server 2012 R2 Backup utility makes it easy to implement a backup plan for many network environments.

> Although the Windows Server 2012 R2 Backup utility provides the basic functionality required to back up your files, you may want to investigate third-party products that provide additional functionality. These applications can provide options for specific types of backups (such as those for Exchange Server and SQL Server) as well as disaster recovery options, networking functionality, centralized management, and support for more advanced hardware.

Backup Types

One of the most important issues you will have to deal with when you are performing backups is keeping track of which files you have backed up and which files you need to back up. Whenever a backup of a file is made, the archive bit for the file is set. You can view the attributes of system files by right-clicking them and selecting Properties. By clicking the Advanced button in the Properties dialog box, you will access the Advanced Attributes dialog box. Here you will see the option Folder Is Ready For Archiving. Figure 3.2 shows an example of the attributes for a folder.

FIGURE 3.2   Viewing the archive attributes for a folder

Although it is possible to back up all of the files in the file system during each backup operation, it's sometimes more convenient to back up only selected files (such as those that have changed since the last backup operation). When performing backups, you can back up to removable media (DVD) or to a network location.

It is recommended by Microsoft to do a backup to a network location. The reason for this is that if your company suffers from a disaster (fire, hurricane, and so forth), your data can all still be lost—including the backup. If you back up to a removable media source, a copy of the backup can be taken offsite. This protects against a major disaster.

 Although Windows Server 2012 R2 does not support all of these backup types, it's important to understand the most common backup types. Most administrators use third-party software for their backups. That's why it's important to know all of the different types.

Several types of backups can be performed:

Normal Normal backups (also referred to as *system* or *full backups*) back up all of the selected files and then mark them as backed up. This option is usually used when a full system backup is made. Windows Server 2012 R2 supports this backup.

Copy *Copy backups* back up all of the selected files but do not mark them as backed up. This is useful when you want to make additional backups of files for moving files offsite or you want to make multiple copies of the same data for archival purposes.

Incremental *Incremental backups* copy any selected files that are marked as ready for backup (typically because they have not been backed up or they have been changed since the last backup) and then mark the files as backed up. When the next incremental backup is run, only the files that are not marked as having been backed up are stored. Incremental backups are used in conjunction with normal (full) backups.

The most common backup process is to make a full backup and then make subsequent incremental backups. The benefit to this method is that only files that have changed since the last full or incremental backup will be stored. This can reduce backup times and disk or tape storage space requirements.

When recovering information from this type of backup method, a system administrator must first restore the full backup and then restore each of the incremental backups.

Differential *Differential backups* are similar in purpose to incremental backups with one important exception: Differential backups copy all files that are marked for backup but do not mark the files as backed up. When restoring files in a situation that uses normal and differential backups, you need only restore the normal backup and the latest differential backup.

Daily *Daily backups* back up all of the files that have changed during a single day. This operation uses the file time/date stamps to determine which files should be backed up and does not mark the files as having been backed up.

Backing Up System State Data

When you are planning to back up and restore Active Directory, be aware that the most important component is known as the *system state data*. System state data includes the components upon which the Windows Server 2012 R2 operating system relies for normal operations. The Windows Server 2012 R2 Backup utility offers you the ability to back up the system state data to another type of media (such as a hard disk or network share).

Specifically, it will back up the following components for a Windows Server 2012 R2 domain controller:

Active Directory   The *Active Directory data store* is at the heart of Active Directory. It contains all of the information necessary to create and manage network resources, such as users and computers. In most environments that use Active Directory, users and system administrators rely on the proper functioning of these services in order to do their jobs.

Boot Files   *Boot files* are the files required for booting the Windows Server 2012 R2 operating system and can be used in the case of boot file corruption.

COM+ Class Registration Database   The *COM+ class registration database* is a listing of all the COM+ class registrations stored on the computer. Applications that run on a Windows Server 2012 R2 computer might require the registration of various share code components. As part of the system state backup process, Windows Server 2012 R2 stores all of the information related to Component Object Model+ (COM+) components so that it can be quickly and easily restored.

Registry   The Windows Server 2012 R2 *registry* is a central repository of information related to the operating system configuration (such as desktop and network settings), user settings, and application settings. Therefore, the registry is absolutely vital to the proper functioning of Windows Server 2012 R2.

Sysvol Directory   The *Sysvol directory* includes data and files that are shared between the domain controllers within an Active Directory domain. Many operating system services rely on this information in order to function properly.

Bare-Metal Backups and Restores

One of the options you have in Windows Server 2012 R2 is to do a *bare-metal restore (BMR)*. This is a restore of a machine after the machine has been completely wiped out and formatted. This type of restore is done usually after a catastrophic machine failure or crash.

Windows Server 2012 R2 gives you the ability to back up all of the files needed for a bare-metal restore by choosing the Bare Metal Recovery check box (see Figure 3.3).

FIGURE 3.3   Bare Metal Recovery option

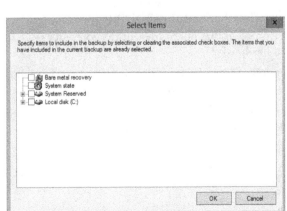

When you choose the Bare Metal Recovery option in Windows Server 2012 R2, all of the suboptions (System State, System Reserved, and Local Disk) automatically get checked.

When preparing your network for a bare-metal backup, you want to make sure you have everything you need on hand to complete this type of restore. You may want to keep a copy of the server software, server drivers, and so forth, on hand and ready to go, just in case you have to do a full restore.

Scheduling Backups

In addition to specifying which files to back up, you can schedule backup jobs to occur at specific times. Planning *when* to perform backups is just as important as deciding *what* to back up. Performing backup operations can reduce overall system performance; therefore, you should plan to back up information during times of minimal activity on your servers.

To add a backup operation to the schedule, you can simply click the Add button in the Specify Backup Time window.

Restoring System State Data

In some cases, the Active Directory data store or other system state data may become corrupt or unavailable. This could be because of many different reasons. A hard disk failure might, for example, result in the loss of data. Or the accidental deletion of an OU and all of its objects might require a restore operation to be performed.

The actual steps involved in restoring system state data are based on the details of what has caused the data loss and what effect this data loss has had on the system. In the best-case scenario, the system state data is corrupt or inaccurate, but the operating system can still boot. If this is the case, all you must do is boot into a special *Directory Services Restore Mode (DSRM)* and then restore the system state data from a backup. DSRM is available only on a domain controller. This process will replace the current system state data with that from the backup. Therefore, any changes that have been made since the last backup will be completely lost and must be redone.

In a worst-case scenario, all of the information on a server has been lost or a hardware failure is preventing the machine from properly booting. If this is the case, here are the steps you must take in order to recover system state data:

1. Fix any hardware problem that might prevent the computer from booting (for example, replace any failed hard disks).

2. Reinstall the Windows Server 2012 R2 operating system. This should be performed like a regular installation on a new system.

3. Reinstall any device drivers that may be required by your backup device. If you backed up information to the file system, this will not apply.

4. Restore the system state data using the Windows Server 2012 R2 Backup utility. When restoring the system state data on a domain controller, you must specify either an authoritative or nonauthoritative restore.

I'll cover the technical details of performing restores later in this chapter. For now, however, you should understand the importance of backing up information and, whenever possible, testing the validity of backups.

Backing Up and Restoring Group Policy Objects

Group Policy objects (GPOs) are a major part of Active Directory. When you back up Active Directory, GPOs can also get backed up. You also have the ability to back up GPOs through the Group Policy Management Console (GPMC). This gives you the ability to back up and restore individual GPOs.

To back up all GPOs, open the GPMC and right-click the Group Policy Objects container. You will see the option Back Up All. After you choose this option, a wizard will start asking you for the backup location. Choose a location and click Backup.

To back up an individual GPO, right-click the GPO (in the Group Policy Objects container) and choose Backup. Again, after you choose this option, a wizard will start asking you for the backup location. Choose a location and click Backup.

To restore a GPO, it's the same process, except instead of choosing Backup, you will choose either Manage Backups (to restore all GPOs) or Restore (for an individual GPO).

Configure the Boot Configuration Data Store

BCDEdit is another great command-line utility that is used primarily for managing boot configuration data (BCD) stores. A *BCD store* is a set of configuration files that describe an operating system's boot applications and settings. These files essentially replace the Boot.ini file in your local Windows directory. You will notice that the BCDEdit command-line utility is similar to the Bootcfg.exe utility used in earlier versions of Windows operating systems. You can effectively use BCDEdit to create new boot parameters for your Windows boot loader, modify the existing BCD stores, and create new BCD stores as needed. Please note that administrative permissions are required to use BCDEdit to modify a BCD store.

Setting Up an Active Directory Backup

The Windows Server 2012 R2 Backup utility makes it easy to back up the system data (including Active Directory) as part of a normal backup operation. I've already covered the ideas behind the different backup types and why and when they are used.

Exercise 3.1 walks you through the process of backing up the domain controller. To complete this exercise, the local machine must be a domain controller, and you must have a DVD burner or network location to back up the system state.

The Windows Server 2012 R2 Backup utility is not installed by default. If you have already installed the Windows Server 2012 R2 Backup utility, skip to step 9.

EXERCISE 3.1

Backing Up Active Directory

1. To install the Windows Server 2012 R2 Backup utility, press the Windows key and select Administrative Tools ➤ Server Manager.

2. In the center console, click the Add Roles And Features link.

3. At the Select Installation Type screen, choose a role-based or feature-based installation and click Next.

4. The Select Destination Server screen appears. Choose Select A Server From The Server Pool and choose your server under Server Pool. Click Next.

5. Click Next at the Select Server Roles screen.

6. At the Select Features screen, scroll down and check the box next to Windows Server Backup. Click Next.

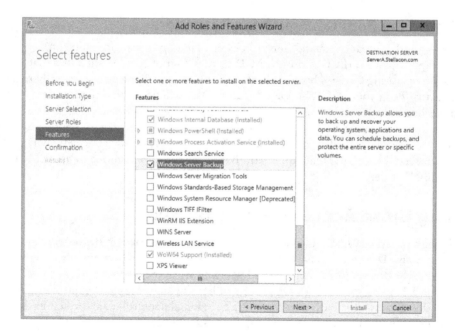

7. At the Confirmation screen, click the check box to restart the destination server automatically. This will bring up a dialog box. Click Yes and then click the Install button.

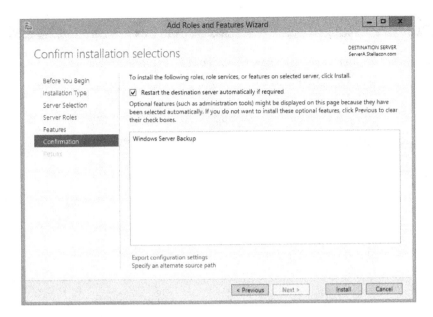

8. Click the Close button when finished. Close Server Manager.

9. Open Windows Backup by pressing the Windows key and selecting Administrative Tools
    ➤ Windows Server Backup.

10. On the left side, click Local Backup. Then, under Actions, click Backup Once.

11. When the Backup Once Wizard appears, click Different Options and click Next.

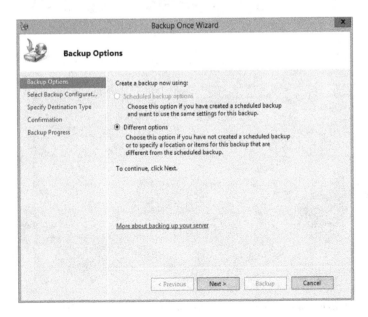

EXERCISE 3.1 *(continued)*

12. At the Select Backup Configuration screen, choose Custom and click Next.

13. Click the Add Items button. Choose System State and click OK. Click Next.

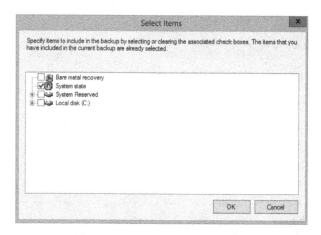

14. At the Specify Destination Type, choose Remote Shared Folder. Click Next.

15. Put in the shared path you want to use and click Next.

16. At the Confirmation screen, click the Backup button.

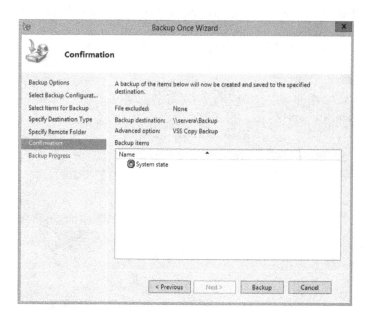

17. Once the backup is complete, close the Windows Server Backup utility.

Restoring Active Directory

Active Directory has been designed with fault tolerance in mind. For example, it is highly recommended by Microsoft that each domain have at least two domain controllers. Each of these domain controllers contains a copy of the Active Directory data store. Should one of the domain controllers fail, the available one can take over the failed server's functionality. When the failed server is repaired, it can then be promoted to a domain controller in the existing environment. This process effectively restores the failed domain controller without incurring any downtime for end users because all of the Active Directory data is replicated to the repaired server in the next scheduled replication.

In some cases, you might need to restore Active Directory from a backup. For example, suppose a system administrator accidentally deletes several hundred users from the domain and does not realize it until the change has been propagated to all of the other domain controllers. Manually re-creating the accounts is not an option because the objects' security identifiers will be different (and all permissions must be reset). Clearly, a method for restoring from backup is the best solution. You can elect to make the Active Directory restore authoritative or nonauthoritative, as described in the following sections.

Overview of Authoritative Restore

Restoring Active Directory and other system state data is an important process should system files or the Active Directory data store become corrupt or otherwise unavailable. Fortunately, the Windows Server 2012 R2 Backup utility allows you to restore data easily from a backup, should the need arise.

I mentioned earlier that in the case of the accidental deletion of information from Active Directory, you might need to restore Active Directory from a recent backup. But what happens if there is more than one domain controller in the environment? Even if you did perform a restore, the information on this domain controller would be seen as outdated, and it would be overwritten by the data from another domain controller. This data from the older domain controller is exactly the information you want to replace. The domain controller that was reloaded using a backup would have an older timestamp, and the other domain controllers would re-delete the information from the backup.

Fortunately, Windows Server 2012 R2 and Active Directory allow you to perform what is called an *authoritative restore*. The authoritative restore process specifies a domain controller as having the authoritative (or master) copy of the Active Directory data store. When other domain controllers communicate with this domain controller, their information will be overwritten with Active Directory data stored on the local machine.

Now that you have an idea of how an authoritative restore is supposed to work, let's move on to looking at the details of performing the process.

Performing an Authoritative Restore

When you are restoring Active Directory information on a Windows Server 2012 R2 domain controller, make sure Active Directory services are not running. This is because the restore of system state data requires full access to system files and the Active Directory data store. If you attempt to restore system state data while the domain controller is active, you will see an error message.

In general, restoring data and operating system files is a straightforward process. It is important to note that restoring a system state backup will replace the existing registry, Sysvol, and Active Directory files so that any changes you made since the last backup will be lost.

In addition to restoring the entire Active Directory database, you can also restore only specific subtrees within Active Directory using the restoresubtree command in the ntdsutil utility. This allows you to restore specific information, and it is useful in case of accidental deletion of isolated material.

Following the authoritative restore process, Active Directory should be updated to the time of the last backup. Furthermore, all other domain controllers for this domain will have their Active Directory information overwritten by the results of the restore operation. The result is an Active Directory environment that has been recovered from media.

Overview of Nonauthoritative Restore

Now that you understand why you would use an authoritative restore and how it is performed, it's an easy conceptual jump to understand a *nonauthoritative restore*. Remember that by making a restore authoritative, you are simply telling other domain controllers in the domain to recognize the restored machine as the newest copy of Active Directory for replication purposes. If you have only one domain controller, the authoritative restore process becomes moot; you can simply skip the steps required to make the restore authoritative and begin using the domain controller immediately after the normal restore is complete.

If you have more than one domain controller in the domain and you need to perform a nonauthoritative restore, simply allow the domain controller to receive Active Directory database information from other domain controllers in the domain using normal replication methods.

Active Directory Recycle Bin

The Active Directory recycle bin is a great feature that allows administrators to restore an Active Directory object that has been deleted.

Let's say you have a junior administrator who has been making changes to Active Directory for hours. The junior admin then deletes an OU from Active Directory. You would then have to reload the OU from a tape backup, or even worse, you may have to reload the entire Active Directory (depending on your backup software), thus losing the hours of work the junior admin has completed.

The problem here is that when you delete a security object from Active Directory, the object's security ID (SID) gets removed. All users' rights and permissions are associated with the users' SID number and not their account name. This is where the AD recycle bin can help.

The *Active Directory recycle bin* allows you to preserve and restore accidentally deleted Active Directory objects without the need of using a backup.

The Active Directory recycle bin works for both the Active Directory Domain Services (AD DS) and Active Directory Lightweight Directory Services (AD LDS) environments.

By enabling (disabled by default) the Active Directory recycle bin, any deleted Active Directory objects are preserved, and Active Directory objects can be restored, in their entirety, to their same condition immediately before the deletion. This means all group memberships and access rights that the object had before deletion will remain intact.

To enable the Active Directory recycle bin, you must do the following (you must be a member of the Schema Admins group):

1. Run the `adprep /forestprep` command to prepare the forest on the server that holds the schema master to update the schema.

2. Run the `adprep /domainprep /gpprep` command to prepare the domain on the server that holds the infrastructure operations master role.

3. If a read-only domain controller (RODC) is present in your environment, you must also run the `adprep /rodcprep` command.

4. Make sure that all domain controllers in your Active Directory forest are running Windows Server 2012 R2 or at least Windows Server 2008 R2.

5. Make sure that the forest functional level is set to Windows Server 2012 R2 or at least Windows Server 2008 R2.

Restartable Active Directory

Administrators have the ability to stop and restart Active Directory in the Windows Server 2012 R2 operating system without the need to reboot the entire system. Administrators can perform these actions by using either the Microsoft Management Console (MMC) snap-ins or the command line.

With *Restartable Active Directory Services*, an administrator has the ability to stop Active Directory Services so that updates and other tasks can be applied to a domain controller. One task that an administrator can perform while Active Directory is stopped is an offline defragmentation of the database.

One of the advantages of a restartable Active Directory is that other services running on the same server do not depend on Active Directory to continue to function properly while Active Directory is stopped. An administrator has the ability to stop and restart the Active Directory Domain Services in the Local Services MMC snap-in.

Offline Maintenance

As mentioned, sometimes you have to be offline to do maintenance. For example, you need to perform authoritative and nonauthoritative restores while the domain controller is offline. The main utility administrators use for offline maintenance is `ntdsutil`.

Ntdsutil.exe

The primary method by which system administrators can do offline maintenance is through the `ntdsutil` command-line tool. You can launch this tool by simply entering **ntdsutil** at a command prompt. The ntdsutil command is both interactive and context sensitive. That is, once you launch the utility, you'll see an ntdsutil command prompt. At this prompt, you can enter various commands that set your context within the application. For example, if you enter **domain management,** you'll be able to enter domain-related commands. Several operations also require you to connect to a domain, a domain controller, or an Active Directory object before you perform a command.

Table 3.1 describes the domain-management commands supported by the ntdsutil tool. You can access this functionality by typing the command at a command prompt.

TABLE 3.1   Ntdsutil offline maintenance commands

Ntdsutil domain management command	Purpose
Help or ?	Displays information about the commands that are available within the Domain Management menu of the ntdsutil utility
compact to (at the file maintenance prompt)	Allows you to compact the Active Directory database (offline defragmentation)
metadata cleanup	Removes metadata from decommissioned domain controllers
Set DSRM Password	Resets the Directory Service Restore mode administrator account password

Active Directory Database Mounting Tool

One issue that an administrator may run into when trying to restore Active Directory is the need to restore several backups to compare the Active Directory data that each backup contains. Windows Server 2012 R2 has a utility called the Active Directory database mounting tool (Dsamain.exe) that can resolve this issue.

The Dsamain.exe tool can help the recovery processes by giving you a way to compare data as it exists in snapshots (taken at different times) so that you have the ability to decide which Active Directory database to restore.

Creating snapshots on a regular basis will allow you to have enough data so that you can keep accurate records of how the Active Directory database changes over time. The ntdsutil utility allows you to take snapshots by using the ntdsutil snapshot operation.

You are not required to run the ntdsutil snapshot operation to use Dsamain.exe. You have the ability to use a backup of the Active Directory database.

You must be a member of the Domain Admins group or the Enterprise Admins group to view any snapshots taken because these snapshots contain sensitive Active Directory data.

Compact the Directory Database File (Offline Defragmentation)

One task you have probably done for years is defrag the operating systems that you run. Defragging a system helps return free space from data to the hard drive, and the defragmentation utility has been available since Windows NT.

You can also use the defragmentation process to compact the Active Directory database while it's offline. Offline defragmentation helps return free disk space and check Active Directory database integrity.

To perform an offline defragmentation, you use the ntdsutil command. When you perform a defragmentation of the Active Directory database, a new compacted version of the database is created. This new database file can be created on the same machine (if space permits) or on a network location. After the new file is created, copy the compacted Ntds.dit file to the original location.

It is a good practice, if space allows, to maintain a copy of the older, original database file. You can either rename the older database file and keep it in its current location or copy the older database file to an alternate location.

Monitoring Replication

At times you may need to keep an eye on how your replication traffic is working on your domain controllers. I will cover the replication utility that you can use to help determine whether there are problems on your domain.

Repadmin Utility

The Repadmin utility is included when you install Windows Server 2012 R2. This command-line tool helps administrators diagnose replication problems between Windows domain controllers.

Repadmin allows administrators to view the replication topology of each domain controller as seen from the domain controller's perspective. Administrators can also use Repadmin to create the replication topology manually. By manually creating the replication topology, administrators can force replication events between domain controllers and view the replication metadata vectors.

To access the Repadmin utility, open a command prompt using an elevated privilege (Run ➤ CMD). At the command prompt, type **Repadmin.exe**, and all of the available options will appear.

Using the ADSI Editor

Another utility that allows you to manage objects and attributes in Active Directory is the Active Directory Service Interfaces Editor (ADSI Edit). ADSI Edit allows you to view every object and attribute in an Active Directory forest.

One advantage to using the Adsiedit.msc MMC snap-in is that this tool allows you to query, view, create, and edit attributes that are not exposed through other Active Directory Microsoft Management Console (MMC) snap-ins.

ADSI Edit allows you to administer an AD LDS instance. To do this, you must first connect and bind to the instance. After you connect and bind to the instance, you can administer the containers and objects within the instance by browsing to the containers or objects and then right-clicking them. To complete this task, you must be a member of the Administrators group for the AD LDS instance.

Wbadmin Command-Line Utility

The wbadmin command allows you to back up and restore your operating system, volumes, files, folders, and applications from a command prompt.

You must be a member of the Administrators group to configure a backup schedule. You must be a member of the Backup Operators or the Administrators group (or you must have been delegated the appropriate permissions) to perform all other tasks using the wbadmin command.

To use the wbadmin command, you must run wbadmin from an elevated command prompt (to open an elevated command prompt, click Start, right-click Command Prompt, and then click Run As Administrator). Table 3.2 describes some of the wbadmin commands.

TABLE 3.2   Wbadmin commands

Command	Description
wbadmin enable backup	Configures and enables a daily backup schedule
wbadmin disable backup	Disables your daily backups
wbadmin start backup	Runs a one-time backup
wbadmin stop job	Stops the currently running backup or recovery operation
wbadmin get items	Lists the items included in a specific backup
wbadmin start recovery	Runs a recovery of the volumes, applications, files, or folders specified
wbadmin get status	Shows the status of the currently running backup or recovery operation
wbadmin start systemstaterecovery	Runs a system state recovery
wbadmin start systemstatebackup	Runs a system state backup
wbadmin start sysrecovery	Runs a recovery of the full system state

Configure Windows Azure Backups

Microsoft continues to offer robust cloud solutions to assist administrators with effective backup options. With Windows Server 2012 R2, you can integrate with Windows Azure Online Services to store short-term backup data to an off-premises location. This solution comes with additional costs for storing the data after the initial free trial. The cost model is relatively straightforward, and it is comparable to other cloud storage solutions that are currently available. To run backup jobs from your organization to the Microsoft Azure cloud solution, your environment must be running System Center 2012 with Data Protection Manager.

Data Protection Manager

System Center 2012 *Data Protection Manager (DPM)* is an application that runs on the server and allows disk-based and tape-based data protection and recovery. This recovery is for all the computers in the Active Directory domain. One of the nice features of DPM is that all replication, synchronization, and recovery point creation is done by DPM.

Because you are able to use DPM and set up recoverability for your computers, if a system needs to be recovered, DPM provides reliable protection and rapid recovery of the computer's data either by the system administrator and/or by end users.

DPM uses multiple features to help keep the computers in your network safe. These features include replication, the Volume Shadow Copy Service (VSS) infrastructure, and a policy-driven engine. DPM helps provide protection and fast data recovery for businesses of all sizes.

Windows Azure Backup Prerequisites

Before you can start using the Windows Azure backup services, you must first have a few prerequisites set up within your environment. The following are the deployment prerequisites that you will need to accomplish the task:

- A Windows Server 2012 R2 server running Data Protection Manager in System Center 2012 R2.
- An active Windows Azure account with the Windows Azure Backup feature enabled.
- The Windows Azure backup agent must be installed on the DPM servers that you want to back up, and the DPM servers must have at least 2.5GB of free space reserved for caching. At least 15GB to 20GB of free space is recommended.
- A management certificate that will be uploaded to the backup vault in Windows Azure Backup.

  Please note the following in regard to the certificate parameters:

    - To upload to the certificate to the vault, you must export it as a .cer format file that contains the public key.
    - The certificate should be an x.509 v3 certificate.
    - The key length should be at least 2,048 bits.
    - The certificate must have a valid ClientAuthentication EKU.

- The certificate should be valid currently, with a validity period that does not exceed 3 years.

- The certificate should reside in the Personal certificate store of your local computer.

- The private key should be included during installation of the certificate.

- You can create a self-signed certificate using the makecert tool or use any valid SSL certificate issued by a certification authority (CA) trusted by Microsoft whose root certificates are distributed via the Microsoft Root Certificate Program.

 Make sure to take full advantage of the Microsoft Azure free trial when preparing for your exam. You can start your free trial by following this web link: http://azure.microsoft.com/en-us/pricing/free-trial/.

Configure Backup Vaults for Windows Azure Backup

The Windows Azure backup vault is where your data will be stored in the cloud. After you obtain a Windows Azure account, you will be able to create and manage your cloud backups from the Windows Azure Management Portal. Before you can start storing data using Windows Azure, you must first configure the backup vault by following four easy configuration steps:

1. Obtain a management certificate that will be used by Windows Azure:

   - You can either use an existing management certificate or obtain one by using makecert.exe. If you want to register a server that was not used to run makecert.exe, you must export the .pfx file (containing the private key) from that server, copy it to the server that you want to register, and import it to the Personal certificate store on that computer.

2. Create a backup vault in Windows Azure:

   a. Log in to the Windows Azure Management Portal.

   b. Click Recovery Services and then click Create New. Point to Backup Vault and then click Quick Create.

   c. Name the Vault, specify the geographic region, enter your Windows Azure subscription, and then click Create Backup Vault. It usually takes only a few minutes for the backup vault to finish building. Notifications are provided at the bottom of the management portal.

3. Upload a management certificate to Windows Azure:

   a. Log in to the Windows Azure Management Portal.

   b. Click Recovery Services, click the backup vault you want to certify, and then open the Quick Start page by clicking the Quick Start icon.

   c. On the Quick Start page, click Manager Certificate. A dialog box will appear allowing you to browse your computer for the appropriate certificate that has been staged for upload. Select and upload that certificate.

4. Download and Install the Windows Azure Backup Agent onto each of your DPM servers that you want to back up:

   a. Log in to the Windows Azure Management Portal.

   b. Select Download Agent from the Quick Start page.

   c. Select the appropriate agent for your deployment to start the Agent Installation Wizard.

   d. Complete the installation wizard, keeping all defaults.

Register DPM Servers with the Backup Vault

Now that your Windows Azure Backup Vault is fully configured and all of your DPM servers have agents installed, it's time to register your DPM servers with the backup vault.

1. Launch the Windows Azure Backup application from one of your DPM servers.

2. Click the Register Server task in the Action pane to start the Register Server Wizard.

3. Follow the wizard, making appropriate selections suitable for your particular environment.

4. If the process is successful, a registration confirmation message is displayed, and you can close the wizard.

That's all there is to it. If you have completed these steps properly, you are ready to configure backup jobs to run from your DPM servers to your backup vault in Microsoft Azure. Make sure to spend lots of time running through all of the available options found in the Microsoft Azure Management Portal. The exam is likely to cover multiple scenarios surrounding the configuration and troubleshooting of backups using Microsoft Azure.

Understanding Shadow Copies

An excellent way to protect your shared folders is by using *shadow copies* (Volume Snapshot Service [VSS]). Shadow copies allow an administrator to back up shared folders to a remote location. Shadow copies are designed to help recover files that were accidentally deleted, that were overwritten, or that have become corrupt. One major advantage to shadow copies is that open files can be backed up. This means that even if users are currently working on files in a shared folder that has shadow copies enabled, the shadow copies will continue to function.

Once administrators have configured and enabled shadow copies (using the Computer Management snap-in), network users can restore earlier versions of files. After the initial shadow copy of the shared folder is created, only changes are copied and not the entire file.

You can enable shadow copies of entire volumes.

The following are some of the settings that you can configure when setting up shadow copies:

Schedule   You have the ability to set the schedule of the shadow copies. You can set this schedule to run daily, weekly, monthly, once, at system startup, at logon, or when the system is idle. You can also set the time at which the shadow copy will run.

Storage Locations   An administrator needs to set the location of the shadow copy backup. If you are on a network, it is a good idea to place the shadow copy on a network drive.

Maximum Size   You can set a maximum size on your shadow copies, or you can specify that they have no size limit. One of the predetermined settings is 64 shadow copies per volume.

In Exercise 3.2, you'll set up a volume to make shadow copies every Monday at 7 a.m. To set up the shadow copies, you will use the Computer Management MMC snap-in.

EXERCISE 3.2

Configuring a Shadow Copy on a Volume

1. Open Computer Management by pressing the Windows key and selecting Administrative Tools ➤ Computer Management.

2. Expand Storage and then right-click Disk Management. Choose All Tasks ➤ Configure Shadow Copies.

3. When the Shadow Copies dialog box appears, click the Settings button.

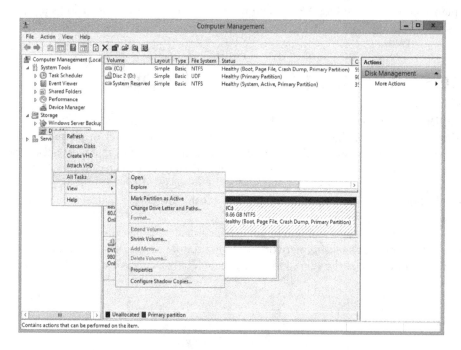

4. When the Settings windows appears, click the Schedule button.

5. In the Schedule window, set the schedule task to weekly and the start time for 7 a.m. Uncheck all of the days-of-the-week boxes except Mon. Click OK.

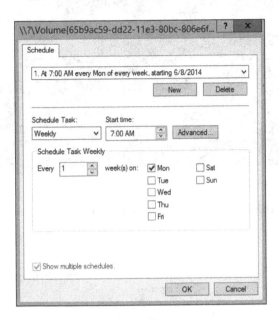

6. When the Settings window reappears, click OK.

7. If the Enable button is enabled, click it. Then click OK.

8. Exit the Computer Management MMC.

To recover a previous version of a file from a shadow copy, you use the \\servername\ sharename path. The operating system determines how you will gain access to the shared folders and shadow copies. Shadow copies are built into Windows XP (SP1), Windows Vista, Windows 7, Windows 8, Windows Server 2003, Windows Server 2008/2008 R2, Windows Server 2012, and Windows Server 2012 R2. If you are using a different Microsoft operating system, you need to download the Shadow Copy Client Pack from the Microsoft download center.

VssAdmin Command

Another way to create, configure, and manage shadow copies is by using the vssadmin.exe command-line utility (see Figure 3.4). The vssadmin.exe command allows you to create, delete, list, and resize shadow copies and shadow storage.

FIGURE 3.4 vssadmin.exe command-line utility

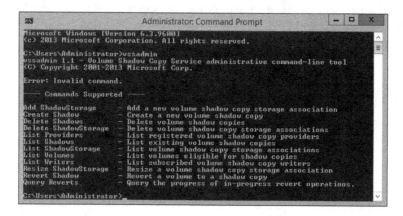

Table 3.3 describes the vssadmin.exe command and the different commands associated with the vssadmin utility.

TABLE 3.3 Vssadmin.exe commands

Command	Description
Add ShadowStorage	Adds a new volume shadow copy storage association
Create Shadow	Creates a new volume shadow copy
Delete Shadows	Deletes volume shadow copies
Delete ShadowStorage	Deletes the volume shadow copy storage associations
List Providers	Lists registered volume shadow copy providers
List Shadows	Lists existing volume shadow copies
List ShadowStorage	Lists volume shadow copy storage associations
List Volumes	Lists volumes eligible for shadow copies
List Writers	Lists subscribed volume shadow copy writers
Resize ShadowStorage	Resizes a volume shadow copy storage association
Revert Shadow	Reverts a volume to a shadow copy
Query Reverts	Queries the progress of in-progress revert operations

Using Advanced Boot Options

The Windows Server 2012 R2 advanced startup options can be used to troubleshoot errors that keep Windows Server 2012 R2 from successfully booting.

> To access the Windows Server 2012 R2 advanced startup options, start or reboot the computer and press the F8 key after the firmware POST process but before Windows Server 2012 R2 is loaded. This will bring up the Advanced Boot Options menu, which offers numerous options for booting Windows Server 2012 R2.

These advanced startup options are covered in the following three sections (see Figure 3.5).

FIGURE 3.5   Advanced Boot Options screen

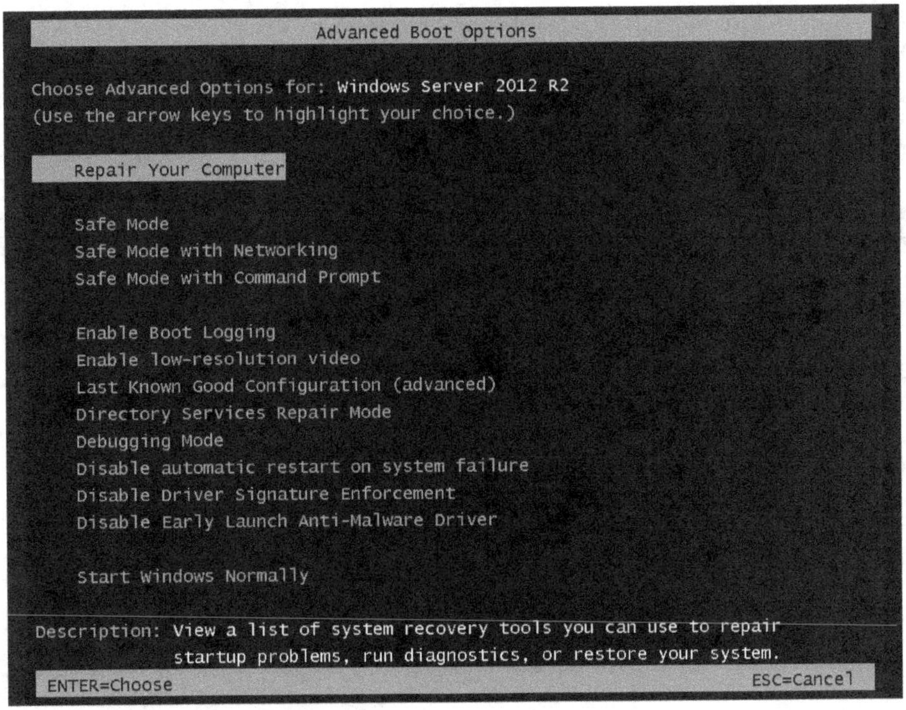

```
                         Advanced Boot Options

Choose Advanced Options for: Windows Server 2012 R2
(Use the arrow keys to highlight your choice.)

    Repair Your Computer

    Safe Mode
    Safe Mode with Networking
    Safe Mode with Command Prompt

    Enable Boot Logging
    Enable low-resolution video
    Last Known Good Configuration (advanced)
    Directory Services Repair Mode
    Debugging Mode
    Disable automatic restart on system failure
    Disable Driver Signature Enforcement
    Disable Early Launch Anti-Malware Driver

    Start Windows Normally

Description: View a list of system recovery tools you can use to repair
            startup problems, run diagnostics, or restore your system.
  ENTER=Choose                                          ESC=Cancel
```

Starting in Safe Mode

When your computer will not start, one of the fundamental troubleshooting techniques is to simplify the configuration as much as possible. This is especially important when you do not know the cause of your problem and you have a complex configuration. After you have simplified the configuration, you can determine whether the problem is in the basic configuration or is a result of your complex configuration.

If the problem is in the basic configuration, you have a starting point for troubleshooting. If the problem is not in the basic configuration, you should proceed to restore each configuration option you removed, one at a time. This helps you to identify what is causing the error.

If Windows Server 2012 R2 will not load, you can attempt to load the operating system through *Safe Mode*. When you run Windows Server 2012 R2 in Safe Mode, you are simplifying your Windows configuration as much as possible. Safe Mode loads only the drivers needed to get the computer up and running.

The drivers that are loaded with Safe Mode include basic files and drivers for the mouse, monitor, keyboard, hard drive, standard video driver, and default system services. Safe Mode is considered a diagnostic mode, so you do not have access to all of the features and devices in Windows Server 2012 R2 that you have when you boot normally, including networking capabilities.

A computer booted to Safe Mode will show Safe Mode in the four corners of your desktop.

If you boot to Safe Mode, check all of your computer's hardware and software settings in Device Manager and try to determine why Windows Server 2012 R2 will not boot properly. After you take steps to fix the problem, try to boot to Windows Server 2012 R2 as you normally would.

In Exercise 3.3, you will boot your computer to Safe Mode.

EXERCISE 3.3

Booting Your Computer to Safe Mode

1. If your computer is currently running, restart the system.

2. During the boot process, press the F8 key to access the Advanced Boot Options menu.

3. Highlight Safe Mode and press Enter.

4. When Windows Server 2012 R2 starts, log in.

5. You will see a Help And Support dialog box letting you know what Safe Mode is. Exit Help And Support.

6. You should see that a network connection is not available in the lower-right corner.

7. Don't restart your computer yet; you will do this as a part of the next exercise.

Enabling Boot Logging

Boot logging creates a log file that tracks the loading of drivers and services. When you choose the Enable Boot Logging option from the Advanced Boot Options menu, Windows

Server 2012 R2 loads normally, not in Safe Mode. This allows you to log all of the processes that take place during a normal boot sequence.

This log file can be used to troubleshoot the boot process. When logging is enabled, the log file is written to \WINDOWS\Ntbtlog.txt (see Figure 3.6).

FIGURE 3.6 Ntbtlog.txt file

In Exercise 3.4, you will create and access a boot log file.

EXERCISE 3.4

Using Boot Logging

1. Restart your computer.

2. During the boot process, press the F8 key to access the Advanced Boot Options menu.

3. Highlight Enable Boot Logging and press Enter.

4. When Windows Server 2012 R2 starts, log in.

5. Click the Folders icon on the bottom left of the desktop and browse to C:\WINDOWS\ Ntbtlog.txt. Double-click this file.

6. Examine the contents of your boot log file.

7. Shut down your computer and restart it without using Advanced Boot Options.

The boot log file is cumulative. Each time you boot to Safe Mode, you are writing to this file. This enables you to make changes, reboot, and see whether you have fixed any problems. If you want to start from scratch, you should manually delete this file and reboot to an Advanced Boot Options menu selection that supports logging.

Using Other Advanced Boot Options Menu Modes

In this section, you will learn about additional Advanced Boot Options menu modes. These include the following:

Safe Mode With Networking   This is the same as the Safe Mode option, but it adds networking features. You might use this mode if you need networking capabilities to download drivers or service packs from a network location.

Safe Mode With Command Prompt   This starts the computer in Safe Mode, but after you log in to Windows Server 2012 R2, only a command prompt is displayed. This mode does not provide access to the desktop. Experienced troubleshooters use this mode.

Enable Low-Resolution Video (640×480)   This loads a standard VGA driver without starting the computer in Safe Mode. You might use this mode if you changed your video driver, did not test it, and tried to boot to Windows Server 2012 R2 with a bad driver that would not allow you to access video. The Enable VGA mode bails you out by loading a default driver, providing access to video so that you can properly install (and test!) the correct driver for your computer.

 Safe Mode starts Windows Server 2012 R2 at a resolution of 800×600.

Last Known Good Configuration (Advanced)   This boots Windows Server 2012 R2 by using the registry information that was saved the last time the computer was successfully booted. You would use this option to restore configuration information if you improperly configured the computer and did not successfully reboot it. When you use the *Last Known Good Configuration* option, you lose any system configuration changes that were made since the computer last successfully booted.

Directory Services Restore Mode   This option is used for domain controllers only, and it is not relevant to Windows Server 2012 R2 unless it is a domain controller.

Debugging Mode   This runs the Kernel Debugger, if it is installed. The Kernel Debugger is an advanced troubleshooting utility.

Disable Automatic Restart On System Failure   This prevents Windows from restarting when a critical error causes Windows to fail. This option should be used only when Windows fails every time you restart so that you are not able to access the desktop or any configuration options.

Disable Driver Signature Enforcement   This allows drivers to be installed even if they do not contain valid signatures.

Start Windows Normally   This boots to Windows Server 2012 R2 in the default manner. This option is on the Advanced Boot Options menu in case you accidentally hit F8 during the boot process but really wanted to boot Windows Server 2012 R2 normally.

Windows Recovery Environment

When your Windows Server 2012 R2 machine fails to start, it will automatically enter into the *Windows Recovery Environment (Windows RE)*. This environment is an extensible recovery platform based on Windows Preinstallation Environment (Windows PE).

When your server starts in the Windows RE, the Startup Repair tool starts the diagnosis, and it will begin to help you repair the system. The Windows RE is also an environment in which you can use various tools to help you do a manual system recovery. The boot options for the Windows RE are as follows:

- Start recovery, troubleshooting, or diagnostic tools

- Boot from a device

- Access the Firmware menu

- Choose which operating system to boot, if multiple operating systems are installed on the same computer

Administrators also have the ability to configure a hardware button to run an alternate boot path that includes the Windows RE. This gives administrators the ability to help their users get to the Windows RE menus more easily, which allows your users to recover their PCs easily in the event of a corrupted system.

There are certain instances where Windows RE will automatically try to repair the system:

- Two successive failed attempts to start Windows

- Two successive unexpected shutdowns that occur within two minutes of boot completion

- A Secure Boot error (except for issues related to `Bootmgr.efi`)

- A BitLocker error on touch-only devices

Configure Site-Level Fault Tolerance

Disaster recovery is a key piece of maintaining a solid corporate infrastructure. Companies will rely heavily on the ability to configure fault tolerance, redundancy, and replication within the environment to ensure production uptime across the organization. Windows Server 2012 R2 has quite a few new features to help administrators accomplish these tasks in a failover clustered environment.

Hyper-V in Windows Server 2012 R2 gives you the power you need to be truly fault tolerant. Using the Hyper-V Replica feature, you can keep entire replicated copies of your virtual machines readily available to keep your production environment online when virtual machines fail. The nice thing about the replica VM is that it doesn't share storage with the primary VM like you are used to seeing with a traditional failover cluster. The replica starts off with a full cloned copy of the primary VM's virtual hard disk and then updates itself automatically through replication frequency from the primary VM. These automatic updates are configurable to occur anywhere from 30 seconds to 15 minutes.

To set up a Hyper-V replica properly, you must first configure the server-level replication settings for both physical Hyper-V hosts that will make up this failover configuration. One host will act as the primary, and the other will serve as the replica. You must enable replication on the replica host before you can replicate VMs from the primary host. These configuration settings are found in the Hyper-V Manager settings navigation pane under Replication Configuration. Check the box Enable This Computer As A Replica Server and then make your authentication, port, and storage selections, as shown in Figure 3.7. The authentication, port, and storage selections must be configured on both physical Hyper-V hosts.

FIGURE 3.7: Hyper-V settings

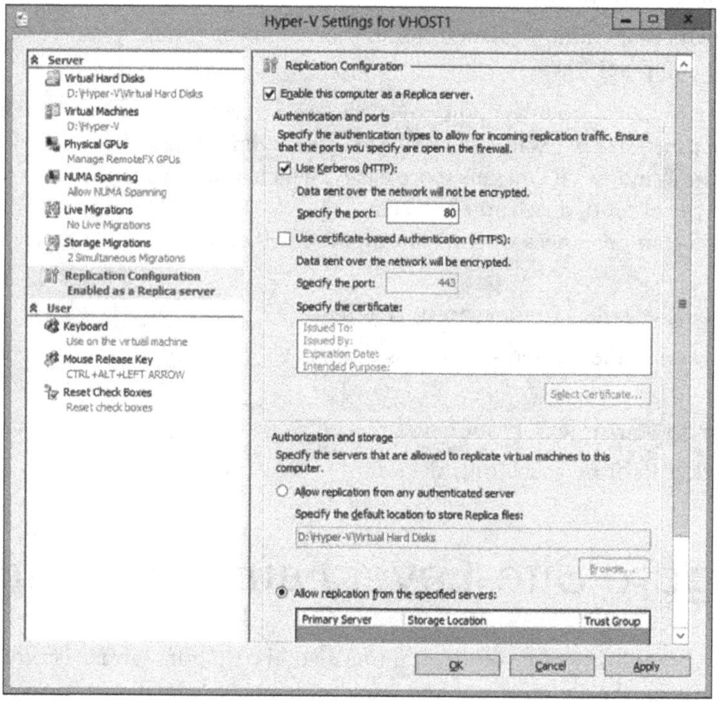

Once the Hyper-V hosts have been configured, you can enable replication on the VMs running on the primary Hyper-V host. Simply right-click a virtual machine running on the primary host and select the new Enable Replication option to start the Enable

Replication Wizard. Once you are finished configuring failover settings using the wizard, that VM is now considered to be fault tolerant between your two physical Hyper-V hosts. You should initiate a test failover action by launching the Hyper-V Manager on the replica host, right-clicking a replica VM, clicking Replication, and then clicking Test Failover. Testing failover is the only way you know for sure that your configuration settings are correct.

In addition to having the ability to create Hyper-V replicas, Windows Server 2012 R2 also has the ability to perform Hyper-V Extended Replication. Hyper-V Extended Replication is a new feature that allows administrators to extend the replication boundaries from the primary and replica hosts to an actual third site location. For example, you have a Hyper-V primary host in Denver replicating to a Hyper-V replica host in Tampa. Using Hyper-V Extended Replication, you can configure the Tampa replica host to replicate to a third Hyper-V host located at your London office. This feature gives you an added level of fault tolerance within your environment.

The component that manages how the cluster databases are updated within a failover cluster environment is known as the *Global Update Manager*. Whenever the state of the cluster changes, such as when a node goes down or offline, all of the other nodes in the cluster must acknowledge the change before those changes can be written to the cluster database. The Global Update Manager has three configurable settings available to you through Windows PowerShell using the following command:

```
(Get-Cluster).DatabaseReadWriteMode
```

The three configurable Global Update Manager settings are as follows:

0 = All (Write) And Local (Read)   This is the default setting in Windows Server 2012 R2 for all cluster workloads except Hyper-V. It requires that all of the cluster nodes acknowledge the update before the change is committed to the database. Database reads occur on the local node.

1 = Majority (Read And Write)   This is the default setting for Windows Server 2012 R2 Hyper-V failover clusters. It requires that only a majority of nodes acknowledge the update before the change is committed to the database. Database read involves comparing the most recent timestamp from the majority of available nodes and using the most recent data.

2 = Majority (Write) And Local (Read)   This mode also requires that the majority of the cluster nodes acknowledge the update before committing the change to the database. The difference is that database read occurs on the local node, which means the data may be stale.

Microsoft recommends that you use mode 0 only when you have a requirement to make sure that the cluster database is consistent between all nodes in the cluster. For example, you would want to use mode 0 only when using availability groups in a Microsoft Exchange Server 2013 or Microsoft SQL Server 2012 environment to ensure that all of the cluster nodes acknowledge the change before the update is committed to the database. You cannot afford mismatched or stale data within a SQL or Exchange failover clustered environment. Having this situation could result in serious performance issues within the cluster.

Using the Startup Repair Tool

If your Windows Server 2012 R2 computer will not boot because of missing or corrupted system files, you can use the *Startup Repair tool* to correct these problems. Startup Repair cannot repair hardware failures. Additionally, Startup Repair cannot recover personal files that have been corrupted, damaged by viruses, or deleted. To ensure that you can recover your personal files, you should use the Backup utility previously discussed in this chapter.

To use the Startup Repair tool, follow these steps:

1. Boot your computer using the Windows Server 2012 R2 media.

2. When the Install Windows dialog box appears, select the language, the time and currency format, and the keyboard or input method. Click Next to continue.

3. The Install Now button appears in the center of the screen. Click Repair Your Computer in the lower-left corner.

4. Select the operating system to recover and click Next. If you do not see your operating system, you might need to load your hard disk drivers by clicking the Load Drivers button.

5. The System Recovery Options dialog box appears. You can choose one of the following options:
   - Startup Repair
   - System Restore
   - Windows Complete PC Restore
   - Windows Memory Diagnostic Tool
   - Command Prompt
   - Choose Startup Repair to continue.

6. Startup Repair checks your computer for problems and attempts to repair them. After Startup Repair has finished, click Shut Down or Restart.

If you were not provided the Windows Server 2012 R2 media when you purchased your computer, the computer manufacturer might have placed the files on a recovery partition—or they might have replaced the Startup Repair tool with one of their own. Check with the manufacturer for more information.

If Startup Repair is unable to correct the problem, you might have to reinstall Windows Server 2012 R2. This should be done as a last resort. This is a reason why you should always back up your Windows Server 2012 R2 machine.

Summary

In this chapter, you learned about the different ways to recover and protect your Windows Server 2012 R2 machine from hardware and software issues. I discussed using the Advanced Boot Options, such as Last Known Good Configuration, Safe Mode, debugging mode, and VGA mode. You can use these Advanced Boot Options for troubleshooting multiple software and hardware related issues within your environment.

Other important items that need to be completed on a Windows Server 2012 R2 machine are backups and restores. Backing up a Windows Server 2012 R2 machine protects it in the event of a hardware or software failure. Don't find yourself caught in the situation where a machine fails, and you don't have a fresh backup copy to restore data from. Take the time to back up all of the data that you care about.

Another way to protect data is by the use of shadow copies. Shadow copies allow you to keep previous versions of data and revert to that previous version in the event of a problem. Shadow copies are very convenient when you need to restore a file quickly.

Exam Essentials

Understand the various backup types available with the Windows Server 2012 R2 Backup utility.   The Windows Server 2012 R2 Backup utility can perform full and incremental backup operations. Some third-party backup utilities also support differential and daily backups. You can use each of these operations as part of an efficient backup strategy.

Know how to back up Active Directory.   The data within the Active Directory database on a domain controller is part of the system state data. You can back up the system state data to a file using the Windows Server 2012 R2 Backup utility.

Know how to restore Active Directory.   Restoring the Active Directory database is considerably different from other restore operations. To restore some or the entire Active Directory database, you must first boot the machine into Directory Services Restore mode.

Understand the importance of an authoritative restore process.   You use an authoritative restore when you want to restore earlier information from an Active Directory backup and you want the older information to be propagated to other domain controllers in the environment.

Understand offline maintenance using ntdsutil.   The ntdsutil command-line tool is a primary method by which system administrators perform offline maintenance. Understand how to launch this tool by entering **ntdsutil** at a command prompt.

Review Questions

1. You need to ensure that you can recover your Windows Server 2012 R2 configuration and data if the computer's hard disk fails. What should you do?

   A. Create a complete PC Backup.

   B. Create a backup of all file categories.

   C. Perform an automated system recovery (ASR) backup.

   D. Create a system restore point.

2. After you update multiple drivers on your Windows Server 2012 R2 machine, the machine hangs at the logon screen, and you can't log into the machine. You need to get this computer up and running as quickly as possible. Which of the following repair strategies should you try first to correct your problem?

   A. Restore your computer's configuration with your last backup.

   B. Boot your computer with the Safe Mode option.

   C. Boot your computer with the Last Known Good Configuration option.

   D. Boot your computer to the recovery console and manually copy the old driver back to the computer.

3. You are the system administrator for a large organization that uses Windows Server 2012 R2 and Windows 8. You have a Windows 8 machine that needs to be configured with a normal backup schedule to restore sensitive data in the event of a catastrophic failure. At a worst case interval, you need to be able to perform a full restore from within the last 24 hours of a failure. What type of backup should you schedule?

   A. Normal

   B. Differential

   C. Incremental

   D. Daily

4. You are the network administrator for a small company. You manage the computers for the Marketing department, all of which are running the Windows Server 2012 R2 operating system. You are making several configuration changes to the manager's computer to enhance performance. Before you make any changes, you want to create a restore point that can be used if any problems arise. How do you manually create a restore point?

   A. By using the System Restore utility

   B. By using the Shadow Copies tab of the System Properties dialog box

   C. By using the System Configuration utility

   D. By using the Startup Repair tool

5. Your computer uses a SCSI adapter that supports a SCSI drive, which contains your Windows 8 system and boot partitions. After updating the SCSI driver, you restart your computer, but Windows 8 will not load. You need to get this computer up and running as quickly as possible. Which of the following repair strategies should you try first to correct your problem?

   A. Restore your computer's configuration with your last backup.

   B. Boot your computer with the Last Known Good Configuration.

   C. Boot your computer with the Safe Mode option.

   D. Boot your computer to the recovery console and manually copy the old driver back to the computer.

6. You enable the Boot Logging option on the Advanced Boot Options menu. Where can you find the log file that is created?

   A. \Windows\netlog.txt

   B. \Windows\System32\netlog.txt

   C. \Windows\ntbtlog.txt

   D. \Windows\System32\netboot.log

7. After you updated Will's computer, his system files became corrupted because of a virus and now need to be restored. Which of the following processes should you use to fix the problem?

   A. Restore a backup.

   B. Restore an image.

   C. Use the Startup Repair tool.

   D. Boot to Safe Mode.

8. You are unable to boot your Windows Server 2012 R2 computer, so you decide to boot the computer to Safe Mode. Which of the following statements regarding Safe Mode is false?

   A. When the computer is booted to Safe Mode, there is no network access.

   B. Safe Mode loads all of the drivers for the hardware that is installed on the computer.

   C. When you run Safe Mode, boot logging is automatically enabled.

   D. When you run Safe Mode, the screen resolution is set to 800×600.

9. You need to back up the existing data on a computer before you install a new application. You also need to ensure that you are able to recover individual user files that are replaced or deleted during the installation. What should you do?

   A. Create a System Restore point.

   B. Perform an automated system recovery (ASR) backup and restore.

   C. In the Windows Server Backup utility, click the Backup Once link.

   D. In the Backup And Restore Center window, click the Back Up Computer button.

10. Your data recovery strategy must meet the following requirements:

- Back up all data files and folders in C:\Data.
- Restore individual files and folders in C:\Data.
- Ensure that data is backed up to and restored from external media.

What should you do?

A. Use the Previous Versions feature to restore the files and folders.

B. Use the System Restore feature to perform backup and restore operations.

C. Use the NTBackup utility to back up and restore individual files and folders.

D. Use the Windows Server Backup to back up and restore files.

Chapter

4

Configure Advanced Network Services

THE FOLLOWING 70-412 EXAM OBJECTIVES ARE COVERED IN THIS CHAPTER:

✓ **Implement an advanced Dynamic Host Configuration Protocol (DHCP) solution**

- Create and configure superscopes and multicast scopes
- Implement DHCPv6
- Configure high availability for DHCP including DHCP failover and split scopes
- Configure DHCP Name Protection
- Configure DNS registration

✓ **Implement an advanced DNS solution**

- Configure security for DNS including DNSSEC, DNS Socket Pool, and cache locking
- Configure DNS logging
- Configure delegated administration
- Configure recursion
- Configure netmask ordering
- Configure a GlobalNames zone
- Analyze zone level statistics

✓ **Deploy and manage IPAM**

- Provision IPAM manually or by using Group Policy
- Configure server discovery

- Create and manage IP blocks and ranges
- Monitor utilization of IP address space
- Migrate to IPAM
- Delegate IPAM administration
- Manage IPAM collections
- Configure IPAM database storage

In this chapter, you will take a deep dive into configuring network services using the new features and functionality provided by Windows Server 2012 R2. Unlike the 70-410 exam, the 70-412 exam will require that you have the skills and knowledge to configure advanced network configurations beyond just their initial installations and setup.

This chapter will discuss and demonstrate some of the most common advanced network configuration options that you will see both on the exam and in the field. Once you have completed this chapter, you will have a better understanding of how to configure advanced network services surrounding DHCP, DNS, and IPAM in a Windows Server 2012 R2 environment.

Working with Advanced DHCP Configuration Options

DHCP makes the life of an administrator easy when it comes to managing the IP addresses of devices within an organization. Could you imagine having to keep track of each device and that device's IP manually? With Windows Server 2012 R2's DHCP high availability and load balancing options available, life gets even easier. The next few sections will cover how to implement advanced DHCP solutions in detail.

Create and Configure Superscopes

A *superscope* enables the DHCP server to provide addresses from more than one scope to clients on the same physical subnet. This is helpful when clients within the same subnet have more than one IP network and thus need IPs from more than one address pool. Microsoft's DHCP Management Console allows you to manage IP address assignment in the superscope, though you must still configure other scope options individually for each child scope. In Exercise 4.1 you will configure a superscope from two preexisting scopes.

Remember that only one superscope can exist per server and that a superscope requires at least two preconfigured scopes.

EXERCISE 4.1

Creating a Superscope

1. Open the DHCP Management Console.

2. Right-click IPv4 and choose the New Superscope command to launch the New Superscope Wizard. Click Next.

3. On the Superscope Name page, name your superscope and click the Next button.

4. The Select Scopes page appears, listing all scopes on the current server. Select the two scopes you want to use for a superscope and then click the Next button.

5. The wizard's summary page appears. Click the Finish button to create your scope.

6. Verify that your new superscope appears in the DHCP Management Console to complete this exercise.

Deleting a Superscope

You can delete a superscope by right-clicking it and choosing the Delete command. A superscope is just an administrative convenience, so you can safely delete one at any time—it doesn't affect the "real" scopes that make up the superscope.

Adding a Scope to a Superscope

To add a scope to an existing superscope, find the scope you want to add, right-click it, and choose Action ➤ Add To Superscope. A dialog box appears, listing all of the superscopes known to this server. Pick the one to which you want the current scope appended and click the OK button.

Removing a Scope from a Superscope

To remove a scope from a superscope, open the superscope and right-click the target scope. The pop-up menu provides a Remove From Superscope command that will do the deed.

Activating and Deactivating Superscopes

Just as with regular scopes, you can activate and deactivate superscopes. The same restrictions and guidelines apply. You must activate a superscope before it can be used, and you must not deactivate it until you want all of your clients to lose their existing leases and be forced to request new ones.

To activate or deactivate a superscope, right-click the superscope name and select Activate or Deactivate, respectively, from the pop-up menu.

Create and Configure Multicast Scopes

Multicasting occurs when one machine communicates to a network of subscribed computers rather than specifically addressing each computer on the destination network.

It's much more efficient to *multicast* a video or audio stream to multiple destinations than it is to unicast it to the same number of clients, and the increased demand for multicast-friendly network hardware has resulted in some head scratching about how to automate the multicast configuration.

In the following sections, you will learn about MADCAP, the protocol that controls multicasting, and about how to build and configure a multicast scope.

Understanding the Multicast Address Dynamic Client Allocation Protocol

DHCP is usually used to assign IP configuration information for *unicast* (or one-to-one) network communications. With multicast, there's a separate type of address space assigned from 224.0.0.0 through 239.255.255.255. Addresses in this space are known as *Class D addresses*, or simply *multicast addresses*. Clients can participate in a multicast just by knowing (and using) the multicast address for the content they want to receive. However, multicast clients also need to have an ordinary IP address.

How do clients know what address to use? Ordinary DHCP won't help because it's designed to assign IP addresses and option information to one client at a time. Realizing this, the Internet Engineering Task Force (IETF) defined a new protocol: *Multicast Address Dynamic Client Allocation Protocol (MADCAP)*. MADCAP provides an analog to DHCP but for multicast use. A MADCAP server issues leases for multicast addresses only. MADCAP clients can request a multicast lease when they want to participate in a multicast.

DHCP and MADCAP have some important differences. First you have to realize that the two are totally separate. A single server can be a DHCP server, a MADCAP server, or both; no implied or actual relation exists between the two. Likewise, clients can use DHCP and/or MADCAP at the same time—the only requirement is that every MADCAP client has to get a unicast IP address from somewhere.

Remember that DHCP can assign options as part of the lease process, but MADCAP cannot. The only thing MADCAP does is to assign multicast addresses dynamically.

Building Multicast Scopes

Building a multicast scope is similar to building a unicast scope, but it requires a few different configuration settings when going through the wizard. Exercise 4.2 walks you through creating and activating a new multicast scope.

EXERCISE 4.2

Creating and Activating a New Multicast Scope

1. Open the DHCP Management Console.

2. Right-click IPv4 and choose New Multicast Scope to launch the New Multicast Scope Wizard. Click the Next button on the welcome page.

EXERCISE 4.2 *(continued)*

3. On the Multicast Scope Name page, provide a name and description for your multicast scope. Click Next.

4. The IP Address Range page appears. Enter a start IP address of **224.0.0.0** and an end IP address of **224.255.0.0**. Adjust the TTL to 1 to make sure no multicast packets escape your local network segment. Click Next.

5. On the Add Exclusions page of the wizard, add any IP Exclusions or leave this page blank. Click Next.

6. Keep the defaults on the Lease Duration page. Click Next.

7. Ensure the Activate Scope Now radio button is toggled to Yes. Click Finish to complete the creation and activation of your new multicast scope.

8. Verify that your new multicast scope appears in the DHCP Management Console to complete this exercise.

Setting Multicast Scope Properties

Once you create a multicast scope, you can adjust its properties by right-clicking the scope name and selecting Properties.

The Multicast Scope Properties dialog box has two tabs. The General tab (see Figure 4.1) allows you to change the scope's name, its start and end addresses, its Time To Live (TTL) value, its lease duration, and its description—in essence, all of the settings you provided when you created it in the first place.

FIGURE 4.1 General tab of the Multicast Scope Properties dialog box

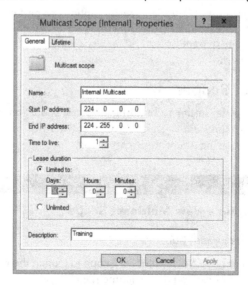

The Lifetime tab (see Figure 4.2) allows you to limit how long your multicast scope will be active. By default, a newly created multicast scope will live forever, but if you're creating a scope to provide MADCAP assignments for a single event (or a set of events of limited duration), you can specify an expiration time for the scope. When that time is reached, the scope disappears from the server but not before making all of its clients give up their multicast address leases. This is a nice way to make sure the lease cleans up after itself when you're finished with it.

FIGURE 4.2   Lifetime tab of the Multicast Scope Properties dialog box

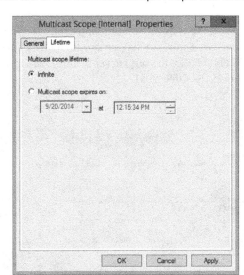

Implement DHCPv6

In Windows Server 2012 R2, administrators can create and manage both IPv4 and IPv6 DHCP scopes for their organization. Even though they are managed separately, they have the same capabilities of being able to configure reservations, exclusions, and other DHCP options. Unlike an IPv4 client, a DHCPv6 client uses a device unique identifier (DUID) instead of a MAC address to get an IP address from the DHCP server.

DHCPv6 supports both stateful address configuration and stateless address configuration. An easy way to think of the difference between a stateful configuration and a stateless configuration is that, with a stateful configuration, the DHCPv6 client receives its IPv6 address and its additional DHCP options from the DHCPv6 server. With a stateless configuration, the IPv6 client can automatically assign itself an IPv6 address without ever having to communicate with the DHCPv6 server. The stateless configuration process is also known as *DHCPv6 autoconfiguration*. Exercise 4.3 will walk you through the process of creating and activating a new DHCPv6 scope.

EXERCISE 4.3

Creating and Activating a New DHCPv6 Scope

1. Open the DHCP Management Console.

2. Right-click IPv6 and choose the New Scope command. The New Scope Wizard appears. Click the Next button.

3. On the Welcome to the New Scope Wizard page, click the Next button.

4. On the Scope Name page, provide a name and description for your new DHCPv6 scope. Click the Next button.

5. On the Scope Prefix page, input the corresponding prefix for your organization's IPv6 network settings. In the event that you have more than one DHCPv6 server, you can set a preference value that will indicate your server priority. The lower the preference value, the higher the server priority. Click Next.

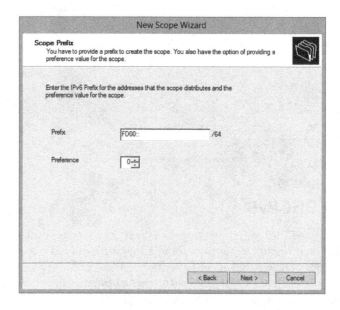

6. On the Add Exclusions page of the wizard, you can configure either a single IP exclusion or a range of IPs to exclude from obtaining an address automatically. Exclusions should include any device or range of devices that have been manually set with a static IP on that particular scope. Click Next.

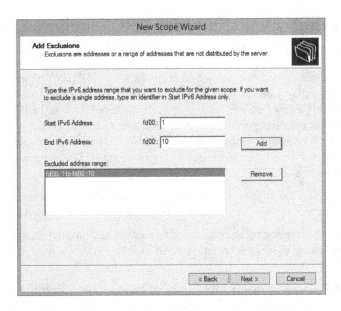

7. Keep the default selections on the Scope Lease page. Click Next.

8. Make sure the Activate Scope Now radio button is toggled to Yes. Click Finish to complete the creation and activation of your new DHCPv6 scope.

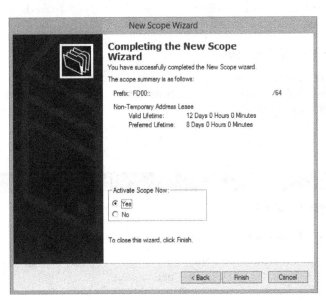

9. Verify that your new scope appears in the DHCP Management Console to complete this exercise.

Configure High Availability for DHCP Including DHCP Failover and Split Scopes

DHCP failover provides load balancing and redundancy for DHCP services, enabling administrators to deploy a highly resilient DHCP service for their organization. The idea is to share your DHCP IPV4 scopes between two Windows Server 2012 R2 servers so that if one of the failover partners goes down, then the other failover partner will continue providing DHCP services throughout the environment. DHCP failover supports large-scale DHCP deployments without the challenges of a split-scope DHCP environment.

Here are a few of the benefits that DHCP failover provides:

Multisite   DHCP failover supports a deployment architecture that includes multiple sites. DHCP failover partner servers do not need to be located at the same physical site.

Flexibility   DHCP failover can be configured to provide redundancy in hot standby mode; or, with load balancing mode, client requests can be distributed between two DHCP servers.

Seamless   DHCP servers share lease information, allowing one server to assume the responsibility for servicing clients if the other server is unavailable. DHCP clients can keep the same IP address when a lease is renewed, even if a different DHCP server issues the lease.

Simplicity   A wizard is provided to create DHCP failover relationships between DHCP servers. The wizard automatically replicates scopes and settings from the primary server to the failover partner.

Configuring DHCP Failover

One of the nice things about DHCP failover is that the configured scope is replicated between both clustered DHCP nodes whether or not you are running the cluster in hot standby or load balancing mode. If one server fails, the other can manage the entire pool of IP addresses on behalf of the environment. Exercise 4.4 provides step-by-step DHCP failover configuration in Windows Server 2012 R2.

EXERCISE 4.4

Configuring DHCP Failover

1.   Open the DHCP Management Console.

2.   Right-click IPv4 and choose the Configure Failover command to launch the Configure Failover Wizard. Click Next on the Introduction page.

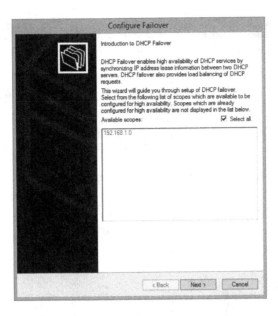

3. On the Specify The Partner Server To Use For Failover page, select your partner DHCP server from the drop-down menu or by browsing the Add Server directory. Click Next.

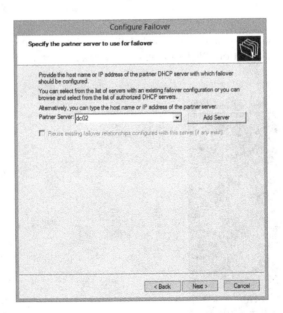

4. On the Create A New Failover Relationship page, provide a relationship name, select the Load Balance mode from the drop-down, and provide a shared secret password that will be used to authenticate the DHCP failover relationship between the two servers in the failover cluster. Click Next.

EXERCISE 4.4 *(continued)*

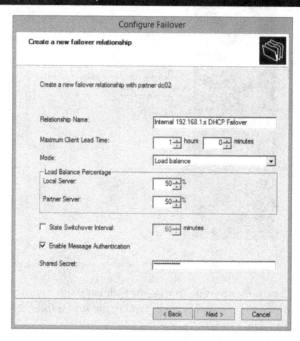

5. Review your configuration settings and click the Finish button to configure your new DHCP failover configuration. Click Close upon successful completion.

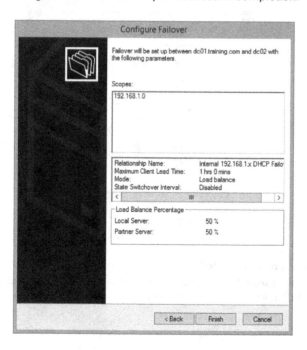

6. After the wizard successfully completes on the primary DHCP server, verify that the new failover scope has been created and activated on the secondary DHCP server in the DHCP Management Console to complete this exercise.

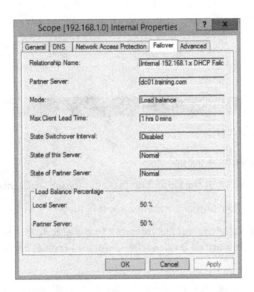

You can always go back in and change the properties of the failover scope if you want. Test both hot standby and load balancing modes to decide which deployment configuration option best suits your organization's needs. Expect to see exam scenarios discussing both DHCP failover configuration modes and the differences between them.

DHCP Split Scopes

Even though you have the capabilities of DHCP failover in Windows Server 2012 R2, for exam purposes you will need to understand how DHCP split scopes work. Split scopes are configurable only on IPv4 IP addresses and cannot be configured on IPv6 scopes. The idea of DHCP split scopes is to have two stand-alone DHCP servers that are individually responsible for only a percentage of the IP addresses on a particular subnet.

For example, DHCP Server 1 would be responsible for 70 percent of the IP addresses, and DHCP Server 2 would be responsible for the other 30 percent of IP addresses. The two DHCP servers in a split-scope configuration do not share any lease information between one another, and they do not take over for one another in the event that one of the two DHCP servers fail. As you can see, a split-scope configuration is less fault tolerant than a full DHCP failover configuration. However, a split scope configuration does split the load of DHCP leases and renewals between two servers providing a basic level of native load balancing in a Windows Server 2012 R2 environment.

DHCP Allow and Deny Filtering

One of the nice things about DHCP is that administrators can use allow or deny filtering to control which devices get an IP address and which devices do not on your network. DHCP filtering is controlled by recording a client's MAC address in a list and then enabling either the Allow or Deny filter. One thing to keep in mind about DHCP filtering is that by enabling the allow list, you automatically deny DHCP addresses to any client computer not on the list. In Exercise 4.5, you will configure DHCP filtering by adding a client machine to the Deny filter by MAC address.

EXERCISE 4.5

Configuring DHCP Filtering

1. Open the DHCP Management Console.

2. Expand IPv4 until you reach the Deny filter object in your DHCP hierarchy.

3. Right-click the Deny filter object and select New Filter.

4. Enter the MAC address of the device you want to exclude from your network, provide a description such as **Unwanted Device**, click Add, and then click Close.

5. Right-click the Deny filter and select Enable to complete this exercise.

One of the good things about these filters is that you can move devices from one filter to the other quite easily at any time by right-clicking the device in the list and selecting either Move To Allow or Move To Deny. Test both Allow and Deny filters thoroughly while preparing for the exam. You will most likely see multiple scenarios surrounding DHCP filtering.

Configure DHCP Name Protection

DHCP name protection is an additional configuration option that administrators should consider when working DHCP within their environment. Name protection protects a DHCP leased machine's name from being overwritten by another machine with the same name during DNS dynamic updates so that you can configure a Windows 2012 R2 DHCP server to verify and update the DNS records of a client machine during the lease renewal process. If the DHCP server detects that a machine's DNS A and PTR records already exist in the environment when a DHCP update occurs, then that DHCP update will fail on that client machine, making sure not to overwrite the existing server name. There are just a few simple steps needed in order to configure DHCP name protection. Exercise 4.6 will walk you through these steps.

EXERCISE 4.6

Enabling DHCP Name Protection

1. Open the DHCP Management Console.

2. Right-click IPv4 and select Properties.

3. The Server Properties dialog box appears. Click the DNS tab.

4. Verify that Enable DNS Dynamic Updates According To The Settings Below is checked, and verify that the radio button labeled Dynamically Update DNS A And PTR Records Only If Requested By The DHCP Clients is selected.

5. Verify that Discard A And PTR Records When Lease Is Deleted is checked. If not, then check it.

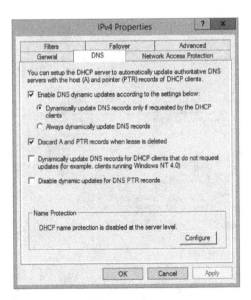

6. Click Configure under Name Protection, and select Enable Name Protection.

7. Click OK twice to complete this exercise.

Configure DNS Registration

Another great feature of Windows Server 2012 R2 DHCP server is the ability to perform registration of DNS records with the DNS server on behalf of its clients. The DHCP server has the flexibility to register DNS clients based on Host A records only instead of being forced to use PTR records during DNS registration. This functionality reduces the number of registration failures that are directly due to the absence of suitable reverse and forward lookup zones on the DNS server.

In addition, you can now also create a DHCP policy that will register only certain clients that match a specific DNS suffix. Together, these new Windows Server 2012 R2 features further integrate DNS and DHCP so that administrators have cleaner control over how clients are registered on their networks. Exercise 4.7 will demonstrate disabling dynamic updates for DNS PTR records in DHCP.

EXERCISE 4.7

Disabling Dynamic Updates

1. Open the DHCP Management Console.

2. Right-click IPv4 and select Properties.

3. Navigate to the DNS tab.

4. Check the box Disable Dynamic Updates For DNS PTR Records.

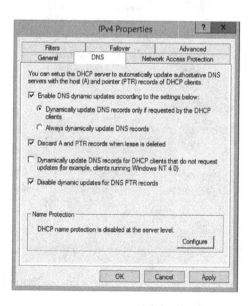

5. Click Apply and OK to complete this exercise.

All of the new DHCP features provided to you by Windows Server 2012 R2 are worth examining. DHCP failover is a big win for administrators. I'm quite sure that many Windows customers will be changing their DHCP infrastructure from split scopes to a load balanced or hot standby configuration in the near future.

The Ins and Outs of DNS

This chapter will expand on what you have already learned over the course of the next few sections. It will focus on hardening your environment with DNS security options, DNS logging and analysis, and a few other advanced configuration options that you will most likely see on the 70-412 exam. DNS is a core network service about which every administrator should have a full understanding. Make it a point to be able to complete each lab from memory to prepare fully for your test.

DNS Security

Security is a main focal point for almost every organization. Since DNS is a core network service that has its hands in every piece of your infrastructure, it is extremely important that you take the time to make sure this environment's DNS is as secure as possible. Let's take a look at few major configuration options for securing DNS on your network.

DNSSEC

Domain Name System Security Extensions (DNSSEC) is a suite of extensions that add security to the Domain Name System (DNS) protocol by enabling DNS responses to be validated. DNSSEC works by securing a DNS zone with a process called *zone signing*. When a client machine queries a record in a zone that is signed by DNSSEC, the DNS server returns both the record and the record's digital signature. When you sign a DNS zone using DNSSEC, the following new resource records become available within the environment:

Resource Record Signature (RRSIG) Record   This is the additional record that is returned to a client for validity upon a DNS query. This record is stored in the DNSSEC signed zone.

Next Secure (NSEC/NSEC3) Record   This record provides proof that a queried record does not exist in the zone. If a client queries a nonexistent record, then the DNS server returns a NSEC record.

DNSKEY   This record is used for cryptographic verification of the RRSIG records.

DNSSEC is usually used in high-security environments. The main security advantage of DNSSEC is that it prevents attacks where clients on your network are fed false DNS information. In addition to the new resource records, when you deploy DNSSEC, the following cryptographic keys are created within the environment:

Zone Signing Key (ZSK)   This cryptographic key is used to sign individual host records within a DNSSEC-implemented DNS zone.

Key Signing Key (KSK)   This cryptographic key is used to sign all DNSKEY records.

Trust Anchor   This cryptographic key is used to validate the DNSKEY record in a DNSSEC protected zone. The trust anchor is replicated to all domain controllers in the forest when you deploy DNSSEC with an Active Directory Integrated zone.

Together, these records and keys provide administrators with enhanced security on their DNS networks. The first DNS server within your environment that you implement with DNSSEC is referred to as the *DNSSEC key master*. It's the key master's job to generate and manage the keys that are signed within a DNSSEC protected zone. Using Group Policy, administrators can set client rules that will ensure that those clients will accept records only from a DNSSEC protected zone. In Exercise 4.8, you will use DNSSEC to sign a zone.

EXERCISE 4.8

Configuring DNSSEC

1. Open DNS Manager.

2. Right-click a forward lookup zone, scroll down to DNSSEC, and click Sign The Zone to launch the Zone Signing Wizard.

3. On the DNS Security Extensions (DNSSEC) page, click Next.

4. On the Signing Options page, select Use Default Settings To Sign The Zone and click Next.

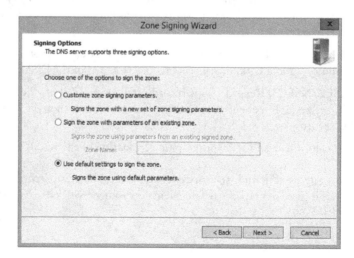

5. On the DNS Security Extensions (DNSSEC) page, click Next.

6. On the Signing the Zone page, click Finish.

7. Verify that the new DNSSEC records and keys have been generated in the zone to complete this exercise.

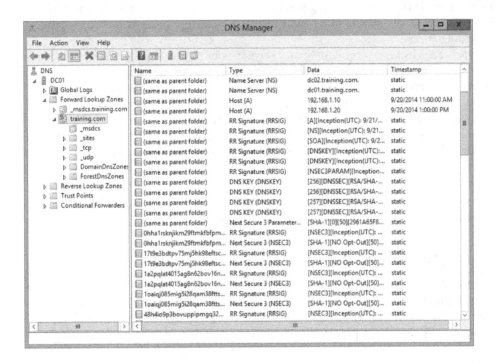

DNS Socket Pool

DNS socket pooling is another great security technology that helps reduce cache-tampering and spoofing attacks by randomizing which source port is used when issuing DNS queries to remote DNS servers. Port randomization makes it difficult for an attacker to spoof the DNS server with an invalid record. By default, Windows Server 2012 R2 uses a socket pool of 2,500. The maximum configuration is 10,000. Administrators can use the dnscmd command-line utility to adjust the DNS socket pool size within their environment. The following is an example of expanding the pool to 5,000 via the command line. Make sure to restart the DNS service after making a change.

```
dnscmd /config /socketpoolsize 5000
```

DNS Cache Locking

DNS cache locking allows an administrator to control when the information stored in the DNS server's cache can be overwritten. When a DNS record is queried, that query is cached by the DNS server based on that record's Time To Live settings. If that same record is queried again before the TTL has expired, the cached information on the DNS server is overwritten. If DNS cache locking is enabled, the DNS server will not overwrite the cached information on new queries of the same record. The feature protects DNS from cache poisoning attacks.

DNS cache locking is configured as a percent value. For example, let's say you configure DNS cache locking at a defined value of 80 percent. This means the DNS server will not overwrite a record's cached information for 80 percent of the duration of that record's TTL. Just like DNS socket pools, DNS cache locking can be configured using the dnscmd command-line utility. By default, DNS cache locking is set to 100 percent. The following is an example of changing the default DNS cache locking percentage to 80 percent via the command line. Make sure and restart the DNS service after making a change.

```
dnscmd /config /cachelockingpercent 80
```

Having all of these additional DNS security tools at your disposal will greatly assist you in hardening your environment and making your network more secure overall.

Configure DNS Logging

Since DNS is such a crucial piece of every organization's infrastructure, it has a dedicated event log that tracks all of the actions that are completed by the DNS Server service, as shown in Figure 4.3. By default, in Windows Server 2012 R2, the DNS Server event logs automatically track audit events correlated to the DNS Server service. An audit event is logged each time DNS settings are changed. A few examples of audit events include zone transfers, zone signing, and dynamic updates.

Windows Server 2012 R2 comes with a new set of enhanced DNS Logging and Diagnostic Tools that provide administrators with Analytical and Debug logs in addition to the Audit logs enabled already. Analytical and Debug logs enable activity tracking that logs an event every time the DNS server sends or receives information. A few examples of Analytical log events include response success, response failure, and internal lookup CNAME.

To take full advantage of these additional tools, you must first install a Windows hotfix that will add change auditing and query logging to your DNS server. Analytical and Debug logs are not enabled by default. You can download and install the hotfix from the following location: http://support.microsoft.com/kb/2956577.

Once you have successfully installed the Windows hotfix, you can enable Analytical and Debug logs in the Window Event Viewer. Exercise 4.9 will demonstrate the process on enabling these additional DNS logs.

FIGURE 4.3 DNS Server Event Viewer log

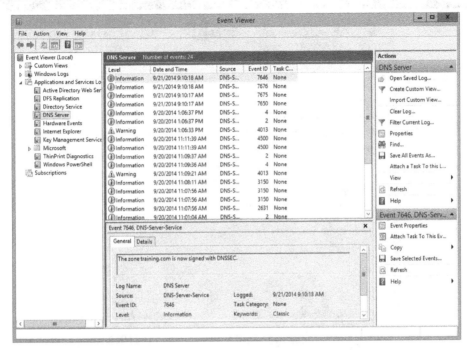

EXERCISE 4.9

Enabling DNS Diagnostic Logging

1. Open Event Viewer.

2. Navigate to Applications And Services Logs ➤ Microsoft ➤ Windows ➤ DNS-Server.

3. Right-click and change your view to Show Analytic And Debug Logs. The Analytical log will be displayed.

4. Right-click the Analytical log and select Properties.

5. On the Log Properties page, select the Do Not Overwrite Events radio button, check the box to enable logging, and then click Apply.

EXERCISE 4.9 *(continued)*

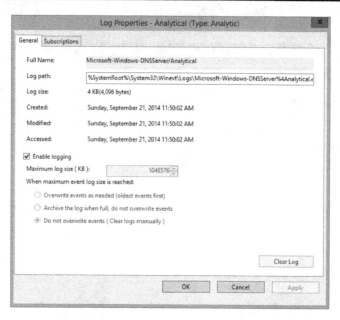

6. Click OK to close log properties. You should now see detailed DNS Analytical events populate in the log.

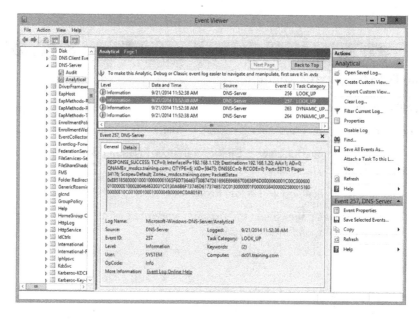

7. Close the Event Viewer to complete this exercise.

DNS logging is a great way to manage and troubleshoot what DNS is doing on your network. Administrators can easily isolate and fix most DNS related issues by checking the event logs. It's even easier when you have the enhanced DNS diagnostic tools enabled.

Configure Delegated Administration

As you are well aware, DNS is highly integrated with Active Directory Domain Services (ADDS). Since the relationship between these two technologies is so close, Active Directory has a built-in security group called DNS Admins to help delegate DNS administration within an environment without having to expose full Domain Admins level privileges to a user account. An administrator would use this security group to separate roles and responsibilities between users.

For example, let's say you have an administrator who is required to manage DNS records, but it is not their responsibility to manage user accounts. Instead of just throwing that administrator in the Domain Admins security group and granting them permissions they don't need, place that administrator's user account in the DNSAdmins security group. This will ensure that you are managing environmental permissions properly, and it will eliminate the possibility of that administrator making changes to things not within their responsibility. You can then use the DNSAdmins group to restrict/allow access to DNS servers on your network just like any other security group.

Configure Recursion

DNS recursion is automatically configured by default in Windows Server 21012 R2. When a client asks a DNS server for a record that isn't stored in a zone that is hosted by that particular DNS server, the DNS server performs a recursive query by going out and finding the result of that query and passing it back to the client if it can be found. This is a nice service for the DNS server to perform, but unfortunately it leaves your network open to denial-of-service (DoS) attacks. In a DoS attack, false or invalid record requests are repeatedly sent to the DNS server, causing it to become increasingly slowed down and even crash completely if it gets too overburdened by requests. To avoid such attacks, it is recommended that DNS recursion be turned off. Exercise 4.10 will walk you through disabling DNS recursion on a DNS server.

EXERCISE 4.10

Disabling DNS Recursion

1. Open DNS Manager.

2. Right-click a DNS server of your choice and click Properties.

3. Navigate to the Advanced tab of the Properties window.

4. Check the box to disable recursion.

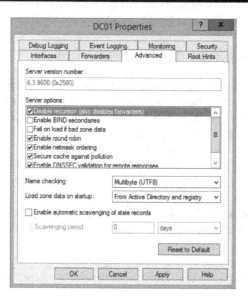

5.   Click Apply and OK to complete this exercise.

Configure Netmask Ordering

Netmask ordering is another DNS feature that comes automatically enabled by default on Windows Server 2012 R2. Basically, this feature makes sure that if a client requests a host record from the DNS server, the DNS server will always return a host record from that client's subnet if one lives there. The DNS server will examine the first three octets of the client's IP address against the record request, assuming that the closest available response would come from that client's subnet.

DNS uses a round-robin rotation to load balance traffic between multiple server IP addresses that happen to share a single DNS name. For example, you have a hostname of www.stellacon.com that maps to three different servers across multiple subnets to help load-balance requests and improve performance within your environment. The IP addresses to each server are as follows:

172.100.10.10

172.100.20.10

172.100.30.10

A client machine with an IP of 172.100.10.150 submits a record request to the DNS server for a lookup on www.stellacon.com. Because of netmask ordering, the DNS server will return the IP of 172.100.10.10 for that client to use. Without netmask ordering enabled, the DNS server could have returned IPs for either of the other two servers, depending on where the next request would fall in this round-robin rotation.

Imagine if the other two servers in the previous example were physically located halfway around the world. Your client's connection could be severely degraded compared to the connection you would have on your local subnet. DNS netmask ordering ensures that your clients get the best possible connection available. Verifying that netmask ordering is enabled is done on the same advanced properties page as disabling DNS recursion (shown in Exercise 4.10).

Configure a GlobalNames Zone

A *GlobalNames zone* is a DNS zone in which the host records that live in that zone use short, single-labeled names instead of a fully qualified domain name (FQDN) to communicate on the network. This is similar to the way administrators use Windows Internet Name Service (WINS) as a name resolution protocol alternative to DNS. GlobalName zones are not intended to support peer-to-peer networks and workstation name resolution, and they don't support dynamic DNS updates. In Exercise 4.11, you will configure a DNS GlobalNames zone.

EXERCISE 4.11

Configuring a GlobalNames Zone

1. Open DNS Manager.

2. Right-click one of your DNS servers and click New Zone to start the New Zone Wizard.

3. Click Next on the Welcome page.

4. On the Zone Type page, make sure that Primary Zone and the Store Zone in Active Directory (available only if DNS server is a writeable domain controller) are selected and then click Next.

5. Click To All DNS Servers In This Forest and then click Next.

6. Click Forward Lookup Zone and then click Next.

7. In Zone Name, type **GlobalNames** and then click Next.

8. Click Do Not Allow Dynamic Updates and then click Next.

9. Click Finish to create the GlobalNames zone and complete this exercise.

Analyze Zone-Level Statistics

Windows Server 2012 R2 introduces a set of new features for gathering and analyzing DNS server statistics. Having this level of granularity for DNS statistics is useful for troubleshooting DNS-related issues. Using PowerShell, an administrator can now easily get the following statistics on every authoritative zone within the environment.

Zone Update Statistics   Provides information on zone dynamic update transactions

   DynamicUpdateReceived   The total number of dynamic update requests received by the DNS server

   DynamicUpdateRejected   The total number of dynamic updates rejected by the DNS server

Zone Query Statistics   Provides the following information

   QueriesReceived   The number of queries received

   QueriesResponded   The number of queries responded successfully (with a valid DNS response)

   QueriesFailure   The number of queries not responded successfully

   QueriesNameError   The number of queries that responded with an NXDOMAIN or EMPTY AUTH response

Zone Transfer Statistics   Provides information about the zone transfer transactions

   RequestReceived   The total number of zone transfer requests received by the DNS Server service when operating as a primary server for a specific zone

   RequestSent   The total number of zone transfer requests sent by the DNS Server service when operating as a secondary server for a specific zone

   ResponseReceived   The total number of zone transfer requests received by the DNS Server service when operating as a secondary server for a specific zone

   SuccessReceived   The total number of zone transfers received by the DNS Server service when operating as a secondary server for a specific zone

   SuccessSent   The total number of zone transfers successfully sent by the DNS Server service when operating as a master server for a specific zone

Use the following PowerShell syntax to analyze and view complete DNS zone-level statistics within your environment:

Get-DnsServerStatistics –ZoneName yourdomain.com

IPAM Administration 101

One of the great features of Windows Server 2012 R2 is the *IP Address Management (IPAM)* utility. IPAM is a built-in utility that allows an administrator to discover, monitor, audit, and manage the TCP/IP schema used on your network. IPAM provides an administrator with the ability to observe and administer the servers that are running the Dynamic Host Configuration Protocol (DHCP) and the Domain Name System. IPAM includes some of the following advantages:

Automatic IP Address Infrastructure Discovery   IPAM has the ability to discover automatically the domain's DHCP servers, DNS servers, and domain controllers. IPAM can do the discovery for any of the domains you specify. Administrators also have the ability to enable or disable management of these servers using the IPAM utility.

Management of DHCP and DNS Services   IPAM gives administrators the capability to monitor and manage Microsoft DHCP and DNS servers across an entire network using the IPAM console.

Custom IP Address Management   Administrators now have the ability to customize the display of IP addresses and tracking and utilization data. IPAM allows the IP address space to be organized into IP address blocks, IP address ranges, and individual IP addresses. To help you organize the IP address space further, built-in or user-defined fields are also assigned to the IP addresses.

Auditing and Tracking of IP Address   IPAM allows administrators to track and audit IP addresses through the use of the IPAM console. IPAM allows IP addresses to be tracked using DHCP lease events and user logon events. These events are collected from the Network Policy Server (NPS) servers, domain controllers, and DHCP servers. Administrators can track IP data by following the IP address, client ID, hostname, or username.

As an administrator, you should understand a few things before installing the IPAM feature. When setting up an IPAM server, you must *not* install IPAM on a domain controller. There are three main methods to deploy an IPAM server.

Distributed   This method allows an IPAM server deployment at every site in an enterprise network.

Centralized   This method allows only one IPAM server in an enterprise network.

Hybrid   This method uses a central IPAM server deployment along with dedicated IPAM servers at each site in the enterprise network.

   Remember, when installing IPAM in any of the scenarios mentioned, you cannot install the IPAM feature on an Active Directory domain controller.

Provision IPAM Manually or by Using Group Policy

If configured, IPAM automatically communicates on your domain. IPAM will try to locate your DNS servers, DHCP servers, and domain controllers as long as those servers are within the searching scope that you have configured. An administrator can configure whether the servers (DNS, DHCP, and domain controllers) are managed by IPAM or unmanaged. Please note that this will work only with Microsoft products; it won't find Infoblox or Unix-based DNS/DHCP.

If you want your servers to be managed by IPAM, you must make sure you set up the network and the servers properly. For example, you will need to configure the security settings and firewall ports properly on the servers (DNS, DHCP, and domain controllers) in order to allow IPAM to access these servers and perform its configuration and monitoring. You can configure these server settings in one of two ways: manually or automatically through the use of a Group Policy object (GPO).

Exercise 4.12 will show you how to install the IPAM feature. You will install and configure the IPAM feature using Server Manager. This exercise has to be done on a member server.

EXERCISE 4.12

Installing the IPAM Feature

1. Open Server Manager.

2. Click the number 2 link, Add Roles And Features.

3. Choose a role-based or feature-based installation and click Next.

4. Choose your server and click Next.

5. On the Roles screen, just click Next.

6. On the Features screen, click the box for the IP Address Management (IPAM) server. Click the Add Features button when the box appears. Click Next.

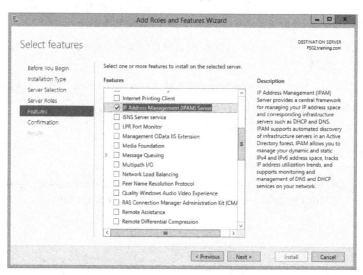

7. At the Confirmation screen, click the Install button.

8. Once the installation is complete, click the Close button.

9. While in Server Manager, click the IPAM link on the left side. This opens the IPAM Overview page.

10. Click number 2, Provision The IPAM Server.

11. Click Next at the Before You Begin screen.

12. Make your database selection on the Configure Database screen and click Next.

13. At the Select Provisioning Method screen, choose GPO and put in a GPO suffix name. I used IPAM1 for the GPO suffix name. This is a unique name to help identify the IPAM.

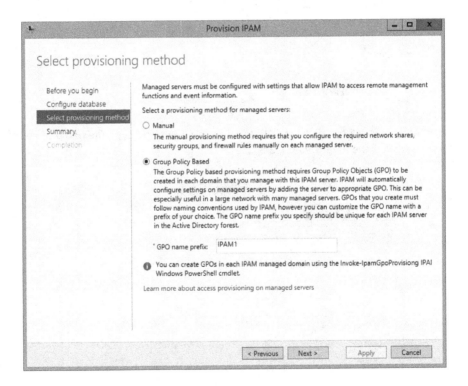

14. At the Summary screen, click the Apply button.

15. Once the process is completed, click the Close button.

16. Under Manage on the IPAM overview screen, choose Add Server.

EXERCISE 4.12 *(continued)*

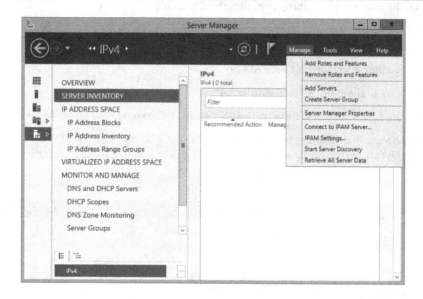

17. In the Add Servers box, click the DNS tab. In the search box, type the name of your DNS server and click the magnifying glass.

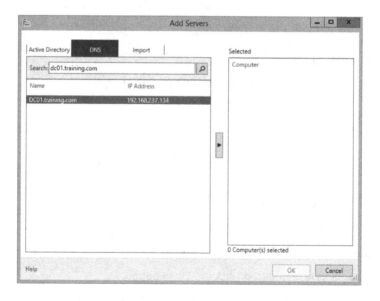

18. Under Name, double-click the server name. The server will be added to the right-side box. Click OK. Close Server Manager.

Configure Server Discovery

Once you have successfully installed and provisioned the IPAM feature on your Windows Server 2012 R2 machine, you can begin server discovery. One of the great things about IPAM is that you can define multiple domains within the same forest to be managed by a single IPAM server. Once initiated, server discovery will automatically search for all of the machines running on the specified domain. Administrator privileges are required for the domain against which you are running server discovery. Exercise 4.13 will walk you through the server discovery process.

EXERCISE 4.13

Configuring IPAM Server Discovery

1.   Open Server Manager and select IPAM.

2.   On the IPAM Overview page, select option 3, Configure Server Discovery.

3.   On the Configure Server Discovery page, select and add the domains you want to discover and click OK.

4.   On the IPAM Overview page, select option 4, Start Server Discovery. The task will run in the background. You will receive notification once server discovery has completed.

5.   On the IPAM home page, select Server Inventory to review the now-completed server discovery of the requested domain. Servers found by server discovery will be in a blocked status until those servers have applied the GPO configured from Exercise 4.12.

Create and Manage IP Blocks and Ranges

In IPAM, IP address space is divided into addresses, ranges, and blocks. Blocks are groups of ranges, and ranges are groups of IPs. Here you will find a breakdown of each IP Management space found within IPAM:

IP Addresses   Individual IP addresses map to a single IP address range. When you map an IP address to a range, it enables actions to be taken on a range that affect all IP addresses in the range, such as adding, updating, or deleting IP address fields.

IP Address Ranges   IP address ranges are smaller chunks of IP addresses that typically correspond to a DHCP scope. IP address ranges are contained within, or "mapped to," IP address blocks. IP address ranges cannot map to multiple IP address blocks, and ranges that map to the same block cannot overlap.

IP Address Blocks   IP address blocks are large chunks of IP addresses that are used to organize address space at a high level. For example, you might use one IP address block for all private IP addresses in your organization and another block for public IP addresses. You can think of IP address blocks as containers that hold IP address ranges. IP address blocks are not deployed and managed on the network like IP address ranges or individual IP addresses.

When you have an IPAM managed DHCP server, the IP address ranges found within the scopes of that DHCP server are automatically entered into the IPAM database during the discovery process. Individual IP addresses and IP blocks are not automatically added to the IPAM database. Exercise 4.14 will demonstrate how to add an IP address space manually.

EXERCISE 4.14

Manually Add IPAM IP Address Space

1.   Open Server Manager and select IPAM.

2.   Select IP Address Inventory.

3.   Right-click IPv4 and select Add IP Address.

4.   Enter the IP address of the device that is to be managed by IPAM. Keep all other defaults.

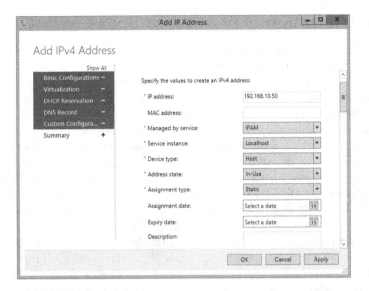

5. Click Apply.

6. On the Summary page, verify that the task completed successfully.

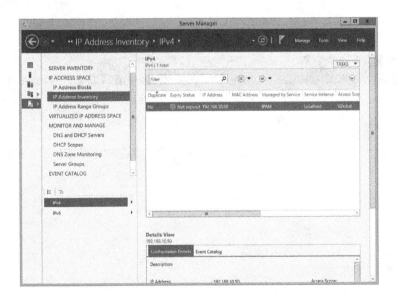

7. Click OK to complete this exercise. Your new IP address is now managed by IPAM. You can now both create and delete DHCP reservations and DNS records for this IP address space from inside the IPAM management console. Similar steps are used to create IP address ranges and blocks. Find the wizard for each under the Tasks menu in the IPAM navigation window.

Monitor Utilization of IP Address Space

It is essential for network administrators to be able to monitor and manage their IP address infrastructure well. This grows increasingly difficult as your network gets bigger and becomes more complex. Unfortunately, quite a few administrators still rely on spreadsheets and basic database applications for IP tracking and usage. The problem is that manual tracking is time-consuming and prone to error.

IPAM tracks the service status of the DNS and DHCP servers on the network. By aggregating multiple DHCP servers, the multiserver management (MSM) module enables an administrator to perform editing and configuration of important properties on multiple DHCP servers and scopes. It also facilitates surveillance and tracking of DHCP service status and utilization of DHCP scopes. IPAM allows for monitoring the condition of a DNS zone on multiple DNS servers by exposing the collected status of a zone across all authoritative DNS servers.

IPAM also comes with its own event catalog that allows administrators to track both DHCP and DNS correlated events. The nice thing about this event log is that you can easily search by client hostname, client ID, username, or IP address for a full list of both DNS- and DHCP-related events on that client. You can also export these event logs to an Excel workbook. The Event Catalog is found toward the bottom of the IPAM hierarchical navigation window, as shown in Figure 4.4.

FIGURE 4.4   IPAM event catalog

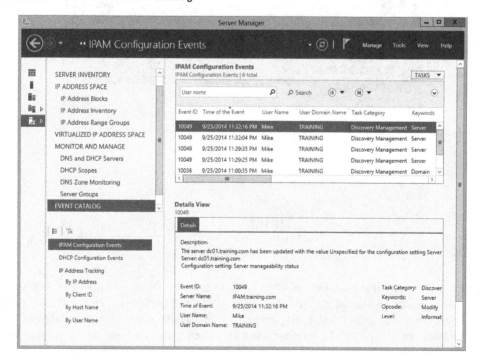

Migrate to IPAM

The situation may arise in which you must migrate your IPAM database infrastructure either from a Windows Internal Database (WID) to a Microsoft SQL database or from one SQL server to another. New to Windows Server 2012 R2, IPAM comes with the functionality to migrate an IPAM database via PowerShell. The `Move-IpamDatabase` cmdlet is used to complete this operation. When this cmdlet is run, a new IPAM schema is created, and then all of the IP address information is copied over. You can also use the `Get-IpamDatabase` cmdlet to review and compare pre- and postdatabase configuration settings during an IPAM database migration.

Delegate IPAM Administration

The delegation of IPAM administration is similar to the delegation of DNS. When IPAM is installed and provisioned, new security groups become available to administrators to configure role-based administration within your IPAM infrastructure. The five new security groups for IPAM administration are as follows:

IPAM Administrators   Members of this group have full permissions to manage and administer an IPAM infrastructure.

IPAM IP Audit Administrators   Members of this group can perform common IPAM management tasks and can carry out IPAM audits.

IPAM ASM Administrators   Members of this group can perform tasks related to IP address space management (ASM) functionality.

IPAM MSM Administrator   Members of this group can perform tasks across multiple IPAM servers through the IPAM multiserver management (MSM) functionality.

IPAM Users   Members of this group can only view information about server discovery, ASM, and MSM in IPAM. They can also view operational events, but they have no access to tracking or auditing information.

In addition to these new security groups, IPAM comes with a new Access Control feature, which allows administrators to get even more granular with IPAM permissions by using up to eight different preconfigured roles. You can also create your own custom IPAM administration roles for full IPAM permissions flexibility within your environment. Figure 4.5 illustrates the new Access Control panel for IPAM delegation of administration. Take the time to add and remove users from each of these groups and roles to get used to IPAM permission sets.

FIGURE 4.5 IPAM Access Control

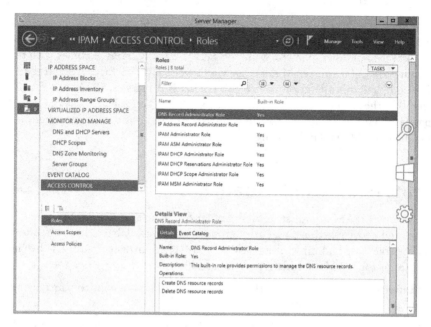

Manage IPAM Collections

In IPAM, server groups are logical groups used to organize managed DHCP and DNS servers. Servers are members of a server group based on values of custom fields that are assigned to the server. Having servers of the same type sorted into their own IPAM collections makes it easier to manage your server lists within the IPAM Management Console. Drop-down menus will allow you to filter server and task lists by IPAM service categories such as DNS or DHCP servers.

Configure IPAM Database Storage

There are two possible IPAM database storage solutions. An administrator can use either a Windows Internal Database (WID) or a dedicated Microsoft SQL Server Instance for their IPAM configuration. For smaller networks, a WID back end will work just fine for the initial IPAM deployment. If in the future the need arises to expand past a WID to a SQL database, then you already know that IPAM comes with migration functionality just for that situation. The database configuration options are chosen during the provisioning steps of an IPAM deployment.

Fully deploy and test the capabilities of the IPAM feature set to help track and forecast IP address utilization within your organization. IPAM is great way to discover, monitor, and manage all of the TCP/IP devices on your network.

Summary

This chapter talked about the advanced configuration options of DHCP, DNS, and IPAM. You learned step-by-step how to configure core network services and features. These features allow administrators to manage network devices easily in a large or complex environment. Understanding how DHCP, DNS, and IPAM all work together is essential for ensuring success when taking the exam. Focus your attention on completing the labs found within the chapter and learning the ins and outs of each management console for DHCP, DNS, and IPAM administration.

Exam Essentials

Understand DHCP Failover DHCP failover (and load sharing) is one of the hottest new features in Windows Server 2012 R2. It is easy to deploy, and it provides an added level of redundancy when compared to using a DHCP split-scope configuration.

Know How to Configure DHCP Name Protection DHCP name protection protects DNS Host A records from being overwritten by other client's Host A records during DNS dynamic updates. DHCP name protection is configured using the DHCP Management Console.

Understand IP Address Management IPAM allows administrators to track and audit IP addresses through the use of the IPAM console. IPAM allows IP addresses to be tracked using DHCP lease events and user logon events.

Know How to Provision IPAM and Configure Server Discovery IPAM is managed and monitored in Server Manager. Know that there are two separate provisioning models—manual and GPO—and know how to configure each. Know how to configure IPAM server discovery.

Understand Security for DNS Hardening your DNS infrastructure is important. Know how to configure and use DNSSEC, socket pooling, and cache locking to make your network more secure.

Know How to Configure and Use DNS Logging DNS logging gives administrators a more granular inside view at what DNS is actually doing on the network. DNS logging helps administrators troubleshoot DNS issues within the environment.

Know How to Analyze DNS Zone-Level Statistics Administrators can use PowerShell to troubleshoot DNS-related issues further. You can generate and export multiple reports that will help you analyze DNS queries, requests, and dynamic updates.

Know How to Delegate Both DNS and IPAM Administration Active Directory has specific security groups for delegating DNS administration, and IPAM has its own internal delegation of administration. A user does not need to be a member of the Domain Admins group in order to manage these services.

Review Questions

1. You are the network administrator for a midsize computer company. You have a single Active Directory forest, and you have a requirement to implement DHCP for the organization. You need to ensure that your DHCP deployment configuration is both fault-tolerant and redundant. Out of the options provided, which is the most reliable DHCP configuration that you could implement?

   A. DHCP split scope

   B. DHCP multicast scope

   C. DHCP failover

   D. DHCP super scope

2. You are a systems administrator for a large computer company. You have a multidomain Active Directory forest, and you have a requirement to implement advanced DNS security options for the organization. Which three security options could you configure to make DNS more secure on your network? (Choose three.)

   A. DNSSEC

   B. DNS registration

   C. DNS cache locking

   D. DNS socket pooling

3. You are the network administrator for a software development company. Your DNS infrastructure consists of multiple DNS servers that are geographically disparate. You need to ensure that when clients perform DNS queries, those queries will always be sent to the closest DNS server for lookup services. What must be enabled for this to take place on your network?

   A. DNS logging

   B. DNS delegated administration

   C. DNS recursion

   D. DNS netmask ordering

4. You are an IT manager for an enterprise storage solutions company. You have just hired a new team member to your network staff with the primary responsibility of managing DNS for your organization. It will not be this administrator's responsibility to manage any other active directory services for the company. Which security group would best fit this administrator's responsibilities?

   A. Domain Admins

   B. Enterprise Admins

   C. Schema Admins

   D. DNSAdmins

5. You are the network administrator for a toy company. Your DHCP infrastructure includes the use of DNS dynamic updates. You need to ensure that DNS host A records are not over-written by new DNS devices with the same hostname during DNS dynamic updates. Which DHCP configuration option would fulfill this requirement?

   A. Configure DNS Registration

   B. Configure DHCP Name Protection

   C. Configure DHCP High Availability

   D. Implement A DHCPv6 Scope

6. You are the infrastructure team lead for a high-tech hardware development company. You need to delegate some of the teams IPAM administration responsibilities between team members. You decide that Noelle will be managing IPAM address spaces, but she will not be managing IP address tracking and auditing. Which IPAM security group would best fit Noelle's new responsibilities?

   A. IPAM Administrators

   B. IPAM Users

   C. IPAM ASM Administrators

   D. IPAM MSM Administrators

7. You are the network administrator for a large communications company. You have recently decided to implement IPAM within your organization with the release of Windows Server 2012 R2. You want to set up your IPAM infrastructure so that one primary server can manage your entire enterprise. Which IPAM deployment method would fulfill this require-ment?

   A. Isolated

   B. Centralized

   C. Hybrid

   D. Distributed

8. You are the systems administrator for an advanced space exploration research facility. Your DNS infrastructure needs to accommodate the use of short, single-labeled DNS hostnames instead of the usual FQDN. Which advanced network configuration option would accom-modate this requirement?

   A. Configure DNS Recursion

   B. Configure DHCP Name Protection

   C. Configure IPAM Server Discovery

   D. Configure A GlobalNames Zone

9. You are the lead network administrator for a web hosting company. You have recently made the decision to implement IPAM within your organization. You have already installed and provisioned the IPAM feature on your dedicated Windows Server 2012 R2 server. What is the next logical step in your IPAM deployment?

    A. Create a new IP block

    B. Delegate IPAM administration

    C. Configure server discovery

    D. Create a new IP range

10. You are a systems administrator for the Stellacon Corporation. Because of the unusual growth of TCP/IP devices on your corporate network over the last year, you need to scale out your IPAM database capabilities. You are currently using a Windows Internal Database (WID) for your IPAM infrastructure, and you want to migrate your IPAM database to a Microsoft SQL Server. Which PowerShell cmdlet would you use to verify current IPAM database configuration settings?

    A. `Get-IpamDatabase`

    B. `Show-IpamDatabaseConfig`

    C. `Show-IpamStatistics`

    D. `Get-IpamMigrationSettings`

Chapter 5

Configure the Active Directory Infrastructure

THE FOLLOWING 70-412 EXAM OBJECTIVES ARE COVERED IN THIS CHAPTER:

✓ **Configure a forest or a domain**

- Implement multi-domain and multi-forest Active Directory environments including interoperability with previous versions of Active Directory
- Upgrade existing domains and forests including environment preparation and functional levels
- Configure multiple user principal name (UPN) suffixes

✓ **Configure Trusts**

- Configure external, forest, shortcut, and realm trusts
- Configure trust authentication
- Configure SID filtering
- Configure name suffix routing

✓ **Configure Sites**

- Configure sites and subnets
- Create and configure site links
- Manage site coverage
- Manage registration of SRV records
- Move domain controllers between sites

✓ **Manage Active Directory and SYSVOL replication**

- Configure replication to Read-Only Domain Controllers (RODCs)

- Configure Password Replication Policy (PRP) for RODCs

- Monitor and manage replication

- Upgrade SYSVOL replication to Distributed File System Replication (DFSR)

Microsoft has designed Active Directory to be an enterprise-wide solution for managing network resources. In previous chapters, you saw how to create Active Directory objects based on an organization's logical design. Domain structure and organizational unit (OU) structure, for example, should be designed based primarily on an organization's business needs.

Now it's time to learn how Active Directory can map to an organization's *physical* requirements. Specifically, you must consider network connectivity between sites and the flow of information between domain controllers (DCs) under less-than-ideal conditions. These constraints determine how domain controllers can work together to ensure that the objects within Active Directory remain synchronized no matter how large and geographically dispersed the network.

Fortunately, through the use of the Active Directory Sites and Services administrative tool, you can quickly and easily create the various components of an Active Directory replication topology. Using this tool, you can create objects called *sites*, place servers in sites, and create connections between sites. Once you have configured Active Directory replication to fit your current network environment, you can sit back and allow Active Directory to make sure that information remains consistent across domain controllers.

This chapter covers the features of Active Directory, which allow system administrators to modify the behavior of replication based on their physical network design. Through the use of sites, system and network administrators will be able to leverage their network infrastructure best to support Windows Server 2012 R2 and Active Directory.

So far, you have learned the steps necessary to install the Domain Name System (DNS) and to implement the first Active Directory domain. Although I briefly introduced multidomain Active Directory structures earlier, I focused on only a single domain and the objects within it.

Many businesses find that using a single domain provides an adequate solution to meet their business needs. By working with *trees* and *forests*, however, large organizations can use multiple domains to organize their environments better.

Overview of Network Planning

Before I discuss sites and replication, you need to understand some basic physical and network concepts.

The Three Types of Networks

When designing networks, system and network administrators use the following terms to define the types of connectivity between locations and servers:

Local Area Networks   A *local area network (LAN)* is usually characterized as a high-bandwidth network. Generally, an organization owns all of its LAN network hardware and software. Ethernet is by far the most common networking standard. Ethernet speeds are generally at least 10Mbps and can scale to multiple gigabits per second. Currently, the standard for Ethernet is the 10 Gigabit Ethernet, which runs at 10 times the speed of Gigabit Ethernet (1GB). Several LAN technologies, including routing and switching, are available to segment LANs and to reduce contention for network resources.

Wide Area Networks   The purpose of a *wide area network (WAN)* is similar to that of a LAN, that is, to connect network devices. Unlike LANs, however, WANs are usually leased from third-party telecommunications carriers and organizations known as *Internet service providers (ISPs)*. Although extremely high-speed WAN connections are available, they are generally costly for organizations to implement through a distributed environment. Therefore, WAN connections are characterized by lower-speed connections and, sometimes, nonpersistent connections.

The Internet   The *Internet* is a worldwide public network infrastructure based on the *Internet Protocol (IP)*. Access to the Internet is available through Internet service providers (ISPs). Because it is a public network, there is no single "owner" of the Internet. Instead, large network and telecommunications providers constantly upgrade the infrastructure of this network to meet growing demands.

Organizations use the Internet regularly to sell and market their products and services. For example, it's rare nowadays to see advertisements that don't direct you to one website or another. Through the use of technologies such as *virtual private networks (VPNs)*, organizations can use encryption and authentication technology to enable secure communications across the Internet.

Exploring Network Constraints

In an ideal situation, a high-speed network would connect all computers and networking devices. In such a situation, you would be able to ensure that any user of your network, regardless of location, would be able to access resources quickly and easily. When you are working in the real world, however, you have many other constraints to keep in mind, including network bandwidth and network cost.

Network Bandwidth

Network bandwidth generally refers to the amount of data that can pass through a specific connection in a given amount of time. For example, in a WAN situation, a T1 may have 1.544Mbps (megabits per second), while a DSL might have a bandwidth of 56Kbps or 57.6Kbps (kilobits per second) or more. On the other hand, your LAN's Ethernet connection may have a bandwidth of 100Mbps. Different types of networks work at different speeds. Therefore, it's imperative that you always consider network bandwidth when thinking about how to deploy domain controllers in your environment.

Network Cost

Cost is perhaps the single largest factor in determining a network design. If cost were not a constraint, organizations would clearly elect to use high-bandwidth connections for all of their sites. Realistically, trade-offs in performance must be made for the sake of affordability. Some factors that can affect the cost of networking include the distance between networks and the types of technology available at locations throughout the world. In remote or less-developed locations, you may not even be able to get access through an ISP or telecom beyond a satellite connection or dial-up, and what is available can be quite costly. Network designers must keep these factors in mind, and they must often settle for less-than-ideal connectivity.

You have considered the monetary value of doing business. Now let's consider another aspect of cost. When designing and configuring networks, you can require certain devices to make data-transport decisions automatically based on an assigned network cost. These devices are commonly known as *routers*, and they use routing protocols to make routing decisions. One of the elements a router uses to configure a routing protocol is its ability to adjust the cost of a route. For example, a router may have multiple ways to connect to a remote site, and it may have multiple interfaces connected to it, each with different paths out of the network to which it is connected locally. When two or more routes are available, you can set up a routing protocol that states that the route with the lower cost is automatically used first.

Another cost is personnel. Do you have the personnel to do the job, or do you need to hire a consultant? Remember that even if you use individuals already on staff, they will be spending time on these projects. When your IT team is working on a project, this is a cost because they cannot also be working on day-to-day tasks.

All of these factors play an important role when you make your Active Directory implementation decisions.

Overview of Active Directory Replication and Sites

Now I need to address two topics that not only are covered heavily on the Microsoft exams but are two areas that all IT administrators should understand. Understanding Active Directory replication and sites can help you fine-tune a network to run at peak performance.

Replicating Active Directory

Regardless of the issues related to network design and technological constraints, network users have many different requirements and needs that must be addressed. First, network resources, such as files, printers, and shared directories, must be made available.

Similarly, the resources stored within Active Directory, and its security information in particular, are required for many operations that occur within domains.

With these issues in mind, take a look at how you can configure Active Directory to reach connectivity goals using replication.

Active Directory was designed as a scalable, distributed database that contains information about an organization's network resources. In previous chapters, you saw how you can create and manage domains and how you can use domain controllers to store Active Directory databases.

Even in the simplest of network environments, you generally need more than one domain controller. The major reasons for this are *fault tolerance* (if one domain controller fails, others can still provide services as needed) and performance (the workload can be balanced between multiple domain controllers). Windows Server 2012 R2 domain controllers have been designed to contain read-write copies as well as read-only copies of the Active Directory database. However, the domain controllers must also remain current when objects are created or modified on other domain controllers.

To keep information consistent between domain controllers, you use *Active Directory replication*. Replication is the process by which changes to the Active Directory database are transferred between domain controllers. The result is that all of the domain controllers within an Active Directory domain contain up-to-date information and achieve convergence. Keep in mind that domain controllers may be located very near to each other (for example, within the same server rack), or they may be located across the world from each other. Although the goals of replication are quite simple, the real-world constraints of network connections between servers cause many limitations that you must accommodate. If you have a domain controller on your local LAN, you may find that you have Gigabit Ethernet, which runs at 1000Mbps between your server connections, whereas you may have a domain controller on the other side or a WAN where the network link runs at a fraction of a T1, 56Kbps. Replication traffic must traverse each link to ensure convergence no matter what the speed or what bandwidth is available.

Throughout this chapter, you will study the technical details of Active Directory replication. You will also learn how to use the concept of sites and site links to map the logical structure of Active Directory to a physical network topology to help it work efficiently, no matter the type of link with which you are working.

Understanding Active Directory Site Concepts

One of the most important aspects of designing and implementing Active Directory is understanding how it allows you to separate the logical components of the directory service from the physical components.

The logical components—Active Directory domains, OUs, users, groups, and computers—map to the organizational and business requirements of a company.

The physical components, on the other hand, are designed based on the technical issues involved in keeping the network synchronized (that is, making sure that all parts of the network have the same up-to-date information). Active Directory uses the concept of sites to map to an organization's physical network. Stated simply, a *site* is a collection of well-connected subnets. The technical implications of sites are described later in this chapter.

It is important to understand that no specified relationship exists between Active Directory domains and Active Directory sites. An Active Directory site can contain many domains. Alternatively, a single Active Directory domain can span multiple sites. Figure 5.1 illustrates this very important characteristic of domains and sites.

FIGURE 5.1   Potential relationships between domains and sites

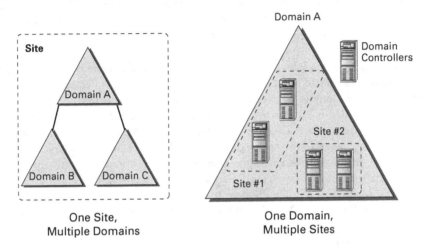

It is important to understand that no specified relationship exists between Active Directory domains and Active Directory sites. An Active Directory site can contain many domains. Alternatively, a single Active Directory domain can span multiple sites. Figure 5.1 illustrates this very important characteristic of domains and sites.

There are two main reasons to use Active Directory sites: service requests and replication.

Service Requests

Clients often require the network services of a domain controller. One of the most common reasons for this is that they need the domain controller to perform network authentication. If your Active Directory network is set up with sites, clients can easily connect to the domain controller that is located closest to them. By doing this, they avoid many of the inefficiencies associated with connecting to distant domain controllers or to those that are located on the other side of a slow network connection. For example, by connecting to a local domain controller, you can avoid the problems associated with a saturated network link that might cause two domain controllers to be out of sync with each other.

Replication

As mentioned earlier, the purpose of Active Directory replication is to ensure that the information stored on all domain controllers within a domain remains synchronized. In environments with many domains and domain controllers, multiple communication paths usually connect them, which makes the synchronization process more complicated. A simple method of transferring updates and other changes to Active Directory involves all of the servers communicating directly with each other as soon as a change occurs; they can all update with the change and reach convergence again. This is not ideal, however, because it places high requirements on network bandwidth and is inefficient for many network environments that use slower and more costly WAN links, especially if all environments update at the same time. Such simultaneous updating could cause the network connection at the core of your network to become saturated and decrease the performance of the entire WAN.

Using sites, Active Directory can automatically determine the best methods for performing replication operations. Sites take into account an organization's network infrastructure, and Active Directory uses these sites to determine the most efficient method for synchronizing information between domain controllers. System administrators can make their physical network design map to Active Directory objects. Based on the creation and configuration of these objects, the Active Directory service can then manage replication traffic in an efficient way.

Whenever a change is made to the Active Directory database on a domain controller, the change is given an update sequence number. The domain controller can then propagate these changes to other domain controllers based on replication settings.

Windows Server 2012 R2 uses a feature called *linked value replication* that is active only when the domain is in the Windows Server 2003, Windows Server 2008, Windows Server 2008 R2, Windows Server 2012, or Windows Server 2012 R2 domain functional level. With linked value replication, only the group member is replicated. This greatly enhances replication efficiency and cuts down on network traffic utilization. Linked value replication is automatically enabled in Windows Server 2003, Windows Server 2008, Windows Server 2008 R2, Windows Server 2012, and Windows Server 2012 R2 functional-level domains.

Planning Your Sites

Much of the challenge of designing Active Directory is related to mapping a company's business processes to the structure of a hierarchical data store. So far, you've seen many of these requirements. What about the existing network infrastructure, however? Clearly, when you plan for and design the structure of Active Directory, you must take into account your LAN and WAN characteristics. Let's see some of the ways that you can use Active Directory sites to manage replication traffic.

Synchronizing Active Directory is extremely important. To keep security permissions and objects within the directory consistent throughout the organization, you must use replication. The Active Directory data store supports *multimaster replication*; that is, data can be modified at any domain controller within the domain because replication ensures that information remains consistent throughout the organization.

Ideally, every site within an organization has reliable, high-speed connections with the other sites. A much more realistic scenario, however, is one in which bandwidth is limited and connections are sometimes either sporadically available or completely unavailable.

Using sites, network and system administrators can define which domain controllers are located on which areas of the network. These settings can be based on the bandwidth available between the areas of the network. Additionally, these administrators can define *subnets*—logically partitioned areas of the network—between areas of the network. Subnets are designed by subdividing IP addresses into usable blocks for assignment, and they are also objects found within the Sites and Services Microsoft Management Console (MMC) in the Administrative Tools folder. Windows Server 2012 R2 Active Directory services use this information to decide how and when to replicate data between domain controllers.

Directly replicating information between all domain controllers might be a viable solution for some companies. For others, however, this might result in a lot of traffic traveling over slow or undersized network links. One way to synchronize data efficiently between sites that have slow connections is to use a *bridgehead server*. Bridgehead servers are designed to accept traffic between two remote sites and then to forward this information to the appropriate servers. Figure 5.2 provides an example of how a bridgehead server can reduce network bandwidth requirements and improve performance. Reduced network bandwidth requirements and improved performance can also be achieved by configuring replication to occur according to a predefined schedule if bandwidth usage statistics are available.

FIGURE 5.2 Using a bridgehead server

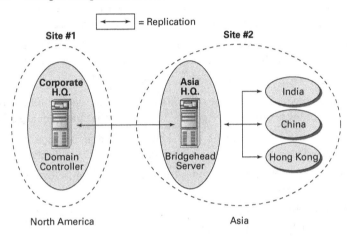

Bridgehead servers do not fit a normal hub-and-spoke WAN topology. Such a topology usually involves a core site (for example, company headquarters) with remote sites as links one off from the core. However, you can use a bridgehead server design to fit a distributed star, where you have a hub-and-spoke topology design with additional spokes coming out of the first set of spokes. Doing so would make some of your spoke sites into smaller core sites. It is at these sites that you would place your bridgehead servers. In Figure 5.2, you can see that your Asia headquarters site is also where you can connect to India, China, and Hong Kong, thus making the Asia headquarters the ideal site for the bridgehead server.

In addition to managing replication traffic, sites offer the advantage of allowing clients to access the nearest domain controller. This prevents problems with user authentication across slow network connections, and it can help find the shortest and fastest path to resources such as files and printers. Therefore, Microsoft recommends that you place at least one domain controller at each site that contains a slow link. Preferably, this domain controller also contains a copy of the global catalog so that logon attempts and resource search queries do not occur across slow links. The drawback, however, is that deploying more copies of the global catalog to servers increases replication traffic.

Through proper planning and deployment of sites, organizations can best use the capabilities of the network infrastructure while keeping Active Directory synchronized.

Understanding Distributed File System Replication

DFS Replication (DFSR) was created to replace the File Replication Service (FRS) that was introduced in the Windows 2000 Server operating systems. DFSR is a state-based, multimaster replication engine that supports replication scheduling and bandwidth throttling. DFSR has the ability to detect insertions, removals, and rearrangements of data in files. This allows DFS Replication to replicate only the changed file blocks when files are updated.

The DFS Replication component uses many different processes to keep data synchronized on multiple servers. To understand the DFSR process, it is helpful to understand some of the following concepts:

- DFSR is a multimaster replication engine, and changes that occur on one of the members are then replicated to all of the other members of the replication group.

- DFSR uses the update sequence number (USN) journal to detect changes on the volume, and then DFSR replicates the changes only after the file is closed.

- Before sending or receiving a file, DFSR uses a staging folder to stage the file.

- When a file is changed, DFSR replicates only the changed blocks and not the entire file. The RDC protocol is what helps determine the blocks that have changed in the file.

- One of the advantages of DFSR is that it is self-healing and can automatically recover from USN journal wraps, USN journal loss, or loss of the DFS Replication database.

- Windows Server 2012 R2 DFSR includes the ability to add a failover cluster as a member of a replication group.

- Windows Server 2012 R2 DFSR allows for read-only replicated folders on a particular member in which users cannot add or change files.

- In Windows Server 2012 R2, it is possible to make changes to the SYSVOL folder of an RODC.

The Dfsrdiag.exe command-line tool includes three Windows Server 2012 R2 command-line switches that provide enhanced diagnostic capabilities for DFSR:

Dfsrdiag.exe ReplState   When you use the ReplState switch, a summary of the replication status across all connections on the specified replication group member is provided. The ReplState switch takes a snapshot of the internal state of the DFSR service, and the updates that are currently being processed (downloaded or served) by the service are shown in a list.

Dfsrdiag.exe IdRecord   When replicating a file or folder, the DFSR service creates an ID record, and an administrator can use this ID record to determine whether a file has replicated properly to a specific member. The IdRecord switch returns the DFSR ID record for the file or folder that you specify by using its path or its unique identifier (UID).

Dfsrdiag.exe FileHash   The FileHash switch, when used against a particular file, will compute and display the hash value that is generated by the DFSR service. An administrator can then look at the hash values to compare two files. If the hash values for the two files are the same, then the two files are the same.

Implementing Sites and Subnets

Now that you have a good idea of the goals of replication, take a look at the following quick overview of the various Active Directory objects that are related to physical network topology.

The basic objects that are used for managing replication include the following:

Subnets   A *subnet* is a partition of a network. As I started to discuss earlier, subnets are logical IP blocks usually connected to other IP blocks through the use of routers and other network devices. All of the computers that are located on a given subnet are generally well connected with each other.

> It is extremely important to understand the concepts of TCP/IP and the routing of network information when you are designing the topology for Active Directory replication.

Sites   An Active Directory site is a logical object that can contain servers and other objects related to Active Directory replication. Specifically, a *site* is a grouping of related subnets. Sites are created to match the physical network structure of an organization. Sites are primarily used for slow WAN links. If your network is well connected (using fiber optics, Category 5 Ethernet, and so on), then sites are not needed.

Site Links   A *site link* is created to define the types of connections that are available between the components of a site. Site links can reflect a relative cost for a network connection and can also reflect the bandwidth that is available for communications.

All of these components work together to determine how information is used to replicate data between domain controllers. Figure 5.3 provides an example of the physical components of Active Directory.

FIGURE 5.3   Active Directory replication objects

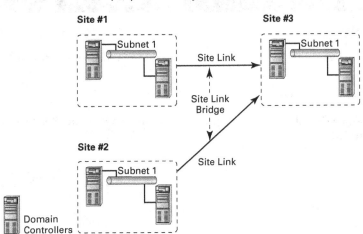

Many issues are related to configuring and managing sites, and all of them are covered in this chapter. Overall, using sites allows you to control the behavior of Active Directory replication between domain controllers. With this background and goal in mind, let's look at how you can implement sites to control Active Directory replication so that it is efficient and in sync.

If you do not have replication set up properly, after a while you will experience problems with your domain controllers. An example of a common replication problem is Event Log event ID 1311, which states that the Windows NT Directory Services (NTDS) Knowledge Consistency Checker (KCC) has found (and reported) a problem with Active Directory replication. This error message states that the replication configuration information in Active Directory does not accurately reflect the physical topology of the network. This error is commonly found on ailing networks that have replication problems for one reason or another.

Creating Sites

The primary method for creating and managing Active Directory replication components is to utilize the Active Directory Sites and Services tool or the MMC found within the Administrative Tools folder. Using this administrative component, you can graphically create and manage sites in much the same way that you create and manage OUs.

Exercise 5.1 walks you through the process of creating Active Directory sites. For you to complete this exercise, the local machine must be a domain controller. Also, this exercise assumes that you have not yet changed the default domain site configuration.

 Do not perform any testing on a production system or network. Make sure you test site configuration in a lab setting only.

EXERCISE 5.1

Creating Sites

1. Open the Active Directory Sites and Services tool from the Administrative Tools program group.

2. Expand the Sites folder.

3. Right-click the Default-First-Site-Name item and choose Rename. Rename the site **CorporateHQ**.

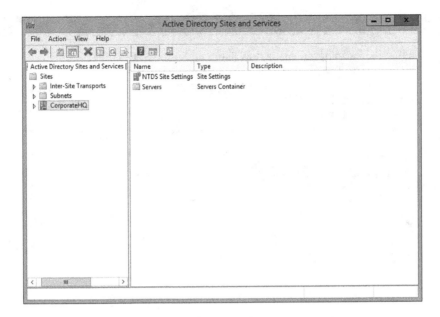

4. Create a new site by right-clicking the Sites object and selecting New Site.

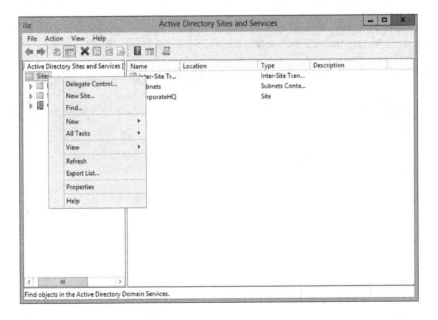

5. In the New Object – Site dialog box, type **Farmington** for the site name. Click the DEFAULTIPSITELINK item, and an information screen pops up. Then click OK to create the site. Note that you cannot include spaces or other special characters in the name of a site.

EXERCISE 5.1 *(continued)*

6. Notice that the Farmington site is now listed under the Sites object.

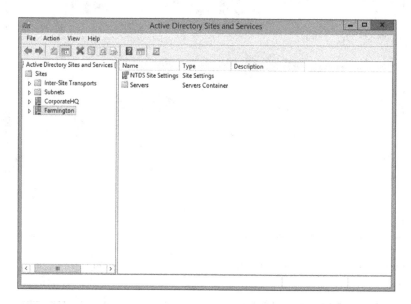

7. Create another new site and name it **Portsmouth**. Again, choose the DEFAULTIPSITE-LINK item. Notice that the new site is listed under the Sites object.

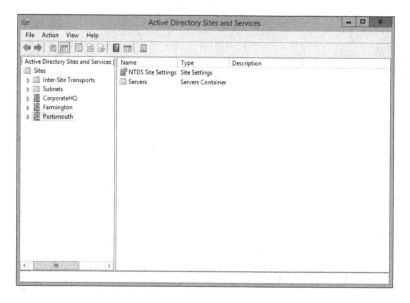

8. When you have finished, close the Active Directory Sites and Services tool.

Creating Subnets

Once you have created the sites that map to your network topology, it's time to define the subnets that define the site boundaries.

Subnets are based on TCP/IPv4 or TCP/IPv6 address information. For example, the IPv4 address may be 10.10.0.0, and the subnet mask may be 255.255.0.0. This information specifies that all of the TCP/IP addresses that begin with the first two octets are part of the same TCP/IP subnet. All of the following TCP/IP addresses would be within this subnet:

- 10.10.1.5

- 10.10.100.17

- 10.10.110.120

The Active Directory Sites and Services tool expresses these subnets in a somewhat different notation. It uses the provided subnet address and appends a slash followed by the number of bits in the subnet mask. In the example in the previous paragraph, the subnet would be defined as 10.1.0.0/16.

Remember that sites typically represent distinct physical locations, and they almost always have their own subnets. The only way for a domain controller in one site to reach a DC in another site is to add subnet information about the remote site. Generally, information regarding the definition of subnets for a specific network environment will be available from a network designer. Exercise 5.2 walks you through the steps that you need to take to create subnets and assign subnets to sites. To complete the steps in this exercise, you must have completed Exercise 5.1.

EXERCISE 5.2

Creating Subnets

1. Open the Active Directory Sites and Services tool from the Administrative Tools program group.

2. Expand the Sites folder. Right-click the Subnets folder and select New Subnet.

3. In the New Object – Subnet dialog box, you are prompted for information about the IPv4 or IPv6 details for the new subnet. For the prefix, type **10.10.1.0/24** (you are staying with the more commonly used IPv4). This actually calculates out to 10.10.1.0 with the mask of 255.255.255.0. Click the Farmington site and then click OK to create the subnet.

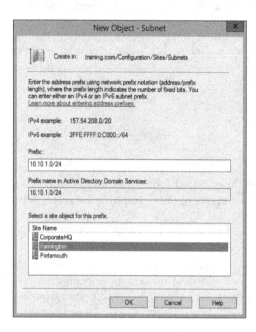

4. In the Active Directory Sites and Services tool, right-click the newly created 10.10.1.0/24 subnet object and select Properties.

5. On the subnet's Properties dialog box, type **Farmington 100MB LAN** for the description. Click OK to continue.

6. Create a new subnet using the following information:

    Address: **160.25.0.0/16**

    Site: **Portsmouth**

    Description: **Portsmouth 100Mbit LAN**

7. Finally, create another subnet using the following information:

    Address: **176.33.0.0/16**

    Site: **CorporateHQ**

    Description: **Corporate 100Mbit switched LAN**

8. When finished, close the Active Directory Sites and Services tool.

So far, you have created the basic components that govern Active Directory sites and subnets. You also linked these two components by defining which subnets belong in which sites. These two steps—creating sites and creating subnets—form the basis of mapping the physical network infrastructure of an organization to Active Directory. Now look at the various settings that you can make for sites.

Configuring Sites

Once you have created Active Directory sites and have defined which subnets they contain, it's time to make some additional configuration settings for the site structure. Specifically, you'll need to assign servers to specific sites and configure the site-licensing options. By placing servers in sites, you tell Active Directory replication services how to replicate information for various types of servers. Later in this chapter, you'll examine the details of working with replication within and between sites.

In Exercise 5.3, you will add servers to sites and configure CorpDC1 options. To complete the steps in this exercise, you must have completed Exercise 5.1 and Exercise 5.2.

EXERCISE 5.3

Configuring Sites

1. Open the Active Directory Sites and Services tool from the Administrative Tools program group.

2. Expand the Sites folder and click and expand the Farmington site.

3. Right-click the Servers container in the Farmington site and select New ➢ Server. Type **FarmingtonDC1** for the name of the server and then click OK.

4. Create a new Server object within the CorporateHQ site and name it **CorpDC1**. Note that this object also includes the name of the local domain controller.

5. Create two new Server objects within the Portsmouth site and name them **PortsmouthDC1** and **PortsmouthDC2**.

6. Right-click the CorpDC1 server object and select Properties. On the General tab of the CorpDC1 Properties box, select SMTP in the Transports Available For Inter-site Data Transfer box and click Add to make this server a preferred IP bridgehead server. Click OK to accept the settings.

7. When you have finished, close the Active Directory Sites and Services tool.

With the configuration of the basic settings for sites out of the way, it's time to focus on the real details of the site topology—creating site links and site link bridges.

Configuring Replication

Sites are generally used to define groups of computers that are located within a single geographic location. In most organizations, machines that are located in close physical proximity (for example, within a single building or branch office) are well connected. A typical example is a LAN in a branch office of a company. All of the computers may be connected using Ethernet, and routing and switching technology may be in place to reduce network congestion.

Often, however, domain controllers are located across various states, countries, and even continents. In such a situation, network connectivity is usually much slower, less reliable, and more costly than that for the equivalent LAN. Therefore, Active Directory replication must accommodate this situation accordingly. When managing replication traffic within Active Directory sites, you need to be aware of two types of synchronization:

Intrasite *Intrasite replication* refers to the synchronization of Active Directory information between domain controllers that are located in the same site. In accordance with the concept of sites, these machines are usually well connected by a high-speed LAN.

Intersite *Intersite replication* occurs between domain controllers in different sites. Usually, this means there is a WAN or other type of low-speed network connection between the various machines. Intersite replication is optimized for minimizing the amount of network traffic that occurs between sites.

In the following sections, you'll look at ways to configure both intrasite and intersite replication. Additionally, you'll see features of Active Directory replication architecture that you can use to accommodate the needs of almost any environment.

Intrasite Replication

Intrasite replication is generally a simple process. One domain controller contacts the others in the same site when changes to its copy of Active Directory are made. It compares the update sequence numbers in its own copy of Active Directory with those of the other domain controllers; then the most current information is chosen by the DC in question, and all domain controllers within the site use this information to make the necessary updates to their database.

Because you can assume that the domain controllers within an Active Directory site are well connected, you can pay less attention exactly to when and how replication takes place. Communications between domain controllers occur using the *Remote Procedure Call (RPC) protocol*. This protocol is optimized for transmitting and synchronizing information on fast and reliable network connections. The RPC protocol provides for fast replication at the expense of network bandwidth, which is usually readily available because most LANs today are running on Fast Ethernet (100Mbps) at a minimum.

Intersite Replication

Intersite replication is optimized for low-bandwidth situations and network connections that have less reliability. Intersite replication offers several features that are tailored toward these types of connections. To begin with, two different protocols may be used to transfer information between sites:

RPC over IP   When connectivity is fairly reliable, IP is a good choice. IP-based communications require you to have a live connection between two or more domain controllers in different sites and let you transfer Active Directory information. RPC over IP was originally designed for slower WANs in which packet loss and corruption may often occur.

Simple Mail Transfer Protocol   *Simple Mail Transfer Protocol (SMTP)* is perhaps best known as the protocol that is used to send and receive email messages on the Internet. SMTP was designed to use a store-and-forward mechanism through which a server receives a copy of a message, records it to disk, and then attempts to forward it to another email server. If the destination server is unavailable, it holds the message and attempts to resend it at periodic intervals.

This type of communication is extremely useful for situations in which network connections are unreliable or not always available. For example, if a branch office in Peru were connected to the corporate office through a dial-up connection that is available only during certain hours, SMTP would be a good choice for communication with that branch.

SMTP is an inherently insecure network protocol. Therefore, if you would like to ensure that you transfer replication traffic securely and you use SMTP for Active Directory replication, you must take advantage of Windows Server 2012's Certificate Services functionality.

Other intersite replication characteristics are designed to address low-bandwidth situations and less-reliable network connections. These features give you a high degree of flexibility in controlling replication configuration. They include the following:

- Compression of Active Directory information. This compression is helpful because changes between domain controllers in remote sites may include a large amount of information and also because network bandwidth tends to be less available and more costly.

- Site links and site link bridges help determine intersite replication topology.

- Replication can occur based on a schedule defined by system administrators.

You can configure intersite replication by using the Active Directory Sites and Services tool. Select the name of the site for which you want to configure settings. Then right-click the NTDS Site Settings object in the right window pane and select Properties. By clicking the Change Schedule button in the NTDS Site Settings Properties dialog box, you'll be able to configure how often replication occurs between sites (see Figure 5.4).

FIGURE 5.4   Configuring intersite replication schedules

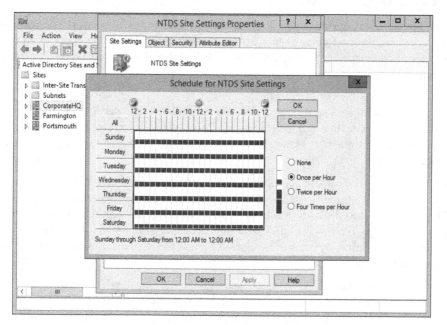

   You will see how to set the replication schedule in Exercise 5.4.

In the following sections, you will see how to configure site links and site link bridges as well as how to manage connection objects and bridgehead servers.

Creating Site Links and Site Link Bridges

The overall topology of intersite replication is based on the use of site links and site link bridges. *Site links* are logical connections that define a path between two Active Directory sites. Site links can include several descriptive elements that define their network characteristics. *Site link bridges* are used to connect site links so that the relationship can be transitive. Figure 5.5 provides an example of site links and site link bridges.

FIGURE 5.5 An example of site links and site link bridges

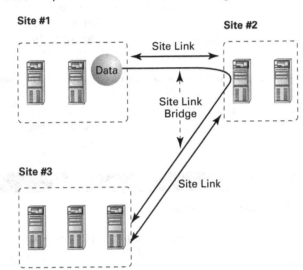

Both of these types of logical connections are used by Active Directory services to determine how information should be synchronized between domain controllers in remote sites. The Knowledge Consistency Checker (KCC) uses this information, which forms a replication topology based on the site topology created. The KCC service is responsible for determining the best way to replicate information within sites.

When creating site links for your environment, you'll need to consider the following factors:

Transporting Information   You can choose to use either RPC over IP or SMTP for transferring information over a site link. You will need to determine which is best based on your network infrastructure and the reliability of connections between sites.

Assigning a Cost Value   You can create multiple site links between sites and assign site links a cost value based on the type of connection. The system administrator determines the cost value, and the relative costs of site links are then used (by the system) to determine the optimal path for replication. The lower the cost, the more likely the link is to be used for replication.

For example, a company may primarily use a T1 link between branch offices, but it may also use a slower and circuit-switched dial-up ISDN connection for redundancy (in case the T1 fails). In this example, a system administrator may assign a cost of 25 to the T1 line and a cost of 100 to the ISDN line. This ensures that the more reliable and higher-bandwidth T1 connection is used whenever it's available but that the ISDN line is also available.

Determining a Replication Schedule   Once you've determined how and through which connections replication will take place, it's time to determine when information should be replicated. Replication requires network resources and occupies bandwidth. Therefore, you need to balance the need for consistent directory information with the need to conserve bandwidth. For example, if you determine that it's reasonable to have a lag time of six hours between when an update is made at one site and when it is replicated to all others, you might schedule replication to occur once in the morning, once during the lunch hour, and more frequently after normal work hours.

Based on these factors, you should be able to devise a strategy that allows you to configure site links.

Exercise 5.4 walks you through the process of creating site links and site link bridges. To complete the steps in this exercise, you must have completed Exercises 5.1, 5.2, and 5.3.

EXERCISE 5.4

Creating Site Links and Site Link Bridges

1. Open the Active Directory Sites and Services tool from the Administrative Tools program group.

2. Expand the Sites, Inter-site Transports, and IP objects. Right-click the DEFAULTIPSITE-LINK item in the right pane and select Rename. Rename the object **CorporateWAN**.

3. Right-click the CorporateWAN link and select Properties. In the General tab of the CorporateWAN Properties dialog box, type **T1 Connecting Corporate and Portsmouth Offices** for the description. Remove the Farmington site from the link by highlighting Farmington in the Sites In This Site Link box and clicking Remove. For the Cost value, type **50** and specify that replication should occur every **60** minutes. To create the site link, click OK.

4. Right-click the IP folder and select New Site Link. In the New Object – Site Link dialog box, name the link **CorporateDialup**. Add the Farmington and CorporateHQ sites to the site link and then click OK.

5. Right-click the CorporateDialup link and select Properties. In the General tab of the CorporateDialup Properties dialog box, type **ISDN Dialup between Corporate and Farmington** for the description. Set the Cost value to **100** and specify that replication should occur every **120** minutes. To specify that replication should occur only during certain times of the day, click the Change Schedule button.

6. In the Schedule For Corporate Dialup dialog box, highlight the area between 8:00 a.m. and 6:00 p.m. for the days Monday through Friday and click the Replication Not Available option. This will ensure that replication traffic is minimized during normal work hours.

7. Click OK to accept the new schedule and then click OK again to create the site link.

8. Right-click the IP object and select New Site Link Bridge. In the New Object – Site Link Bridge dialog box, name the site link bridge **CorporateBridge**. Note that the CorporateDialup and CorporateWAN site links are already added to the site link bridge. Because there must be at least two site links in each bridge, you will not be able to remove these links. Click OK to create the site link bridge.

9. When finished, close the Active Directory Sites and Services tool.

Creating Connection Objects

Generally, it is a good practice to allow Active Directory's replication mechanisms to schedule and manage replication functions automatically. In some cases, however, you may want to have additional control over replication. Perhaps you want to replicate certain changes on demand (for example, when you create new accounts). Or you may want to specify a custom schedule for certain servers.

Connection objects provide you with a way to set up these different types of replication schedules. You can create connection objects with the Active Directory Sites and Services tool by expanding a server object, right-clicking the NTDS Settings object, and selecting New Active Directory Domain Services Connection (see Figure 5.6).

FIGURE 5.6   Creating a new Active Directory Domain Services connection

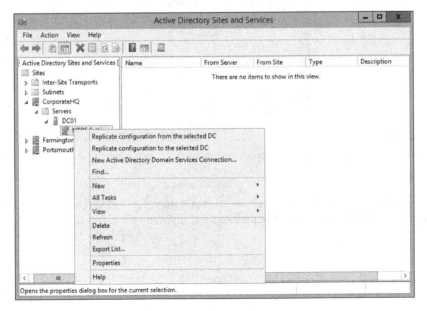

Within the properties of the connection object, which you can see in the right pane of the Active Directory Sites and Services tool, you can specify the type of transport to use for replication (RPC over IP or SMTP), the schedule for replication, and the domain controllers that participate in the replication. Additionally, you can right-click the connection object and select Replicate Now.

Moving Server Objects between Sites

Using the Active Directory Sites and Services tool, you can easily move servers between sites. To do this, simply right-click the name of a domain controller and select Move. You can then select the site to which you want to move the domain controller object.

Figure 5.7 shows the Move Server dialog box. After the server is moved, all replication topology settings are updated automatically. If you want to choose custom replication settings, you'll need to create connection objects manually (as described earlier).

FIGURE 5.7   Choosing a new site for a specific server

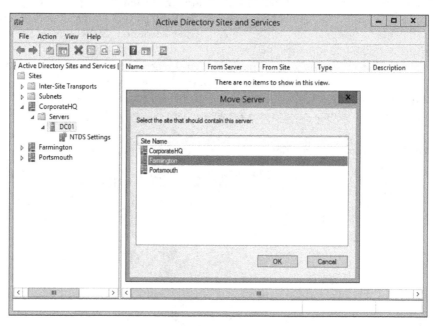

In Exercise 5.5, you move a server object between sites. To complete the steps in this exercise, you must have completed the previous exercises in this chapter.

EXERCISE 5.5

Moving Server Objects Between Sites

1. Open the Active Directory Sites and Services administrative tool.

2. Right-click the server named PortsmouthDC1 and select Move.

3. In the Move Server dialog box, select the Farmington site and then click OK. This moves this server to the Farmington site.

4. To move the server back, right-click PortsmouthDC1 (now located in the Farmington site) and then click Move. Select Portsmouth for the destination site.

5. When finished, close the Active Directory Sites and Services administrative tool.

Creating Bridgehead Servers

By default, all of the servers in one site communicate with all of the servers in another site. You can, however, further control replication between sites by using bridgehead servers. As mentioned earlier in the chapter, using bridgehead servers helps minimize replication traffic, especially in larger distributed star network topologies, and it allows you to dedicate machines that are better connected to receive replicated data. Figure 5.8 provides an example of how bridgehead servers work.

FIGURE 5.8   A replication scenario using bridgehead servers

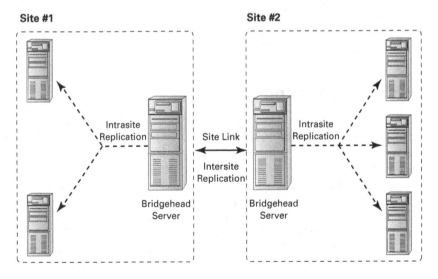

You can use a bridgehead server to specify which domain controllers are preferred for transferring replication information between sites. Different bridgehead servers can be selected for RPC over IP and SMTP replication, thus allowing you to balance the load. To create a bridgehead server for a site, simply right-click a domain controller and select Properties, which brings up the bridgehead server's Properties dialog box (see Figure 5.9). To make the server a bridgehead server, just select one or both replication types (called *transports*) from the left side of the dialog box and click the Add button to add them to the right side of the dialog box.

FIGURE 5.9   Specifying a bridgehead server

RODCs and Replication

I have talked quite a bit about read-only domain controllers (RODCs) throughout the book. It's important that you understand that since RODCs don't actually commit changes against the Active Directory Domain Services (ADDS) database within your environment, then replication to and from your primary domain controller (PDC) and your RODCs can occur only one way. This is referred to as *unidirectional replication.* Any writable domain controller that serves as a replication partner to one of your RODCs will never pull changes from that RODC by design. This helps ensure that no malicious or corrupt changes that are made from an RODC are replicated throughout your entire forest. The RODC performs normal inbound replication for AD DS and Sysvol changes. Any other shares on an RODC that you configure to replicate using DFS Replication would still use bidirectional replication.

RODCs come with additional configuration settings like the *Password Replication Policy (PRP)*. The PRP is used to determine which user's credentials can be cached locally on a specific RODC. By default, an RODC will not cache an Active Directory user's credentials. That would defeat the purpose of an RODC. When a user wants to authenticate to an RODC, the authentication request is forwarded to a writable domain controller for authentication. If the request succeeds, it is then passed back to the RODC, and then that user will be able to log in to the domain.

Nonetheless, it is possible to allow certain user credentials to be cached on an RODC by configuring the PRP. Once a user has been added to the Allowed RODC Password Replication group, then that user's credentials will be cached, and that RODC would be able to authenticate that user locally again in the future. Because the RODC maintains only a subset of user credentials, if the RODC is compromised or stolen, only the user accounts that had been cached on the RODC must have their passwords changed. To configure an RODC PRP, open the properties of an RODC computer object in Active Directory and select the Password Replication Policy tab.

Configuring Server Topology

When you are using environments that require multiple sites, you must carefully consider where you place your servers. In doing so, you can greatly improve performance and end user experience by reducing the time they must spend performing common operations, such as authentication or searching Active Directory for resources.

There are two main issues to consider when you are designing a distributed Active Directory environment. The first is how you should place domain controllers within the network environment. The second is how to manage the use of global catalog servers. Finding the right balance between servers, server resources, and performance can be considered an art form for network and system administrators. In the following sections, you'll look at some of the important considerations that you must take into account when you design a replication server topology.

Placing Domain Controllers

Microsoft highly recommends that you have at least two domain controllers in each domain of your Active Directory environment. As mentioned earlier in this chapter, using additional domain controllers provides the following benefits:

- Increased network performance:
  - The servers can balance the burden of serving client requests.
  - Clients can connect to the server closest to them instead of performing authentication and security operations across a slow WAN link.
- Fault tolerance (in case one domain controller fails, the other still contains a valid and usable copy of the Active Directory database).
- In Windows Server 2012 R2, RODCs help increase security when users connect to a domain controller in an unsecured remote location.

Placing Global Catalog Servers

A *global catalog (GC)* server is a domain controller that contains a copy of all of the objects contained in the forest-wide domain controllers that compose the Active Directory database. Making a domain controller a GC server is simple, and you can change this setting quite easily. That brings us to the harder part—determining which domain controllers should also be GC servers.

Where you place domain controllers and GC servers and how many you deploy are important network planning decisions. Generally, you want to make GC servers available in every site that has a slow link. This means the most logical places to put GC servers are in every site and close to the WAN link for the best possible connectivity. However, having too many GC servers is a bad thing. The main issue is associated with replication traffic—you must keep each GC server within your environment synchronized with the other servers. In a very dynamic environment, using additional GC servers causes a considerable increase in network traffic. Therefore, you will want to find a good balance between replication burdens and GC query performance in your own large multidomain environment.

To create a GC server, simply expand the Server object in the Active Directory Sites and Services tool, right-click NTDS Settings, and select Properties to bring up the NTDS Settings Properties dialog box (see Figure 5.10). To configure a server as a GC server, simply place a check mark in the Global Catalog box.

FIGURE 5.10 Enabling the global catalog on an Active Directory domain controller

🌐 Real World Scenario

Accommodating a Changing Environment

You're a system administrator for a medium-sized business that consists of many offices located throughout the world. Some of these offices are well connected because they use high-speed, reliable links, while others are not so fortunate. Overall, things are going well until your CEO announces that the organization will be merging with another large company and that the business will be restructured. The restructuring will involve opening new offices, closing old ones, and transferring employees to different locations. Additionally, changes in the IT budget will affect the types of links that exist between offices. Your job as the system administrator is to ensure that the network environment and, specifically, Active Directory keep pace with the changes and ultimately outperform them.

An important skill for any technical professional is the ability to adapt quickly and efficiently to a changing organization. When a business grows, restructures, or forms relationships with other businesses, often many IT-related changes must also occur. You may have to create new network links, for example.

Fortunately, Active Directory was designed with these kinds of challenges in mind. For example, you can use the Active Directory Sites and Services administrative tool to reflect physical network changes in Active Directory topology. If a site that previously had 64Kbps of bandwidth is upgraded to a T1 connection, you can change those characteristics for the site link objects. Conversely, if a site that was previously well connected is reduced to a slow, unreliable link, you can reconfigure the sites, change the site link transport mechanisms (perhaps from IP to SMTP to accommodate a nonpersistent link), and create connection objects (which would allow you to schedule replication traffic to occur during the least busy hours).

Suppose further that many of your operations move overseas to a European division. This might call for designating specific domain controllers as preferred bridgehead servers to reduce the amount of replication traffic over costly and slow overseas links.

Sweeping organizational changes inevitably require you to move servers between sites. For example, an office may close and its domain controllers may move to another region of the world. Again, you can accommodate this change by using Active Directory administrative tools. You may change your OU structure to reflect new logical and business-oriented changes, and you can move server objects between sites to reflect physical network changes.

Rarely can the job of mapping a physical infrastructure to Active Directory be "complete." In most environments, it's safe to assume that you will always need to make changes based on business needs. Overall, however, you should feel comfortable that the physical components of Active Directory are at your side to help you accommodate these changes.

Using Universal Group Membership Caching

To understand how Universal Group Membership Caching (UGMC) works, you must first understand how authentication works. When a user tries to authenticate with a domain controller, the first action that takes place is that the domain controller checks with the global catalog to see to which domain the user belongs.

If the domain controller (the one to which the user is trying to authenticate) is not a GC, then the domain controller sends a request to the GC to verify the user's domain. The GC responds with the user's information, and the domain controller authenticates the user (if the user belongs to the same domain as the domain controller).

There are two ways to speed up the authentication process. First, you can make all of the domain controllers global catalogs. But then you end up with a lot of GC replication traffic. This becomes even more of an issue if you have multiple sites. Now replication traffic can be too large for your site link connections.

Thus, if you have a slower site link connection or multiple domains, you can use Universal Group Membership Caching. If you are using UGMC, after a domain controller communicates with the global catalog, the domain controller will then cache the user's credentials for eight hours by default. Now if the user logs off the domain and then logs back into the domain, the domain controller will use the cached credentials and not ask the global catalog. The downside to using UGMC is that it is for authentication only. Global catalogs help speed up Active Directory searches, and they work with Directory Service–enabled applications (applications that have to work with Active Directory) such as Exchange and SQL.

Domain Controller Cloning

Throughout the book, I have talked about why so many organizations are switching to virtualization in their server rooms. Virtualization allows an administrator to take one physical server and turn it into multiple virtual servers by using Windows Server 2012 R2.

In Windows Server 2012 R2, administrators can now easily and safely create replica domain controllers by copying an existing virtual domain controller. Before Windows Server 2012, an administrator would have to deploy a server image that they prepared by using sysprep.exe. After going through the process of using sysprep.exe, the administrator would have to promote this server to a domain controller and then complete additional configuration requirements for deploying each replica domain controller.

Domain controller cloning allows an administrator to deploy rapidly a large number of domain controllers. To set up domain controller cloning, you must be a member of the Domain Admins group or have the equivalent permissions. The administrator must then run Windows PowerShell from an elevated command prompt.

Only Windows Server 2012 or Windows Server 2012 R2 domain controllers that are hosted on a VM-compatible hypervisor can be used as a source for cloning. You should also make sure that the domain controller that you choose to clone is in a healthy state (use computer management to see the computer's state).

The following example is used to create a clone domain controller named TestClone with a static IP address of 10.0.0.5 and a subnet mask of 255.255.0.0. This command also configures the DNS Server and WINS server configurations.

```
New-ADDCCloneConfigFile -CloneComputerName "TestClone" -Static -IPv4Address
"10.0.0.5" -IPv4DNSResolver "10.0.0.1" -IPv4SubnetMask "255.255.0.0" -
PreferredWinsServer "10.0.0.1" -AlternateWinsServer "10.0.0.2"
```

When you are ready to clone a domain controller, I recommend you visit
Microsoft's TechNet site for all of the PowerShell commands needed to
complete this entire process.

Monitoring and Troubleshooting Active Directory Replication

For the most part, domain controllers handle the replication processes automatically.
However, system administrators still need to monitor the performance of Active Directory
replication because failed network links and incorrect configurations can sometimes
prevent the synchronization of information between domain controllers.

You can monitor the behavior of Active Directory replication and troubleshoot the
process if problems occur.

About System Monitor

The Windows Server 2012 R2 System Monitor administrative tool was designed so that
you can monitor many performance statistics associated with using Active Directory.
Included within the various performance statistics that you can monitor are counters
related to Active Directory replication.

Troubleshooting Replication

A common symptom of replication problems is that information is not updated on some or
all domain controllers. For example, a system administrator creates a user account on one
domain controller, but the changes are not propagated to other domain controllers. In most
environments, this is a potentially serious problem because it affects network security and
can prevent authorized users from accessing the resources they require.

You can take several steps to troubleshoot Active Directory replication. These steps are
discussed in the following sections.

Verifying Network Connectivity

For replication to work properly in distributed environments, you must have network
connectivity. Although ideally all domain controllers would be connected by high-speed
LAN links, this is rarely the case for larger organizations. In the real world, dial-up
connections and slow connections are common. If you have verified that your replication

topology is set up properly, you should confirm that your servers are able to communicate. Problems such as a failed dial-up connection attempt can prevent important Active Directory information from being replicated.

Verifying Router and Firewall Configurations

Firewalls are used to restrict the types of traffic that can be transferred between networks. They are mainly used to increase security by preventing unauthorized users from transferring information. In some cases, company firewalls may block the types of network access that must be available for Active Directory replication to occur. For example, if a specific router or firewall prevents data from being transferred using SMTP, replication that uses this protocol will fail.

Examining the Event Logs

Whenever an error in the replication configuration occurs, the computer writes events to the Directory Service and File Replication Service event logs. By using the Event Viewer administrative tool, you can quickly and easily view the details associated with any problems in replication. For example, if one domain controller is unable to communicate with another to transfer changes, a log entry is created.

Verifying That Information Is Synchronized

It's often easy to forget to perform manual checks regarding the replication of Active Directory information. One of the reasons for this is that Active Directory domain controllers have their own read-write copies of the Active Directory database. Therefore, if connectivity does not exist, you will not encounter failures while creating new objects.

It is important to verify periodically that objects have been synchronized between domain controllers. This process might be as simple as logging on to a different domain controller and looking at the objects within a specific OU. This manual check, although it might be tedious, can prevent inconsistencies in the information stored on domain controllers, which, over time, can become an administration and security nightmare.

Verifying Authentication Scenarios

A common replication configuration issue occurs when clients are forced to authenticate across slow network connections. The primary symptom of the problem is that users complain about the amount of time it takes them to log on to Active Directory (especially during a period when there's a high volume of authentications, such as at the beginning of the workday).

Usually, you can alleviate this problem by using additional domain controllers or reconfiguring the site topology. A good way to test this is to consider the possible scenarios for the various clients that you support. Often, walking through a configuration, such as "A client in Domain1 is trying to authenticate using a domain controller in Domain2, which is located across a slow WAN connection," can be helpful in pinpointing potential problem areas.

Verifying the Replication Topology

The Active Directory Sites and Services tool allows you to verify that a replication topology is logically consistent. You can quickly and easily perform this task by right-clicking NTDS Settings within a Server object and choosing All Tasks ➤ Check Replication. If any errors are present, a dialog box alerts you to the problem.

Another way to verify replication is by using the command-line utility Repadmin. Table 5.1 shows some of the Repadmin commands.

TABLE 5.1   Repadmin commands

Command	Description
Repadmin Bridgeheads	Lists the bridgehead servers for a specified site.
Repadmin dsaguid	Returns a server name when given a GUID.
Repadmin failcache	Shows a list of failed replication events.
Repadmin istg	Returns the server name of the Inter-Site Topology Generator (ISTG) server for a specified site. The ISTG manages the inbound replication connection objects for the bridgehead servers in a site.
Repadmin kcc	Forces the Knowledge Consistency Checker (KCC) to recalculate replication topology for a specified domain controller. The KCC modifies data in the local directory in response to system-wide changes.
Repadmin latency	Shows the amount of time between replications.
Repadmin queue	Shows tasks waiting in the replication queue.
Repadmin querysites	Uses routing information to determine the cost of a route from a specified site to another specified site or to other sites.
Repadmin replicate	Starts a replication event for the specified directory partition between domain controllers.
Repadmin replsummary	Displays the replication state and relative health of a forest.
Repadmin showrepl	Displays replication partners for each directory partition on a specified domain controller.

Reasons for Creating Multiple Domains

Before you look at the steps that you must take to create multiple domains, become familiar with the reasons an organization might want to create them.

In general, you should always try to reflect your organization's structure within a single domain. By using organizational units (OUs) and other objects, you can usually create an accurate and efficient structure within one domain. Creating and managing a single domain is usually much simpler than managing a more complex environment consisting of multiple domains.

That being said, you should familiarize yourself with some real benefits and reasons for creating multiple domains and some drawbacks of using them.

Reasons for Using Multiple Domains

You might need to implement multiple domains for several reasons. These reasons include the following considerations:

Scalability   Although Microsoft has designed Active Directory to accommodate millions of objects, this may not be practical for your current environment. Supporting thousands of users within a single domain requires more disk space, greater central processing unit (CPU) usage, and additional network burdens on your domain controllers (computers containing Active Directory security information). To determine the size of the Active Directory domain your network can support, you need to plan, design, test, and analyze within your own environment.

Reducing Replication Traffic   All of the domain controllers in a domain must keep an up-to-date copy of the entire Active Directory database. For small to medium-sized domains, this is generally not a problem. Windows Server 2012 R2 and Active Directory manage all of the details of transferring the database behind the scenes. Other business and technical limitations might, however, affect Active Directory's ability to perform adequate replication. For example, if you have two sites that are connected by a slow network link (or a sporadic link or no link at all), replication is not practical. In this case, you would probably want to create separate domains to isolate replication traffic. Sporadic coverage across the wide area network (WAN) link would come from circuit-switching technologies such as Integrated Services Digital Network (ISDN) technologies. If you didn't have a link at all, then you would have a service provider outage or some other type of disruption. Separate domains mean separate replication traffic, but the amount of administrative overhead is increased significantly.

Because it's common to have WAN links in your business environment, you will always need to consider how your users authenticate to a domain controller (DC). DCs at a remote site are commonly used to authenticate users locally to their local area network (LAN). The most common design involves putting a DC at each remote site to keep authentication traffic from traversing the WAN. If it is the other way around, the authentication traffic may cause users problems if WAN utilization is high or if the link is broken and no other way to the central site is available. The design you are apt to see most often is one in which each server replicates its database of information to each other's server so that the network and its systems converge.

However, it's important to realize that the presence of slow WAN links alone is *not* a good reason to break an organization into multiple domains. The most common solution is to set up site links with the Sites and Services Microsoft Management Console (MMC). When you use this MMC, you can manage replication traffic and fine-tune independently of the domain architecture.

You would want to use a multidomain architecture, such as when two companies merge through an acquisition, for the following reasons:

Meeting Business Needs   Several business needs might justify the creation of multiple domains. Business needs can be broken down even further into organizational and political needs.

One of the organizational reasons for using multiple domains is to avoid potential problems associated with the Domain Administrator account. At least one user needs to have permissions at this level. If your organization is unable or unwilling to trust a single person to have this level of control over all business units, then multiple domains may be the best answer. Because each domain maintains its own security database, you can keep permissions and resources isolated. Through the use of trusts, however, you can still share resources.

A political need for separate domains might arise if you had two companies that merged with two separate but equal management staffs and two sets of officers. In such a situation, you might need to have Active Directory split into two separate databases to keep the security of the two groups separate. Some such organizations may need to keep the internal groups separate by law. A multidomain architecture provides exactly this type of pristinely separate environment.

Many Levels of Hierarchy   Larger organizations tend to have complex internal and external business structures that dictate the need for many different levels of organization. For example, two companies might merge and need to keep two sets of officers who are managed under two different logical groupings. Managing data becomes much easier when you're using OUs, and if you design them correctly, OUs will help you control your network right from one console. You may need only one level of management—your company may be small enough to warrant the use of the default OU structure you see when Active Directory is first installed. If, however, you find that you need many levels of OUs to manage resources (or if large numbers of objects exist within each OU), it might make sense to create additional domains. Each domain would contain its own OU hierarchy and serve as the root of a new set of objects.

Decentralized Administration   Two main models of administration are commonly used: a centralized administration model and a decentralized administration model. In the centralized administration model, a single IT organization is responsible for managing all of the users, computers, and security permissions for the entire organization. In the decentralized administration model, each department or business unit might have its own IT department. In both cases, the needs of the administration model can play a significant role in whether you decide to use multiple domains.

Consider, for example, a multinational company that has a separate IT department for offices in each country. Each IT department is responsible for supporting only the users and computers within its own region. Because the administration model is largely decentralized, creating a separate domain for each of these major business units might make sense from a security and maintenance standpoint.

Multiple DNS or Domain Names   Another reason you may need to use a multidomain architecture is if you want or plan to use multiple DNS names within your organization. If you use multiple DNS names or domain names, you must create multiple Active Directory domains. Each AD domain can have only one *fully qualified domain name (FQDN)*. An FQDN is the full name of a system that consists of a local host, a second-level domain name, and a top-level domain (TLD). For example, `corp.stellacon.com` is an FQDN, `.com` is the TLD, `www` is the host, and `stellacon` is the second-level domain name.

Legality   One final reason you may need to use a multidomain architecture is legality within your organization. Some corporations have to follow state or federal regulations and laws. For this reason, they may need to have multiple domains.

Drawbacks of Multiple Domains

Although there are many reasons why it makes sense to have multiple domains, there are also reasons why you should not break an organizational structure into multiple domains, many of which are related to maintenance and administration. Here are some of the drawbacks to using multiple domains:

Administrative Inconsistency   One of the fundamental responsibilities of most system administrators is implementing and managing security. When you are implementing Group Policy and security settings in multiple domains, you want to be careful to ensure that the settings are consistent. In Windows Server 2012 R2, security policies can be different between and within the same domains. If this is what the organization intended, then it is not a problem. However, if an organization want to make the same settings apply to all users, then each domain requires a separate GPO with similar security settings.

Increased Management Challenges   Managing servers, users, and computers can become a considerable challenge when you are also managing multiple domains because many more administrative units are required. In general, you need to manage all user, group, and computer settings separately for the objects within each domain. The hierarchical structure provided by OUs, on the other hand, provides a much simpler and easier way to manage permissions.

Decreased Flexibility   Creating a domain involves the *promotion* of a DC to the new domain. Although the process is quite simple, it is much more difficult to rearrange the domain topology within an Active Directory environment than it is simply to reorganize OUs. When planning domains, you should ensure that the domain structure will not change often, if at all.

Now that you have examined the pros and cons related to creating multiple domains, it is time to see how to create trees and forests.

Creating Domain Trees and Forests

So far, this chapter has covered some important reasons for using multiple domains in a single network environment. Now it's time to look at how to create multidomain structures such as domain trees and domain forests.

Regardless of the number of domains you have in your environment, you always have a tree and a forest. This might surprise those of you who generally think of domain trees and forests as belonging only to Active Directory environments that consist of multiple domains. However, recall that when you install the first domain in an Active Directory environment, that domain automatically creates a new forest and a new tree.

In the following sections, you will learn how to plan trees and forests and how to promote domain controllers to establish a tree and forest environment.

Planning Trees and Forests

You have already seen several reasons why you might want to have multiple domains within a single company. What you haven't yet seen is how multiple domains can be related to each other and how their relationships can translate into domain forests and trees.

A fundamental commonality between the various domains that exist in trees and forests is that they all share the same Active Directory global catalog (GC). This means that if you modify the Active Directory schema, these changes must be propagated to all of the domain controllers in all of the domains. This is an important point because adding and modifying the structure of information in the GC can have widespread effects on replication and network traffic. Also, you need to ensure that any system you use in the GC role can handle it—you might need to size up the system's hardware requirements. This is especially true if there are multiple domains.

Every domain within an Active Directory configuration has its own unique name. For example, even though you might have a sales domain in two different trees, the complete names for each domain will be different (such as `sales.stellacon1.com` and `sales. stellacon2.com`).

In the following sections, you'll look at how you can organize multiple Active Directory domains based on business requirements.

Using a Single Tree

The concept of domain trees was created to preserve the relationship between multiple domains that share a common contiguous namespace. For example, you might have the following DNS domains (based on Internet names):

- mycompany.com

- sales.mycompany.com

- engineering.mycompany.com

- europe.sales.mycompany.com

Note that all of these domains fit within a single contiguous namespace. That is, they are all direct or indirect children of the mycompany.com domain. In this case, mycompany.com is called the *root domain*. All of the direct children (such as sales.mycompany.com and engineering.mycompany.com) are called *child domains*. Finally, *parent domains* are the domains that are directly above one domain. For example, sales.mycompany.com is the parent domain of europe.sales.mycompany.com. Figure 5.11 provides an example of a domain tree.

FIGURE 5.11 A domain tree

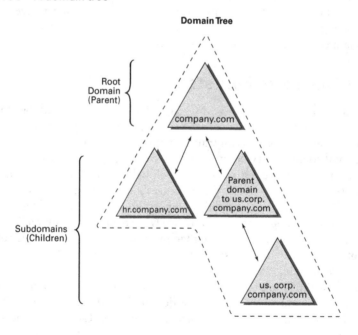

To establish a domain tree, you must first create the root domain for the tree. Then you can add child domains off this root. These child domains can then serve as parents for further subdomains. Each domain must have at least one domain controller, and domain controllers can participate in only one domain at a time. However, you can move a domain controller from one domain to another. To do this, you must first demote a domain controller to a member server and then promote it to a domain controller in another domain.

You will learn how to demote a domain controller later in this chapter in the section "Demoting a Domain Controller."

Domains are designed to be logical boundaries. The domains within a tree are, by default, automatically bound together using a two-way transitive trust relationship, which allows resources to be shared among domains through the use of the appropriate user and group assignments. Because trust relationships are transitive, all of the domains within the tree trust each other. Note, however, that a trust by itself does not automatically grant any security permissions to users or objects between domains. Trusts are designed only to *allow* resources to be shared; you must still go through the process of sharing and managing them. Enterprise administrators must explicitly assign security settings to resources before users can access resources between domains.

Using a single tree makes sense when your organization maintains only a single contiguous namespace. Regardless of the number of domains that exist within this environment and how different their security settings are from each other, they are related by a common name. Although domain trees make sense for many organizations, in some cases the network namespace may be considerably more complicated. You'll look at how forests address these situations next.

Using a Forest

Active Directory forests are designed to accommodate multiple noncontiguous namespaces. That is, they can combine domain trees into logical units. An example might be the following tree and domain structure:

- Tree: Organization1.com
    - Sales.Organization1.com
    - Marketing.Organization1.com
    - Engineering.Organization1.com
    - NorthAmerica.Engineering.Organization1.com
- Tree: Organization2.com
    - Sales.Organization2.com
    - Engineering.Organization2.com.

Figure 5.12 provides an example of how multiple trees can fit into a single forest. Such a situation might occur in the acquisition and merger of companies or if a company is logically divided into two or more completely separate and autonomous business units.

FIGURE 5.12   A single forest consisting of multiple trees

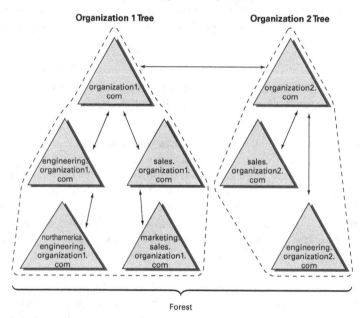

All of the trees within a forest are related through a single forest root domain. This is the first domain that was created in the Active Directory environment. The root domain in each tree creates a transitive trust with the forest root domain. The result is a configuration in which all of the trees within a domain and all of the domains within each tree trust each other. Again, as with domain trees, the presence of a trust relationship does not automatically signify that users have permissions to access resources across domains. It allows only objects and resources to be shared. Authorized network administrators must set up specific permissions.

All of the domains within a single Active Directory forest have the following features in common:

Schema   The *schema* is the Active Directory structure that defines how the information within the data store is structured. For the information stored on various domain controllers to remain compatible, all of the domain controllers within the entire Active Directory environment must share the same schema. For example, if you add a field for an employee benefit plan number, all domain controllers throughout the environment need to recognize this information before you can share information among them.

Global Catalog   One of the problems associated with working in large network environments is that sharing information across multiple domains can be costly in terms of network and server resources. Fortunately, Active Directory uses the global catalog (GC), which serves as a repository for information about a subset of all objects within *all* Active Directory domains in a forest. System administrators can determine what types of information should be added to the defaults in the GC. Generally, they decide to store commonly used information, such as a list of all of the printers, users, groups, and computers. In addition, they can configure specific domain controllers to carry a copy of the GC. Now if you have a question about where to find all of the color printers in the company, for example, all you need to do is to contact the nearest GC server.

Configuration Information   Some roles and functions must be managed for the entire forest. When you are dealing with multiple domains, this means that you must configure certain domain controllers to perform functions for the entire Active Directory environment. I will discuss some specifics of this later in this chapter.

The main purpose of allowing multiple domains to exist together is to allow them to share information and other resources. Now that you've seen the basics of domain trees and forests, take a look at how domains are actually created.

The Promotion Process

A domain tree is created when a new domain is added as the child of an existing domain. This relationship is established during the promotion of a Windows Server 2012 R2 computer to a domain controller. Although the underlying relationships can be quite complicated in larger organizations, the Server Manager's Active Directory Installation Wizard makes it easy to create forests and trees.

Using the Active Directory Installation Wizard, you can quickly and easily create new domains by promoting a Windows Server 2012 R2 stand-alone server or a member server to a domain controller. When you install a new domain controller, you can choose to make it part of an existing domain, or you can choose to make it the first domain controller in a new domain. In the following sections and exercises, you'll become familiar with the exact steps you need to take to create a domain tree and a domain forest when you promote a server to a domain controller.

Creating a Domain Tree

In previous chapters, you learned how to promote the first domain controller in the first domain in a forest, also known as the root. If you don't promote any other domain controllers, then that domain controller simply controls that one domain and only one tree is created. To create a new domain tree, you need to promote a Windows Server 2012 R2 computer to a domain controller. In the Active Directory Installation Wizard, you select the option that makes this domain controller the first machine in a new domain that is a child of an existing domain. As a result, you will have a domain tree that contains two domains—a parent and a child, or two trees if you don't create a child domain.

Before you can create a new child domain, you need the following information:

- The name of the parent domain (for the exercises, you'll use the one you created in the previous chapter.)
- The name of the child domain (the one you are planning to install)
- The file system locations for the Active Directory database, logs, and shared system volume

- DNS configuration information
- The NetBIOS name for the new server
- A domain administrator username and password

Exercise 5.6 walks you through the process of creating a new child domain using Server Manager. This exercise assumes you have already created the parent domain and you are using a server in the domain that is not a domain controller.

EXERCISE 5.6

Creating a New Subdomain

1. Open Server Manager.

2. Click item 2, Add Roles And Features.

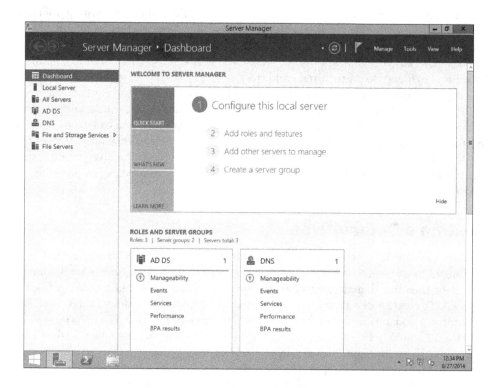

3. Make sure that the Role-Based Or Feature-Based Installation button is selected and click Next.

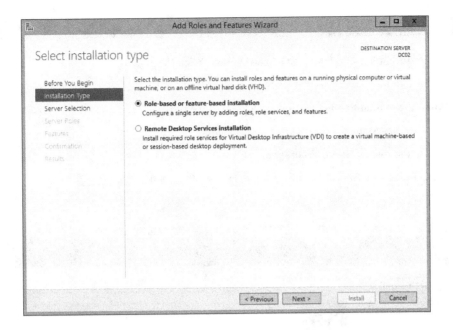

4. At the Select Destination screen, click Next.

5. At the Select Server Roles screen, check the Active Directory Domain Services check box. A box will appear stating that you need to install additional roles. Click the Add Features button. Then click Next.

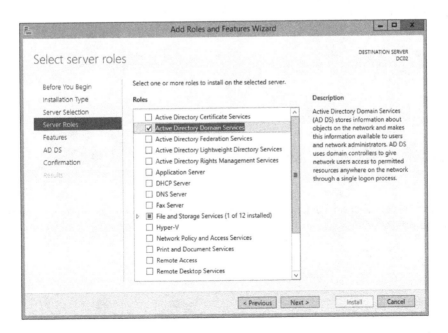

EXERCISE 5.6 *(continued)*

6. At the Add Roles And Features Wizard screen, click Next.

7. At the Confirmation screen, click the Install button.

8. When the installation is complete, click the Close button.

9. Close Server Manager and restart the machine.

10. Log in and restart Server Manager.

11. In the Roles And Server Groups area, click the AD DS link.

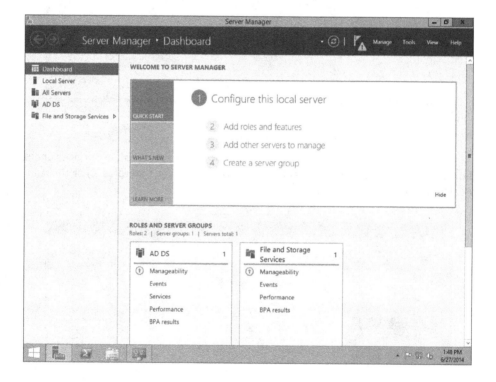

12. In the Servers section, click the More link next to Configuration Required For Active Directory Domain Services.

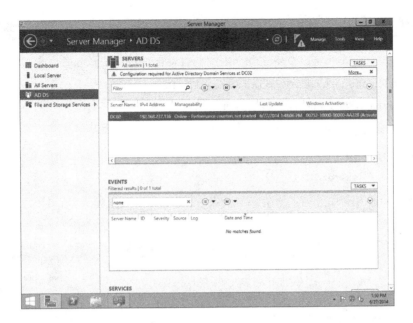

13. At the All Servers Task Details screen, click the Promote This Server To A Domain Controller link.

14. At the Deployment Configuration screen, click the radio button Add A New Domain To An Existing Forest. In the Select Domain Type drop-down, chose Child Domain and then choose your parent domain. In the New Domain Name box, type in the name of your new domain. I used NewHampshire. Click the Next button.

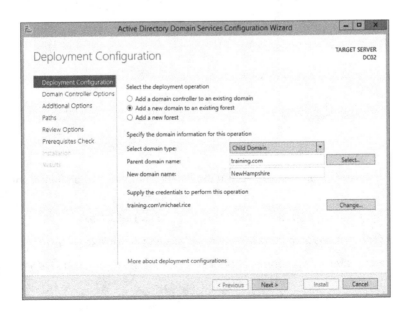

15. At the Domain Controller Options screen, I set the following options:

Domain Functional Level: Windows Server 2012 R2

Domain Name System (DNS) Server: Checked

Global Catalog (GC): Checked

Site Name: CorporateHQ

Password: **P@ssw0rd**

Click Next.

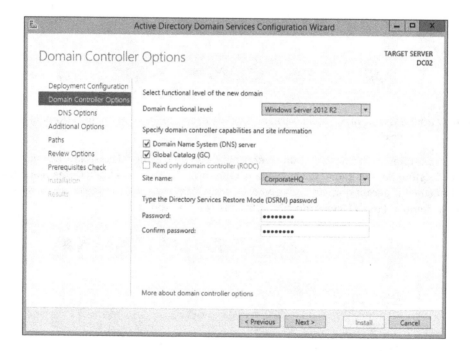

16. At the DNS screen, click Next.

17. At the Additional Options screen, accept the default NetBIOS domain name and click Next.

18. At the Paths screen, accept the default file locations and click Next.

19. At the Review Options screen, verify your settings and click Next.

20. At the Prerequisites Check screen, click the Install button (as long as there are no errors).

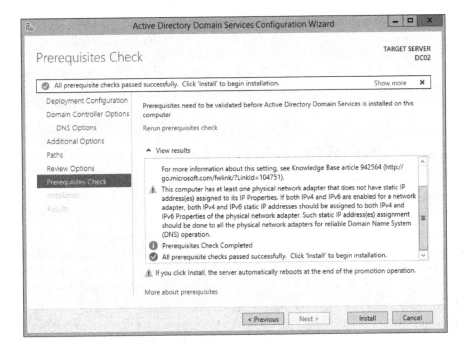

21. After the installation completes, the machine will automatically reboot. Log in as the administrator.

22. Close Server Manager.

Joining a New Domain Tree to a Forest

A *forest* is one or more trees that do not share a contiguous namespace. For example, you could join the organization1.com and organization2.com domains together to create a single Active Directory environment.

Any two trees can be joined together to create a forest, as long as the second tree is installed after the first and the trees have noncontiguous namespaces. (If the namespaces were contiguous, you would actually need to create a new domain for an existing tree.) The process of creating a new tree to form or add to a forest is as simple as promoting a server to a domain controller for a new domain that does *not* share a namespace with an existing Active Directory domain.

The command-line tool adprep.exe is used to prepare a Microsoft Windows 2003, 2008, or 2008 R2 forest or a Windows 2003, 2008, or 2008 R2 domain for the installation of Windows Server 2012 R2 domain controllers.

To add a new domain to an existing forest, you must already have at least one other domain, which is the root domain. Keep in mind that the entire forest structure is destroyed if the original root domain is ever removed entirely. Therefore, you should have at least two domain controllers in the Active Directory root domain; the second serves as a backup in case you have a problem with the first, and it can also serve as a backup solution for disaster recovery and fault tolerance purposes. Such a setup provides additional protection for the entire forest in case one of the domain controllers fails.

Adding Additional Domain Controllers

In addition to the operations you've already performed, you can use the Active Directory Installation Wizard to create additional domain controllers for any of your domains. There are two main reasons to create additional domain controllers:

Fault Tolerance and Reliability   You should always consider the theory of *disaster recovery (DR)* and have a plan, sometimes referred to as a *disaster recovery plan (DRP)*. If you're part of one of those organizations that rely upon their network directory services infrastructures, you need Active Directory to provide security and resources for all users.

For this reason, downtime and data loss are very costly. Through the use of multiple domain controllers, you can ensure that if one of the servers goes down, another one is available to perform the necessary tasks, such as user authentication and resource browsing. Additionally, data loss (perhaps from hard disk drive failure) will not result in the loss or unavailability of network security information because you can easily recover Active Directory information from the remaining, still-functional domain controller.

Performance   The burden of processing login requests and serving as a repository for security permissions and other information can be quite extensive, especially in larger businesses. By using multiple domain controllers, you can distribute this load across multiple systems. Additionally, by strategically placing domain controllers, you can greatly increase response times for common network operations, such as authentication and browsing for resources.

As a rule of thumb, you should always plan and design your infrastructure to have at least two domain controllers per domain. For many organizations, this provides a good balance between the cost of servers and the level of reliability and performance. For larger or more distributed organizations, however, additional domain controllers greatly improve performance.

Demoting a Domain Controller

In addition to being able to promote member servers to domain controllers, the Active Directory Installation Wizard can do the exact opposite, that is, demote domain controllers. You might choose to demote a domain controller for a couple of reasons. First, if you have determined that the role of a server should change (for example, from a domain controller to a member or stand-alone server that you might make into a web server), you can easily demote it to make this happen. Another common reason to demote a domain controller is if you want to move the machine from one domain to another. You cannot do this in a single step: First you need to demote the existing domain controller to remove it from the current domain and then promote it into a new domain. The result is that the server is now a domain controller for a different domain.

To demote a domain controller, you simply access the Active Directory Installation Wizard. The wizard automatically notices that the local server is a domain controller, and it asks you to verify each step you take, as with most things you do in Windows. You are prompted to decide whether you really want to remove this machine from the current domain. Note that if the local server is a global catalog server, you will be warned that at least one copy of the GC must remain available so that you can perform logon authentication.

By default, at the end of the demotion process, the server is joined as a member server to the domain for which it was previously a domain controller. If you demote the last domain controller in the domain, the server becomes a stand-alone server.

Real World Scenario

Planning for Domain Controller Placement

You are the senior system administrator for a medium-sized Active Directory environment. Currently the environment consists of only one Active Directory domain. Your company's network is spread out over 40 different sites throughout North America. Recently, you've received complaints from users and other system administrators about the performance of Active Directory–related operations. For example, users report that it takes several minutes to log on to their machines between 9 a.m. and 10 a.m., when activity is at its highest. Simultaneously, system administrators complain that updating user information within the OUs for which they are responsible can take longer than expected.

Fortunately, Active Directory's distributed domain controller architecture allows you to optimize performance for this type of situation without making dramatic changes to your environment. You decide that the quickest and easiest solution is to deploy additional domain controllers throughout the organization. The domain controllers are generally placed within areas of the network that are connected by slow or unreliable links. For example, a small branch office in Des Moines, Iowa, receives its own domain controller. The process is quite simple: You install a new Windows Server 2012 R2 computer and then run the Active Directory Installation Wizard in Server Manager to make the new machine a domain controller for an existing domain. Once the initial directory services data is copied to the new server, it is ready to service requests and updates of your domain information.

Note that there are potential drawbacks to this solution; for instance, you have to manage additional domain controllers and the network traffic generated from communications between the domain controllers. It's important that you monitor your network links to ensure that you've reached a good balance between replication traffic and overall Active Directory performance. In later chapters, you'll see how you can configure Active Directory sites to map Active Directory operations better to your physical network structure.

WARNING   Removing a domain from your environment is not an operation that you should take lightly. Before you plan to remove a domain, make a list of all of the resources that depend on the domain and the reasons why the domain was originally created. If you are sure that your organization no longer requires the domain, then you can safely continue. If you are not sure, think again, because the process cannot be reversed, and you could lose critical information!

Managing Multiple Domains

You can easily manage most of the operations that must occur *between* domains by using the Active Directory Domains and Trusts administrative tool. On the other hand, if you want to configure settings *within* a domain, you should use the Active Directory Users and Computers tool. In the following sections, you'll look at ways to perform two common domain management functions with the tools just mentioned: managing *single-master operations* and managing *trusts*. You'll also look at ways to manage UPN suffixes in order to simplify user accounts, and you'll examine GC servers in more detail.

Managing Single-Master Operations

For the most part, Active Directory functions in what is known as *multimaster* replication. That is, every domain controller within the environment contains a copy of the Active Directory database that is both readable and writable. This works well for most types of information. For example, if you want to modify the password of a user, you can easily do this on *any* of the domain controllers within a domain. The change is then automatically propagated to the other domain controllers.

However, some functions are not managed in a multimaster fashion. These operations are known as *operations masters*. You must perform single-master operations on specially designated domain controllers within the Active Directory forest. There are five main single-master functions: two that apply to an entire Active Directory forest and three that apply to each domain.

Forest Operations Masters

You use the Active Directory Domains and Trusts tool to configure forest-wide roles. The following single-master operations apply to the entire forest:

Schema Master   Earlier you learned that all of the domain controllers within a single Active Directory environment share the same schema. This ensures information consistency. However, developers and system administrators can modify the Active

Directory schema by adding custom information. A trivial example might involve adding a field to employee information that specifies a user's favorite color.

When you need to make these types of changes, you must perform them on the domain controller that serves as the *Schema Master* for the environment. The Schema Master is then responsible for propagating all of the changes to all of the other domain controllers within the forest.

Domain Naming Master   The purpose of the *Domain Naming Master* is to keep track of all of the domains within an Active Directory forest. You access this domain controller whenever you need to add/remove new domains to a tree or forest.

Domain Operations Masters

You use the Active Directory Users and Computers snap-in to administer roles within a domain. Within each domain, at least one domain controller must fulfill each of the following roles:

Relative ID (RID) Master   Every security object within Active Directory must be assigned a unique identifier so that it is distinguishable from other objects. For example, if you have two OUs named IT that reside in different domains, you must have some way to distinguish easily between them. Furthermore, if you delete one of the IT OUs and then later re-create it, the system must be able to determine that it is not the same object as the other IT OU. The unique identifier for each object consists of a domain identifier and a relative identifier (RID). RIDs are always unique within an Active Directory domain and are used for managing security information and authenticating users. The *RID Master* is responsible for creating these values within a domain whenever new Active Directory objects are created.

PDC Emulator Master   Within a domain, the *PDC Emulator Master* is responsible for maintaining backward compatibility with Windows 95, 98, and NT clients. It is also responsible for processing account lockouts, performing password changes, and validating failed logon authentications within the domain. If a user's logon authentication fails to a bad password on a domain controller, then that domain controller passes the authentication request to the PDC Emulator Master to check and see whether the password that was used matches the password that is most current for that user.

The PDC Emulator Master serves as the default domain controller to process authentication requests if another domain controller is unable to do so. The PDC Emulator Master also receives preferential treatment whenever domain security changes are made.

Infrastructure Master   Whenever a user is added to or removed from a group, all of the other domain controllers should be made aware of this change. The role of the domain controller that acts as an *Infrastructure Master* is to ensure that group membership information stays synchronized within an Active Directory domain.

Unless there is only one domain controller, you should not place the Infrastructure Master on a global catalog server. If the Infrastructure Master and global catalog are on the same domain controller, the Infrastructure Master will not function. If you have only one domain, then all DCs are GCs.

Another service that a server can control for the network is the Windows Time service. The Windows Time service uses a suite of algorithms in the Network Time Protocol (NTP). This helps ensure that the time on all computers throughout a network is as accurate as possible. All client computers within a Windows Server 2012 R2 domain are synchronized with the time of an authoritative computer.

Assigning Single-Master Roles

Now that you are familiar with the different types of single-master operations, take a look at Exercise 5.7. This exercise shows you how to assign these roles to servers within the Active Directory environment. In this exercise, you will assign single-master operations roles to various domain controllers within the environment. To complete the steps in this exercise, you need one Active Directory domain controller.

EXERCISE 5.7

Assigning Single-Master Operations

1. Open the Active Directory Domains and Trusts administrative tool.

2. Right-click Active Directory Domains And Trusts and choose Operations Masters.

3. In the Operations Masters dialog box, note that you can change the operations master by clicking the Change button. If you want to move this assignment to another computer, first you need to connect to that computer and then make the change. Click Close to continue without making any changes.

4. Close the Active Directory Domains and Trusts administrative tool.

5. Open the Active Directory Users and Computers administrative tool.

6. Right-click the name of a domain and select Operations Masters. This brings up the RID tab of the Operations Masters dialog box.

    Notice that you can change the computer that is assigned to the role. To change the role, first you need to connect to the appropriate domain controller. Notice that the PDC and Infrastructure roles have similar tabs. Click Close to continue without making any changes.

7. When you have finished, close the Active Directory Users and Computers tool.

Remember that you manage single-master operations with three different tools. You use the Active Directory Domains and Trusts tool to configure the Domain Name Master role, while you use the Active Directory Users and Computers snap-in to administer roles within a domain. Although this might not seem intuitive at first, it can help you remember which roles apply to domains and which apply to the whole forest. The third tool, the Schema Master role, is a bit different from these other two. To change the Schema Master role, you must install the Active Directory Schema MMS snap-in and change it there.

Managing Trusts

Trust relationships make it easier to share security information and network resources between domains. As was already mentioned, standard transitive two-way trusts are automatically created between the domains in a tree and between each of the trees in a forest. Figure 5.13 shows an example of the default trust relationships in an Active Directory forest.

FIGURE 5.13   Default trusts in an Active Directory forest

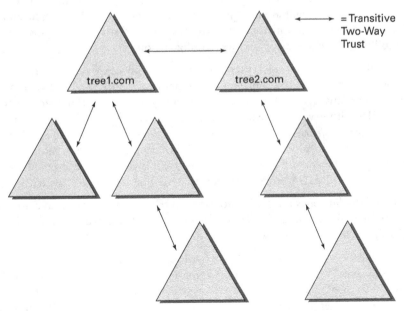

When configuring trusts, you need to consider two main characteristics:

Transitive Trusts By default, Active Directory trusts are *transitive trusts*. The simplest way to understand transitive relationships is through this example: If Domain A trusts Domain B and Domain B trusts Domain C, then Domain A implicitly trusts Domain C. If you need to apply a tighter level of security, trusts can be configured as intransitive.

One-Way vs. Two-Way Trusts can be configured as one-way or two-way relationships. The default operation is to create *two-way trusts* or *bidirectional trusts*. This makes it easier to manage trust relationships by reducing the trusts you must create. In some cases, however, you might decide against two-way trusts. In one-way relationships, the trusting domain allows resources to be shared with the trusted domain but not the other way around.

When domains are added together to form trees and forests, an automatic transitive two-way trust is created between them. Although the default trust relationships work well for most organizations, there are some reasons you might want to manage trusts manually:

- You may want to remove trusts between domains if you are absolutely sure you do not want resources to be shared between domains.

- Because of security concerns, you may need to keep resources isolated.

In addition to the default trust types, you can configure the following types of special trusts:

External Trusts You use *external trusts* to provide access to resources on a Windows NT 4 domain or forest that cannot use a forest trust. Windows NT 4 domains cannot benefit from the other trust types that are used in Windows Server 2012 R2. Thus, in some cases, external trusts could be your only option. External trusts are always nontransitive, but they can be established in a one-way or two-way configuration.

Default SID Filtering on External Trusts When you set up an external trust, remember that it is possible for hackers to compromise a domain controller in a trusted domain. If this trust is compromised, a hacker can use the security identifier (SID) history attribute to associate SIDs with new user accounts, granting themselves unauthorized rights (this is called an *elevation-of-privileges attack*). To help prevent this type of attack, Windows Server 2012 R2 automatically enables SID filter quarantining on all external trusts. SID filtering allows the domain controllers in the trusting domain (the domain with the resources) to remove all SID history attributes that are not members of the trusted domain.

Realm Trusts *Realm trusts* are similar to external trusts. You use them to connect to a non-Windows domain that uses Kerberos authentication. Realm trusts can be transitive or nontransitive, one-way or two-way.

Cross-Forest Trusts *Cross-forest trusts* are used to share resources between forests. They have been used since Windows Server 2000 domains and cannot be nontransitive, but you can establish them in a one-way or a two-way configuration. Authentication requests in either forest can reach the other forest in a two-way cross-forest trust. If you want one forest to trust another forest, you must set it (at a minimum) to at least the forest function level of Windows Server 2003.

Selective Authentication vs. Forest-wide Authentication   Forest-wide authentication on a forest trust means that users of the trusted forest can access all of the resources of the trusting forest. Selective authentication means that users cannot authenticate to a domain controller or resource server in the trusting forest unless they are explicitly allowed to do so. Exercise 5.8 will show you the steps necessary to change forest-wide authentication to selective authentication.

Shortcut Trusts   In some cases, you may actually want to create direct trusts between two domains that implicitly trust each other. Such a trust is sometimes referred to as a *shortcut trust*, and it can improve the speed at which resources are accessed across many different domains. Let's say you have a forest, as shown in Figure 5.14.

FIGURE 5.14   Example of a forest

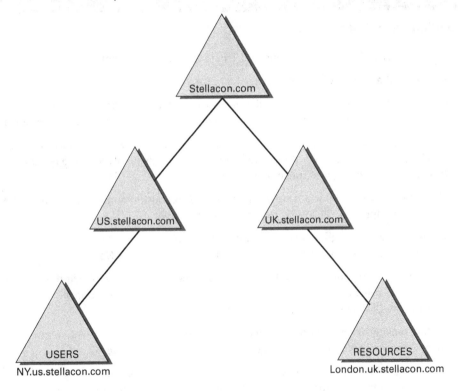

Users in the NY.us.stellacon.com domain can access resources in the London. uk.stellacon.com domain, but the users have to authenticate using the parent domains to gain access (NY.us.stellacon.com to us.stellacon.com to stellacon.com to uk.stellacon.com to finally reach London.uk.stellacon.com). This process can be slow.

An administrator can set up a one-way trust from London.uk.stellacon.com (trusting domain) to NY.us.stellacon.com (trusted domain) so that the users can access the resources directly.

 Perhaps the most important aspect to remember regarding trusts is that creating them only *allows* you to share resources between domains. The trust does not grant any permissions between domains by itself. Once a trust has been established, however, system administrators can easily assign the necessary permissions.

Exercise 5.8 walks you through the steps necessary to manage trusts. In this exercise, you will see how to assign trust relationships between domains. To complete the steps in this exercise, you must have domain administrator access permissions.

EXERCISE 5.8

Managing Trust Relationships

1. Open the Active Directory Domains and Trusts administrative tool.

2. Right-click the name of a domain and select Properties.

3. Select the Trusts tab. You will see a list of the trusts that are currently configured. To modify the trust properties for an existing trust, highlight that trust and click Properties.

4. The Properties window for the trust displays information about the trust's direction, transitivity, and type along with the names of the domains involved in the relationship. Click Cancel to exit without making any changes.

5. To create a new trust relationship, click the New Trust button on the Trusts tab. The New Trust Wizard appears. Click Next to proceed with the wizard.

6. On the Trust Name page, you are prompted for the name of the domain with which the trust should be created. Enter the name of the domain and click Next.

7. On the Trust Type page, you would normally choose the Trust With A Windows Domain option if you know that the other domain uses a Windows domain controller. Choose Realm Trust. Click Next when you have finished.

8. On the Transitivity Of Trust page, you choose whether the trust is transitive or nontransitive. Choose the Nontransitive option and click Next to continue.

9. On the Direction Of Trust page, you select the direction of the trust. If you want both domains to trust each other, you select the Two-Way option. Otherwise, you select either One-Way: Incoming or One-Way: Outgoing, depending on where the affected users are located. For the sake of this exercise, choose One-Way: Incoming and then click Next.

10. On the Trust Password page, you need to specify a password that should be used to administer the trust. Type **P@ssw0rd** and confirm it. Note that if there is an existing trust relationship between the domains, the passwords must match. Click Next to continue.

11. Now you see the Trust Selections Complete page that recaps the selections you have made. Because this is an exercise, you don't actually want to establish this trust. Click Cancel to cancel the wizard without saving the changes.

12. Exit the trust properties for the domain by clicking Cancel.

To Enable Selective Authentication

1. In the console tree, right-click the name of a domain and select Properties.

2. Select the Trusts tab. Under either Domains Trusted By This Domain (Outgoing Trusts) or Domains That Trust This Domain (Incoming Trusts), click the forest trust that you want to administer and then click Properties.

3. On the Authentication tab, click Selective Authentication and then click OK.

Managing UPN Suffixes

User principal name (UPN) suffixes are the part of a user's name that appears after the @ symbol. For example, the UPN suffix of wpanek@stellacon.com would be stellacon.com. By default, the UPN suffix is determined by the name of the domain in which the user is created. In this example, the user wpanek was created in the domain stellacon.com, so the two pieces of the UPN logically fit together. However, you might find it useful to provide an alternative UPN suffix to consolidate the UPNs forest wide.

For instance, if you manage a forest that consists of stellacon.com and stellacon2.com, you might want all of your users to adopt the more generally applicable stellacon.com UPN suffix. By adding additional UPN suffixes to the forest, you can easily choose the appropriate suffix when it comes time to create new users. Exercise 5.9 shows you how to add additional suffixes to a forest.

EXERCISE 5.9

Adding a UPN Suffix

1. Open the Active Directory Domains and Trusts administrative tool.

2. Right-click Active Directory Domains And Trusts in the left side of the window and select Properties.

3. On the UPN Suffixes tab of the Active Directory Domains And Trusts Properties dialog box, enter an alternative UPN suffix in the Alternative UPN Suffixes field. Click the Add button to add the suffix to the list.

4. To remove a UPN suffix, select its name in the list and click the Remove button.

Name Suffix Routing

Name Suffix Routing is a mechanism that is used to manage how authentication requests are routed across Active Directory forests that are joined together by forest trusts. To simplify the administration of authentication requests, when you create a forest trust, all unique name suffixes are routed by default. A *unique name suffix* is a name suffix within a forest, such as a user principal name (UPN) suffix, service principal name (SPN) suffix, or Domain Name System forest, or a domain tree name that is not subordinate to any other name suffix. Name Suffix Routing is managed from the Active Directory Domains and Trusts Administrative Console.

Managing Global Catalog Servers

One of the best features of a distributed directory service like Active Directory is that you can store different pieces of information in different places within an organization. For example, a domain in Japan might store a list of users who operate within a company's Asian operations business unit, while one in New York would contain a list of users who operate within its North American operations business unit. This architecture allows system administrators to place the most frequently accessed information on domain controllers in different domains, thereby reducing disk space requirements and replication traffic.

However, you may encounter a problem when you deal with information that is segmented into multiple domains. The issue involves querying information stored within Active Directory. For example, what would happen if a user wanted a list of all the printers available in all domains within the Active Directory forest? In this case, the search would normally require information from at least one domain controller in each of the domains within the environment. Some of these domain controllers may be located across slow WAN links or may have unreliable connections. The result would include an extremely long wait while retrieving the results of the query, that is, if any results came up without the query timing out.

Fortunately, Active Directory has a mechanism that speeds up such searches. You can configure any number of domain controllers to host a copy of the GC. The GC contains all of the schema information and a subset of the attributes for all domains within the Active Directory environment. Although a default set of information is normally included with the GC, system administrators can choose to add additional information to this data store if it is needed. To help reduce replication traffic and to keep the GC's database small, only a limited subset of each object's attributes is replicated. This is called the *partial attribute set (PAS)*. You can change the PAS by modifying the schema and marking attributes for replication to the GC.

Servers that contain a copy of the GC are known as *GC servers*. Now whenever a user executes a query that requires information from multiple domains, they need only contact the nearest GC server for this information. Similarly, when users must authenticate across domains, they do not have to wait for a response from a domain controller that may be located across the world. The result is that the overall performance of Active Directory queries improves.

Exercise 5.10 walks you through the steps that you need to take to configure a domain controller as a GC server. Generally, GC servers are useful only in environments that use multiple Active Directory domains.

EXERCISE 5.10

Managing GC Servers

1. Open the Active Directory Sites and Services administrative tool.

2. Find the name of the local domain controller within the list of objects, typically under Default First Site Name ➢ Servers, and expand this object. Right-click NTDS Settings, and select Properties.

3. In the NTDS Settings Properties dialog box, type **Primary GC Server for Domain** in the Description field. Note that there is a check box that determines whether this computer contains a copy of the global catalog. If the box is checked, then this domain controller contains a subset of information from all other domains within the Active Directory environment. Select the Global Catalog check box and then click OK to continue.

4. When you have finished, close the Active Directory Sites and Services administrative tool.

Managing Universal Group Membership Caching

Many networks run into problems with available network bandwidth and server hardware limitations. For this reason, it may not be wise to install a GC in smaller branch offices. Windows Server 2012 R2 can help these smaller sites by deploying domain controllers that use *Universal Group Membership Caching (UGMC)*.

Once enabled, Universal Group Membership Caching stores information locally when a user attempts to log on for the first time. With the use of a GC, the domain controller retains the universal group membership for that logged-on user.

The next time that user attempts to log on, the authenticating domain controller running Windows Server 2012 R2 will obtain the universal group membership information from its local cache without the need to contact a GC. By default, the universal group membership information is retained on the domain controller for eight hours.

There are several advantages of using Universal Group Membership Caching:

Faster Logon Times Because the domain controller does not need to contact a global catalog, logon authentication is faster.

Reduced Network Bandwidth The domain controller does not have to handle object replication for all of the objects located in the forest.

Ability to Use Existing Hardware There is no need to upgrade hardware to support a GC.

Exercise 5.11 shows you the steps necessary to configure Universal Group Membership Caching.

EXERCISE 5.11

Managing Universal Group Membership Caching

1. Open the Active Directory Sites and Services administrative tool.

2. Click Sites and then click CorporateHQ. In the right pane, right-click NTDS Settings and choose Properties.

3. In the NTDS Site Settings Properties dialog box, check the box Enable Universal Group Membership Caching and then click OK to continue.

4. When you have finished, close the Active Directory Sites and Services administrative tool.

Upgrading Existing Domains and Forests

Now that you have a new operating system to which you can upgrade, it's important that you take some time to talk about the different ways you can get your infrastructure up-to-date. There are quite a few upgrade paths to consider. Table 5.2 illustrates the most commonly used in-place upgrade paths for upgrading your domain controllers from Windows Server 2008 to Windows Server 2012 R2. The in-place upgrades hold true only for 64-bit versions of Server 2008 to Server 2012 R2. You cannot in-place upgrade domain controllers that run either Windows Server 2003 or a 32-bit version of Windows Server 2008. If your current environmental configurations fall outside of the possibility of an in-place upgrade, then you will need to install new domain controllers on the most up-to-date Windows Server OS and then delete the old ones.

TABLE 5.2   Supported domain controller in-place upgrade paths

If you are running these editions...	You can upgrade to these editions...
Windows Server 2008 Standard with SP2 or Windows Server 2008 Enterprise with SP2	Windows Server 2012 R2 Standard or Windows Server 2012 R2 Datacenter
Windows Server 2008 Datacenter with SP2	Windows Server 2012 R2 Datacenter
Windows Web Server 2008	Windows Server 2012 R2 Standard

Windows Server 2008 R2 Standard with SP1	Windows Server 2012 R2 Standard
or	or
Windows Server 2008 R2 Enterprise with SP1	Windows Server 2012 R2 Datacenter
Windows Server 2008 R2 Datacenter with SP1	Windows Server 2012 R2 Datacenter
Windows Web Server 2008 R2	Windows Server 2012 Standard

When preparing for your domain controller upgrade, make sure you make a full backup of your Active Directory environment prior to the performing the task. If you have never actually performed a full backup and restore of your Active Directory environment, then I recommend doing so by following the instructions in Chapter 3 of this book. You never know if a backup actually works until you perform the restore, and you should never make infrastructure changes without a backup of your current configuration.

In addition to knowing the proper upgrade path and having full backups of your environment, you will also want to take into account domain and forest functional levels. Windows Server 2012 R2 requires a forest functional level of at least Windows Server 2003. This essentially means you cannot add a Windows Server 2012 R2 domain controller to a forest that contains a Windows 2000 machine. You would need to upgrade or eliminate any Windows 2000 machine and then raise the forest functional level to at least Windows Server 2003 in order to accommodate a Windows Server 2012 R2 domain controller. It may seem old, but you'd be surprised how many government organizations still have Windows Server 2000 and Windows Server 2003 running legacy applications in a production environment. You will notice that the issue is far less frequent in commercial settings.

Summary

In this chapter, I discussed the purpose of Active Directory replication. As you have learned, replication is used to keep domain controllers synchronized, and it is important in Active Directory environments of all sizes. Replication is the process by which changes to the Active Directory database are transferred between domain controllers.

This chapter also covered the concepts of sites, site boundaries, and subnets. In addition to learning how to configure them, you learned that subnets define physical portions of your network environment and that sites are defined as collections of well-connected IP subnets. Site boundaries are defined by the subnet or subnets that you include in your site configuration.

I also covered the basics of replication and the differences between intrasite and intersite replication. Additionally, I covered the purpose and use of bridgehead servers in depth. Although replication is a behind-the-scenes type of task, the optimal configuration of sites in distributed network environments results in better use of bandwidth and faster response by network resources. For these reasons, you should be sure you thoroughly understand the concepts related to managing replication for Active Directory.

I covered the placement of domain controllers and global catalog servers in the network and how, when placed properly, they can increase the performance of Active Directory operations.

I also showed how to monitor and troubleshoot replication. The Windows Server 2012 R2 System Monitor administrative tool was designed so that you can monitor many performance statistics associated with using Active Directory.

The chapter also covered the basics of linking multiple domains in trees and forests. You now know why you would want to plan for them and the benefits and drawbacks of using only one domain or of having a multidomain environment. For example, you might decide to have multiple domains if you have an acquisitions-and-mergers situation where you need to keep multiple administrators. In addition, by using multiple domains, organizations can retain separate security databases; however, in such cases, they are also able to share resources between domains.

You can use multiple domains to provide two major benefits for the network directory services—security and availability. These benefits are made possible through Active Directory and the administrative tools that can be used to access it.

System administrators can simplify operations while still ensuring that only authorized users have access to their data. Multiple domains can interact to form Active Directory trees and forests, and you can use the Active Directory Installation Wizard to create new Active Directory trees and forests.

Exam Essentials

Understand the reasons for using multiple domains.   There are seven primary reasons for using multiple domains: They provide additional scalability, they reduce replication traffic, they help with political and organizational issues, they provide many levels of hierarchy, they allow for decentralized administration, they preserve legality, and they allow for multiple DNS or domain names.

Understand the drawbacks of using multiple domains.   With multiple domains, maintaining administrative consistency is more difficult. The number of administrative units multiplies as well, which makes it difficult to keep track of network resources. Finally, it is much more difficult to rearrange the domain topology within an Active Directory environment than it is simply to reorganize OUs.

Know how to create a domain tree.   To create a new domain tree, you need to promote a Windows Server 2012 R2 computer to a domain controller, select the option that makes this domain controller the first machine in a new domain, and make that domain the first domain of a new tree. The result is a new domain tree.

Know how to join a domain tree to a forest.   Creating a new tree to form or add to a forest is as simple as promoting a server to a domain controller for a new domain that does *not* share a namespace with an existing Active Directory domain. To add a domain to an existing forest, you must already have at least one other domain. This domain serves as the root domain for the entire forest.

Understand how to manage single-master operations.   Single-master operations must be performed on specially designated machines within the Active Directory forest. There are five main single-master functions: two that apply to an entire Active Directory forest (Schema Master and Domain Naming Master) and three that apply to each domain (RID Master, PDC Emulator Master, and Infrastructure Master).

Understand how to manage trusts.   When configuring trusts, you'll need to consider two main characteristics: transitivity and direction. The simplest way to understand transitive relationships is through this example: If Domain A trusts Domain B and Domain B trusts Domain C, then Domain A implicitly trusts Domain C. Trusts can be configured as nontransitive so that this type of behavior does not occur. In one-way relationships, the trusting domain allows resources to be shared with the trusted domain. In two-way relationships, both domains trust each other equally. Special trusts include external trusts, realm trusts, cross-forest trusts, and shortcut trusts.

Understand how to manage UPN suffixes.   By default, the name of the domain in which the user is created determines the UPN suffix. By adding additional UPN suffixes to the forest, you can easily choose more manageable suffixes when it comes time to create new users.

Understand how to manage global catalog servers.   You can configure any number of domain controllers to host a copy of the global catalog. The GC contains all of the schema information and a subset of the attributes for all domains within the Active Directory environment. Servers that contain a copy of the GC are known as GC servers. Whenever a user executes a query that requires information from multiple domains, they need only contact the nearest GC server for this information. Similarly, when users must authenticate across domains, they will not have to wait for a response from a domain controller that may be located across the world. The result is increased overall performance of Active Directory queries.

Understand universal group membership caching.   You can enable a domain controller as a Universal Group Membership Caching server. The Universal Group Membership Caching machine will then send a request for the logon authentication of a user to the GC server. The GC will then send the information back to the Universal Group Membership Caching server to be cached locally for eight hours (by default). The user can then authenticate without the need to contact the GC again.

Understand the purpose of Active Directory replication.   Replication is used to keep domain controllers synchronized, and it is important in Active Directory environments of all sizes. Replication is the process by which changes to the Active Directory database are transferred between domain controllers.

Understand the concept of sites, site boundaries, and subnets. Subnets define physical portions of your network environment. Sites are defined as collections of well-connected IP subnets. Site boundaries are defined by the subnet or subnets that you include in your site configuration.

Understand the differences between intrasite and intersite replication. Intrasite replication is designed to synchronize Active Directory information to machines that are located in the same site. Intersite replication is used to synchronize information for domain controllers that are located in different sites.

Understand the purpose of bridgehead servers. Bridgehead servers are designed to accept traffic between two remote sites and then to forward this information to the appropriate servers. One way to synchronize data between sites efficiently that are connected with slow connections is to use a bridgehead server.

Implement site links, site link bridges, and connection objects. You can use all three of these object types to finely control the behavior of Active Directory replication and to manage replication traffic. Site links are created to define the types of connections that are available between the components of a site. Site links can reflect a relative cost for a network connection and can reflect the bandwidth that is available for communications. You can use site link bridges to connect site links so that the relationship can be transitive. Connection objects provide you with a way to set up special types of replication schedules such as immediate replication on demand or specifying a custom schedule for certain servers.

Configure replication schedules and site link costs. You can create multiple site links between sites, and you can assign site links a cost value based on the type of connection. The system administrator determines the cost value, and the relative costs of site links are then used to determine the optimal path for replication. The lower the cost, the more likely the link is to be used for replication. Once you've determined how and through which connections replication will take place, it's time to determine *when* information should be replicated. Replication requires network resources and occupies bandwidth. Therefore, you need to balance the need for consistent directory information with the need to conserve bandwidth.

Determine where to place domain controllers and global catalog servers based on a set of requirements. Where you place domain controllers and global catalog servers can positively affect the performance of Active Directory operations. However, to optimize performance, you need to know the best places to put these servers in a network environment that consists of multiple sites.

Monitor and troubleshoot replication. The Windows Server 2012 R2 System Monitor administrative tool is designed so that you can monitor many performance statistics associated with using Active Directory. In addition to this monitoring, you should always verify basic network connectivity and router and firewall connections and also examine the event logs.

Review Questions

1. You need to deactivate the UGMC option on some of your domain controllers. At which level in Active Directory would you deactivate UGMC?

   A. Server

   B. Site

   C. Domain

   D. Forest

2. You work for an organization with a single domain forest. Your company has one main location and two branch locations. All locations are configured as Active Directory sites, and all sites are connected with the DEFAULTIPSITELINK object. Your connections are running slower than company policy allows. You want to decrease the replication latency between all domain controllers in the various sites. What should you do?

   A. Decrease the Replication interval for the DEFAULTIPSITELINK object.

   B. Decrease the Replication interval for the site.

   C. Decrease the Replication schedule for the site.

   D. Decrease the Replication schedule for all domain controllers.

3. You need to enable three of your domain controllers as global catalog servers. Where would you configure the domain controllers as global catalogs?

   A. Forest, NTDS settings

   B. Domain, NTDS settings

   C. Site, NTDS settings

   D. Server, NTDS settings

4. Daniel is responsible for managing Active Directory replication traffic for a medium-sized organization that has deployed a single Active Directory domain. Currently, the environment is configured with two sites and the default settings for replication. Each site consists of 15 domain controllers. Recently, network administrators have complained that Active Directory traffic is using a large amount of available network bandwidth between the two sites. Daniel has been asked to meet the following requirements:

   - Reduce the amount of network traffic between domain controllers in the two sites.

   - Minimize the amount of change to the current site topology.

   - Require no changes to the existing physical network infrastructure.

   Daniel decides that it would be most efficient to configure specific domain controllers in each site that will receive the majority of replication traffic from the other site. Which of the following solutions meets the requirements?

   A. Create additional sites that are designed only for replication traffic and move the existing domain controllers to these sites.

   B. Create multiple site links between the two sites.

   C. Create a site link bridge between the two sites.

   D. Configure one server at each site to act as a preferred bridgehead server.

5. Which of the following does not need to be created manually when you are setting up a replication scenario involving three domains and three sites?

   A. Sites

   B. Site links

   C. Connection objects

   D. Subnets

6. Which of the following services of Active Directory is responsible for maintaining the replication topology?

   A. File Replication Service

   B. Knowledge Consistency Checker

   C. Windows Internet Name Service

   D. Domain Name System

7. A system administrator for an Active Directory environment that consists of three sites wants to configure site links to be transitive. Which of the following Active Directory objects is responsible for representing a transitive relationship between sites?

   A. Additional sites

   B. Additional site links

   C. Bridgehead servers

   D. Site link bridges

8. You have configured your Active Directory environment with multiple sites and have placed the appropriate resources in each of the sites. You are now trying to choose a protocol for the transfer of replication information between two sites. The connection between the two sites has the following characteristics:

   - The link is generally unavailable during certain parts of the day because of an unreliable network provider.

   - The replication transmission must be attempted whether the link is available or not. If the link was unavailable during a scheduled replication, the information should automatically be received after the link becomes available again.

   - Replication traffic must be able to travel over a standard Internet connection.

   Which of the following protocols meets these requirements?

   A. IP

   B. SMTP

   C. RPC

   D. DHCP

9. A system administrator suspects that there is an error in the replication configuration. How can the system administrator look for specific error messages related to replication?

   A. By using the Active Directory Sites and Services administrative tool

   B. By using the Computer Management tool

   C. By going to Event Viewer ➢ System Log

   D. By going to Event Viewer ➢ Directory Service Log

10. Christina is responsible for managing Active Directory replication traffic for a medium-sized organization. Currently, the environment is configured with a single site and the default settings for replication. The site contains more than 50 domain controllers, and the system administrators are often making changes to the Active Directory database. Recently, network administrators have complained that Active Directory traffic is consuming a large amount of network bandwidth between portions of the network that are connected by slow links. Ordinarily, the amount of replication traffic is reasonable, but recently users have complained about slow network performance during certain hours of the day.

    Christina has been asked to alleviate the problem while meeting the following requirements:

    ■ Be able to control exactly when replication occurs.

    ■ Be able to base Active Directory replication on the physical network infrastructure.

    ■ Perform the changes without creating or removing any domain controllers.

    Which two of the following steps can Christina take to meet these requirements? (Choose two.)

    A. Create and define Connection objects that specify the hours during which replication will occur.

    B. Create multiple site links.

    C. Create a site link bridge.

    D. Create new Active Directory sites that reflect the physical network topology.

    E. Configure one server at each of the new sites to act as a bridgehead server.

Chapter

6

Configure Access and Information Protection Solutions

THE FOLLOWING 70-412 EXAM OBJECTIVES ARE COVERED IN THIS CHAPTER:

✓ **Install and configure Active Directory Certificate Services (AD CS)**

- Describe and explain the new features in Windows Server 2012 Active Directory Certificate Services

- Install and configure Active Directory Certificate Services using Server Manager and Windows PowerShell

- Manage Active Directory Certificate Services using management consoles and Windows PowerShell

- Configure CRL distribution points

- Install and configure Online Responder

- Implement administrative role separation

- Configure CA Disaster recovery

- Manage certificates

- Manage certificate templates

- Implement and manage certificate deployment, validation, and revocation

- Manage certificate renewal

- Manage certificate enrollment and renewal to computers and users using Group Policies

- Configure and manage key archival and recovery

- Manage trust between organizations including Certificate Trust List (CTL)

- Managing Cross certifications and bride CAs

- Monitoring CA Health

✓ **Install and Configure Active Directory Federation Services (AD FS)**

- Implement claims-based authentication including Relying Party Trusts

- Configure authentication policies

- Configure Workplace Join

- Configure multi-factor authentication

✓ **Install and configure Active Directory Rights Management Services (AD RMS)**

- Install a licensing or certificate AD RMS server

- Manage AD RMS Service Connection Point (SCP)

- Manage RMS templates

- Configure Exclusion Policies

- Backup and restore AD RMS

In this chapter, I will discuss certificate services and the importance of securing the corporate *public key infrastructure (PKI)* environment. The Windows 2012 PKI implementation resides in Active Directory Certificate Services. PKI is the collection of technology, protocols, services, standards, and policies that control the issuing and management of public and private keys using digital certificates, which are the core of PKI. Encryption is used to protect data messages. While certificates provide a certain level of security, they are still vulnerable.

Next, I will cover federation services and how to set up relying party trusts with certificates. Finally, I will discuss rights management, which Microsoft created to further protect documents, email, and web pages from unauthorized copying, printing, forwarding, editing, deleting, and so forth.

What's New in Windows Server 2012 R2 with Active Directory Certificate Services?

Active Directory Certificate Services is a server role included in Windows Server 2012 R2. AD CS allows administrators to customize, issue, and manage public key certificates. AD CS issues digital certificates for authentication, encryption and decryption, and signing.

The following are the new features regarding Active Directory Certificate Services (AD CS) in Windows Server 2012 R2:

Server Core and Minimal Server Interface Support   You can install and deploy any of the six AD CS role services to any version of Windows Server 2012 R2, including Server Core and Minimal Server Interface. The Minimal Server Interface looks and feels like a Server Core installation with most of the GUI management utilities intact. Windows Server 2012 R2 Minimal Server Interface reduces the attack surface and lowers the footprint by removing components such as Windows Explorer and Internet Explorer and their supporting libraries.

Site-Aware Certificate Enrollment   Windows 8/8.1 and Windows Server 2012 R2 computers default to using certificate authorities within their sites when requesting certificates. However, you must configure site information on the certificate authorities' objects within Active Directory for the site-awareness feature to be worthwhile. Once configured, computers running Windows 8/8.1 and Windows Server 2012 R2 request certificates from a certificate authority running in the same site as the computer.

Automatic Certificate Renewal for Non-Domain-Joined Computers   Certificate Enrollment Web Services (CES) allows non-domain-joined computers and computers not directly connected to the corporate network to request and retrieve certificates. AD CS in Windows Server 2012 R2 includes the ability for these clients to renew certificates automatically for non-domain-joined computers.

Enforcement of Certificate Renewal with the Same Key   In earlier versions of Windows, clients that received certificates from templates that were configured for renewal with the same key had to renew their certificates using the same key, or renewal would fail.

With Windows 8/8.1 or Windows Server 2012 R2, you can continue this behavior, or you can configure certificate templates to give higher priority to Trusted Platform Module (TPM)–based KSPs for generating keys. Moreover, using renewal with the same key, administrators can rest assured that the key remains on TPM after renewal.

This feature allows you to enforce renewal with the same key, which can reduce administrative costs (when keys are renewed automatically) and increase key security (when keys are stored using TPM-based KSPs).

Internationalized Domain Names (IDNs)   International languages often contain characters that cannot be represented using ASCII encoding, which limits the function of these languages when enrolling for a certificate. Windows Server 2012 R2 now includes support for international domain names.

Default Security Increased on the Certificate Authority Role Service   Certificate authorities running on Windows Server 2012 R2 include increased RPC security. Increased RPC security on the CA requires that all clients must encrypt the RPC communication between themselves and the CA when requesting certificates.

Active Directory Certificate Services Roles

The Active Directory Certificate Services role provides six role services to issue and manage public key certificates in an enterprise environment. These roles are listed in Table 6.1 and described in the following sections.

TABLE 6.1   AD CS roles

Role service	Description
Certificate Authority (CA)	The CA service includes root and subordinate CAs for issuing certificates to users, computers, and services. This role service also manages certificate validity.
Web Enrollment	This is a web-based interface to enable users to enroll, request, and retrieve certificates as well as retrieve certificate revocation lists from a CA using a web browser.

Online Responder (OCSP)	The Online Responder service retrieves revocation status requests for specific certificates and the status of these certificates, and it returns a signed response with the requested certificate status information.
Network Device Enrollment Service (NDES)	NDES enables routers and other non-domain-joined network devices to acquire certificates.
Certificate Enrollment Policy Web Server (CEP)	CEP enables users and computers to inquire about certificate enrollment policy information.
Certificate Enrollment Web Services (CES)	CES enables users and computers to enroll for certificates with the HTTPS protocol. CEP and CES can be used together to support certificate enrollment for non-domain-joined computers and computers not directly connected to the corporate network.

Planning the Certificate Authority Hierarchy

A *certification authority (CA)* is a trusted server designed to grant certificates to individuals, computers, or organizations to certify the identity and other attributes of the certificate subject.

A CA receives a certificate request, verifies the requester's identity data according to the policy of the CA, and uses its private key to apply its digital signature to the certificate. The CA issues the certificate to the subject of the certificate as a security credential within a PKI environment. A CA is also responsible for revoking certificates and publishing a *certificate revocation list (CRL)*.

A CA can be a third-party issuer, such as VeriSign, or you can create your own CA by installing Active Directory Certificate Services. Every CA also has a certificate confirming its identity, issued by another trusted CA or root CAs.

Cryptography

The Cryptography options for a certificate authority provide increased deployment flexibility to those with a more advanced understanding of cryptography. You can implement cryptographic options by using cryptographic service providers (CSPs) or key storage providers (KSPs).

CSPs are hardware and software components of Windows operating systems that provide generic cryptographic functions. CSPs can provide a variety of encryption and signature algorithms. Key storage providers can provide strong key protection on computers running Windows Server 2012/2012 R2, Windows Server 2008/2008 R2, Windows Vista, Windows 7, or Windows 8. Figure 6.1 shows some of the Cryptography options in the AD CS installation.

FIGURE 6.1   Cryptography for CA screen

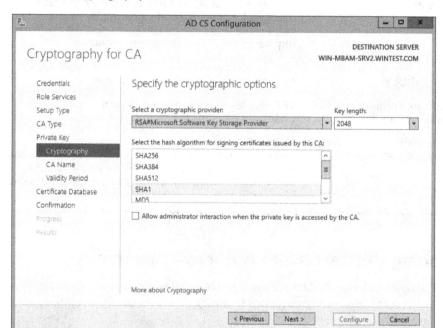

Here are the options:

Select a Cryptographic Provider   Windows Server 2012 R2 provides many CSPs and KSPs, and you can install additional CSPs or KSPs provided by third parties. In Windows Server 2012 R2, the algorithm name is listed in the provider list. All providers with a number sign (#) in the name are cryptography next-generation (CNG) providers. CNG providers can support multiple asymmetric algorithms. CSPs implement only a single algorithm.

Key Length   Each CSP and KSP supports different character lengths for cryptographic keys. Configuring a longer key length hardens against an attack by a hacker to decrypt the key and also degrades the performance of cryptographic operations.

Select The Hash Algorithm For Signing Certificates Used By This CA   The CA uses hash algorithms to sign CA certificates and issues certificates to ensure that an external identity has not tampered with a certificate. Each CSP can support different hash algorithms.

Make sure that your applications, your devices, and all operating systems that may request certificates from this certificate authority support the selected hash algorithm.

Allow Administrator Interaction When The Private Key Is Accessed By The CA   Use this option to help secure the CA and its private key by requiring an administrator to enter a password before every cryptographic operation.

> Exercise caution with this setting because this requires user interaction each time the certificate authority accesses the private key. A certificate authority signs each issued certificate. To sign the issued certificate, the certificate authority must access the private key.

Private Key

A certificate authority uses its assigned certificate to generate and issue certificates. The certificate used by the CA includes a public key and a private key. The private key should be available only to the owner. The public key is publicly available to other entities on the network.

For example, a user's public key can be published within a certificate in a folder so that it is accessible to other people in the organization. The sender of a message can retrieve the user's certificate from Active Directory Domain Services, obtain the public key from the certificate, and then encrypt the message by using the recipient's public key.

Data encrypted with a public key can be decrypted only with the mathematically paired private key. Certificate authorities use their private key to create a digital signature in the certificate when issuing certificates.

Enterprise Certificate Authorities

Enterprise certificate authorities (CAs) publish certificates and CRLs to Active Directory. Enterprise CAs access domain data stored in Active Directory. Enterprise CAs engage certificate templates when issuing certificates. The enterprise CA uses default configuration data in the certificate template to create a certificate with the appropriate attributes for that certificate type.

If you want to enable automatic certificate approval and automatic user certificate enrollment, use enterprise CAs to issue certificates. These features are available only when the CA infrastructure is integrated with Active Directory. Additionally, only enterprise CAs can issue certificates that enable smart card logon because this process requires the CA to map the user account in Active Directory to the smart card certificates.

A *root CA*, sometimes called a *root authority*, is the most trusted CA type in an organization's PKI. The root CA is the only CA that signs its own certificate. The physical security and the certificate issuance policy of a root CA should be tightly reinforced. If the root CA is compromised or if it issues a certificate to an unauthorized identity, any certificate-based security in your organization is compromised by the exposed private key. The best practice is to deploy a second PKI tier to issue certificates from other CAs, called *subordinate CAs* (see Figure 6.2).

FIGURE 6.2 Two-tier PKI hierarchy model

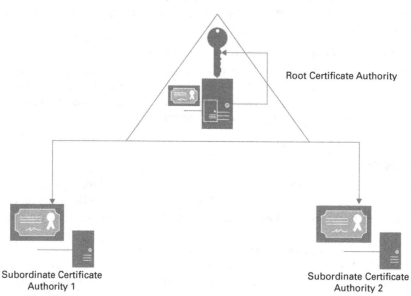

Root Certificate Authority

Subordinate Certificate
Authority 1

Subordinate Certificate
Authority 2

A *subordinate CA* is one that has received its signing certificate by a root CA, third-party CA, or stand-alone CA in your organization. Subordinate CAs normally issue certificates for specific purposes, such as secure email, SSL, Wireless 801.x security, or smart card authentication. Subordinate CAs can also issue certificates to other, more subordinate CAs. A root CA, the subordinate CAs certified by the root, and subordinate CAs certified by other subordinate CAs form a certification hierarchy.

Stand-alone certificate authorities are not integrated into Active Directory and do not support certificate templates. If you deploy stand-alone CAs, you must include all the information about the requested certificate type in the certificate request. By default, all submitted certificate requests to a stand-alone CA are placed in a pending queue, awaiting a CA administrator's approval. Stand-alone CAs can issue certificates automatically upon request, but this is not recommended because the requests are not authenticated.

Because stand-alone CAs are not Active Directory integrated, a stand-alone CA would seem like a less appropriate choice for an enterprise. However, stand-alone root CAs offer a layer of protection when a powered-down stand-alone CA is less likely to be compromised and does not have a footprint in Active Directory. More organizations are deploying *offline stand-alone root CAs* that are brought online only temporarily for re-issuing signing certificates to subordinate CAs. Some organizations permanently keep the offline stand-alone root CA disconnected from the network and distribute signing certificates only via removable media such as CDs, DVDs, or USB flash drives. Offline root CAs have the following characteristics:

- Deployed as a stand-alone root CA

- Deployed on a non-domain-joined server to avoid being offline or powered down for long periods without requiring computer password synchronizations

Real World Scenario

Protect the Offline Root CA

Best practice strongly recommends you securely store and back up the offline stand-alone root CA. A large Medical center implemented their offline stand-alone root CA solution by installing their root CA on a laptop. They routinely kept the laptop in the datacenter until a new administrator discovered and returned laptop to the help desk for repurposing. Needless to say, the laptop was re-imaged, and the entire PKI infrastructure was wiped out. No one was aware until the subordinate CA's certificate had expired a year later and certificates could no longer be issued. You can avoid this catastrophic scenario by securely storing and backing up the offline stand-alone CA.

Two-Tier and Three-Tier Models

It's acceptable for a single enterprise to have multiple PKIs. Multiple PKIs result in one root CA for each PKI and possibly multiple subordinate CAs that chain to their respective roots.

Organizations also may choose a third-tier CA hierarchy model, which involves adding a CA policy server. CA policy servers are designed to implement specific certificate policies that can include certificate life cycle, encryption type, key length, and some approval workflow.

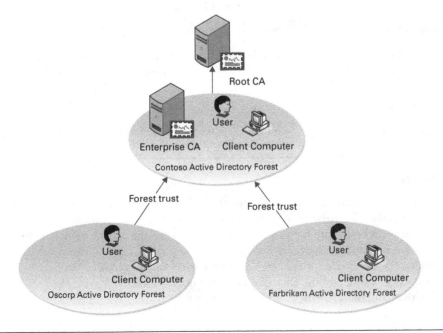

Validity Period

All certificates issued by a certification authority have a validity period. The *validity period* is a time range that specifies how long PKI clients can accept the certificate as an authoritative credential based on the identity stated in the subject of the certificate. This assertion presumes the certificate is not revoked before the validity period ends and the issuing CA remains trusted. The validity period limits the time in which an issued certificate is exposed to the possibility of being compromised (http://technet.microsoft.com/en-us/library/cc740209(v=WS.10).aspx).

All CAs have an expiration date based on its CA certificate's validity ending period. This rule affects the CA's ability to issue certificates and not the validity period of its CA certificate. Because of this rule, organizations must plan for the renewal of every certificate issued to a CA in the certification hierarchy to ensure the existing trust chains and to extend the lifetimes of CAs.

Active Directory Certificate Services enforces a rule that a CA never issues a certificate past the expiration date of its own certificate. Because of this behavior, when a CA's certificate reaches the end of its validity period, all certificates issued by the CA will also expire. Certificates issued by the now-expired CA will not be honored as valid security credentials.

Active Directory Certificate Services allows for the maximum validity periods shown in Table 6.2, which are based on the type of certificate. You configure these validity periods using certificate templates.

TABLE 6.2 AD CS maximum validity periods

Certificate type	Maximum validity period
Root certificate authority	Determined during CA deployment
Subordinate CA Internet Protocol Security Enrollment agent Domain controller	Up to five years, but never more than the root CA's or the issuing CA's validity period
All other certificates	One year, but never more than the root CA's or issuing CA's validity period

Certificate Validation

PKI trust requires a certificate to be validated for both for its expiration and its overall chain of trust. When a certificate user leaves the company, you will want to make sure that no one can use that certificate for authentication and revoke the certificate. Revocation checking is one of the key components of PKI.

Certificate revocation uses certificate revocation lists. CRLs contain a list of certificates that are no longer valid, and the CRL can become large. To solve this, you can access a delta CRL that contains changes or new revocations.

CRLs are accessed through *CRL distribution points (CDPs)*, which are part of a CA role in Windows Server 2012. HTTP, FTP, LDAP, or file-based addresses may be used as URLs. Only newly issued certificates will recognize new changes in the CRL URL; old certificates will use the old URL for revocation list operations.

Online Responders

When a new certificate is issued, the computer queries the issuing CA to find out whether the certificate has been revoked. Traditionally, certificate revocation checking can be done by retrieving certificate revocation lists that are published in Lightweight Directory Access Protocol (LDAP) or Hypertext Transfer Protocol (HTTP) or by using a newer HTTP method named the Online Certificate Status Protocol (OCSP).

OCSP is a lightweight HTTP protocol that responds faster and more efficiently than downloading a traditional CRL. An *online responder* is a trusted server that receives and responds to individual client requests for the status of a certificate. An OCSP responder retrieves CRLs and provides digitally signed real-time certificate revocation status responses to clients based on a given certificate authority's CRL. The amount of data retrieved per request remains constant regardless of the number of revoked certificates.

Online responders process certificate status requests more efficiently than direct access to CRLs in several scenarios (http://technet.microsoft.com/en-us/library/cc725958 .aspx):

- When clients have slow VPN connections or do not have the high-speed connections required to download large CRLs
- When network utilization peaks because revocation-checking activity is high, such as when large numbers of users log on or send signed email simultaneously
- When revocation data for certificates is needed from a non-Microsoft certification authority
- When revocation data is needed to verify individual certificate status requests rather than all revoked or suspended certificates

Installing AD CS

Server Manager provides a graphical user interface to install Active Directory Certificate Services on local and remote computers running Windows Server 2012 R2. The Remote Server Administration Tools for Windows Server 2012 R2 also includes Server Manager, which allows you to run Server Manager on a computer running Windows 8/8.1. In Exercise 6.1, you'll install an AD CS role on the local computer using Server Manager.

EXERCISE 6.1

Installing AD CS Through Server Manager

1. Start Server Manager.

2. Click Manage and click Add Roles And Features

3. The Add Roles And Features Wizard shows the Before You Begin screen. Click Next.

4. Click Role-Based Or Feature-Based Installation on the Select Installation Type screen. Click Next.

5. Click the server on which you want to install Active Directory Certificate Services from the Server Pool list on the Select Destination Server screen. Click Next.

6. Select the Active Directory Certificate Services check box on the Select Server Roles screen.

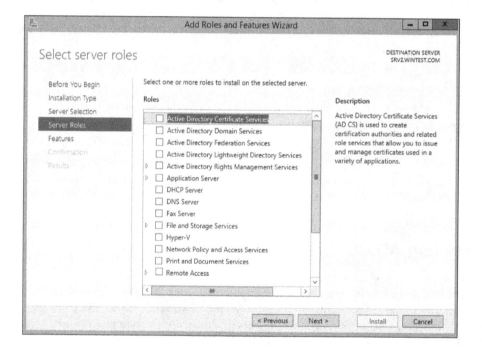

Server Manager prompts you to add more features associated with this role, such as management tools. Leave the default selections. Click Add Features to close the dialog. Click Next on the Select Server Roles screen.

7. Click Next on the Select Features screen.

8. Server Manager displays the Active Directory Certificate Services screen. This screen provides a simple role introduction and noteworthy information, such as that the name of the certificate authority cannot be changed. Click Next.

9. From the Select Role Services screen, select the check boxes next to the AD CS role services you want to install on the computer. Click Next.

10. Read the Confirm Installation Selections screen. This screen provides a list of roles, role services, and features that the current installation prepares on the computer. Click Install to start the installation.

Installation Using Windows PowerShell

A major benefit gained from basing Windows Server 2012 R2's Server Manager on Windows PowerShell is consistency of installation. Server Manager relies on its Windows PowerShell foundation as the underlying engine responsible for installing any of the Active Directory Certificate Services role services. However, you cannot use Server Manager to install roles and features on a Windows Server 2012 R2 core installation.

The Server Manager module for Windows PowerShell provides cmdlets to install, view, and remove features and roles included in Windows Server 2012 R2. You can use these cmdlets on any installation of Windows Server 2012 R2 because it provides Windows PowerShell in all installation types. Also, these cmdlets can install, view, and uninstall Active Directory Certificate Services role services from remote computers running Windows Server 2012 R2.

To view the installation state of Active Directory Certificate Services using Windows PowerShell, follow these steps:

1. Open an elevated Windows PowerShell console. (On Server Core installations, type **PowerShell** in the command console.)

2. In the Windows PowerShell console, type the following command and press Enter:

```
Get-WindowsFeature | where {$_.name -like "adcs*" -or $_.name -like "ad-c*"}
```

The Windows PowerShell cmdlet outputs three columns of information: Display Name, Name, and Install State. The Display Name column is a user-friendly name that describes the feature or service role's use. The Name column represents the name of the component. You use this name with the `Install-WindowsFeature` and `Remove-WindowsFeature` cmdlets. Use the Install State column to determine the installation state of the role or service role.

Typically, the Install State column shows one of three install states: Removed, Available, and Installed. The Removed install state designates that its associated role or feature is not included in the current installation of Windows. You cannot install the associated role or feature without the installation media or Internet connectivity to Windows Update if the feature or role is removed. The Available installation state indicates that the role or feature is staged in the current installation of Windows; however, it is currently not installed. The Installed installation state indicates that the role or feature is installed on the current installation of the computer and is ready, or it has been deployed or configured.

The Active Directory Certificate Services entry from the cmdlet's output represents the parent role. Six child role services appear underneath the parent role. A lowercase *x* appears between the opening and closing square brackets in the parent role if any of the six child role services are installed. The cmdlet also places a lowercase *x* between the opening and closing square brackets for any installed child role service. You should interpret entries without a lowercase *x* between the opening and closing square brackets as not installed. Check the install state to determine whether the role or role service is staged on your installation of Windows.

To install Active Directory Certificate Services using Windows PowerShell, follow these steps:

1. Open an elevated Windows PowerShell console.

2. Use the `Get-WindowsFeature` cmdlet to ensure the Active Directory Certificate Services role's installation state is Available.

3. In the Windows PowerShell console, type the following command and press Enter:

   ```
   Install-WindowsFeature adcs-cert-authority -IncludeManagementTools
   ```

4. Use the `Get-WindowsFeature` cmdlet to verify the installation (see Figure 6.1).

The preceding command instructs the Server Manager module of Windows PowerShell to take the staged binaries for the Certificate Authority role service and install them to the current computer.

> It's important to remember the -IncludeManagementTools argument when installing a feature using Windows PowerShell. The Server Manager module for Windows PowerShell does not install a feature or role management tool by default. The Install-WindowsFeature cmdlet does not install the role management tool without this argument. The Server Manager GUI automatically selects installing the role management tool for you, and it gives you a choice of not to install it before completing the installation.

You can install any of the other child role services using the `Install-WindowsFeature` cmdlet simply by replacing the `adcs-cert-authority` argument with the associated name of the child role service. The following example installs the Active Directory Certificate Services Web Enrollment role service:

```
Install-WindowsFeature adcs-web-enrollment -IncludeManagementTools
```

TIP

The role and feature installation experience is consistent on Windows Server 2012 R2 using the Server Manager module for Windows PowerShell. You can use the same syntax to install a feature or role listed using `Get-WindowsFeature`.

Configuring Active Directory Certificate Services

You begin the Active Directory Certificate Services deployment by starting the AD CS Configuration Wizard (Exercise 6.2). To start the wizard, click the Configure Active Directory Certificate Services On The Destination Server link shown in the Action Flag dialog. The wizard shows the current destination for the role deployment in the Destination Server portion of the screen.

EXERCISE 6.2

Configuring AD CS Through Server Manager

1. After the AD CS installation is successful, click the Configure Active Directory Certificate Services On The Destination Server link.

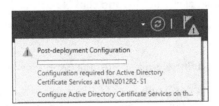

2. The Credentials screen of the AD CS Configuration Wizard displays the required credentials to perform specific AD CS role services deployment. The wizard shows your current credentials in the Credentials portion of the screen. Click Change if your current credentials do not match the credentials needed for the current role service deployment. Otherwise, continue by clicking Next.

3. Select the check boxes for the Certification Authority and Online Responder role services.

4. The Setup Type screen of the AD CS Configuration Wizard shows the two types of certificate authorities you can configure with Active Directory Certificate Services: enterprise or stand-alone. An enterprise certificate authority must run on domain-joined computers and typically remains online to issue certificates or certificate policies. Select Enterprise and click Next.

EXERCISE 6.2 (continued)

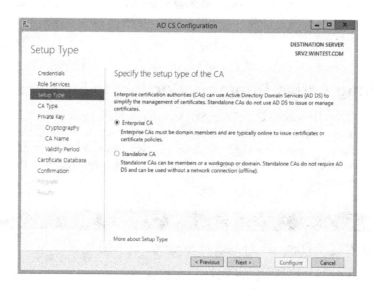

5. In the Setup Type dialog box, select Enterprise CA and click Next.

6. In the CA Type dialog box, click Root CA and click Next.

7. In the Private Key dialog box, verify that Create A New Private Key is selected and click Next.

8. Select the RSA# Microsoft Software Key Storage Provider.

9. Windows Server 2012 includes a number of CSPs and KSPs, and you can install additional CSPs or KSPs provided by third parties. In Windows Server 2012 R2, the provider list includes the name of the algorithm. All providers with a number sign (#) in the name are CNG providers. CNG providers can support multiple asymmetric algorithms. CSPs implement only a single algorithm.

10. Select a key length of 2048.

11. Each CSP and KSP supports different character lengths for cryptographic keys. Configuring a longer key length can enhance security by making it more difficult for a hacker or disgruntled employee to decrypt the key, but it can also slow down the performance of cryptographic operations.

12. Select the SHA1 hash algorithm and click Next.

13. Enter a name for the root CA Server and click Next.

14. In the Certificate Request dialog box, verify that Save A Certificate Request To File On The Target Machine is selected and click Next.

15. In the CA Database dialog box, verify the location for the log files in the Certificate Database Log Location box and click Next.

16. In the Confirmation dialog box, click Configure.

17. In the Results dialog box, click Close.

The CA uses hash algorithms to sign CA certificates and issues certificates to ensure that an external identity has not tampered with a certificate. Each CSP can support different hash algorithms. Make sure your applications, devices, and all operating systems that may request certificates from this certificate authority support the selected hash algorithm.

Use the Create A New Private Key option when creating or reinstalling a certificate authority.

Certificate Authority Name

Names for CAs cannot exceed 64 characters in length. You can create a name by using any Unicode character, but you might want the ANSI character set if interoperability is a concern.

In Active Directory Domain Services (AD DS), the name you specify when you configure a server as a CA (Figure 6.3) becomes the common name of the CA, and this name is reflected in every certificate the CA issues. Because of this behavior, it is important that you do not use the fully qualified domain name (FQDN) for the common name of the CA. Hackers can acquire a copy of a certificate and use the FQDN of the CA to compromise security.

FIGURE 6.3   Specifying the name of the CA

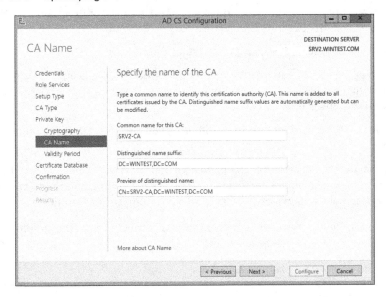

The CA name does not have to be the computer's name. Changing the name after installing Active Directory Certificate Services (AD CS) will invalidate every certificate issued by the CA.

Group Policy Certificate Auto-enrollment

Many certificates can be distributed without the client interaction. These can include most types of certificates issued to computers and services, as well as many certificates issued to users.

To enroll clients automatically for certificates in a domain environment, you must do the following:

- Configure a certificate template with auto-enroll permissions
- Configure an auto-enrollment policy for the domain

Membership in Domain Admins or Enterprise Admins, or equivalent, is the minimum required to complete this procedure. In Exercise 6.3 we are going to configure a group policy to support the auto-enrollment feature.

EXERCISE 6.3

Configure an Auto-enrollment Group Policy for a Domain

1. On a domain controller running Windows Server 2008 R2 or Windows Server 2008, click Start ➤ Administrative Tools ➤ Group Policy Management.

2. In the console tree, double-click Group Policy Objects in the forest and domain containing the Default Domain Policy Group Policy object (GPO) that you want to edit.

3. Right-click the Default Domain Policy GPO and click Edit.

4. In the Group Policy Management Console (GPMC), go to User Configuration ➤ Windows Settings ➤ Security Settings and click Public Key Policies.

5. Double-click Certificate Services Client – Auto-Enrollment.

6. Select the Enroll Certificates Automatically check box to enable auto-enrollment. If you want to block auto-enrollment from occurring, select the Do Not Enroll Certificates Automatically check box.

7. If you are enabling certificate auto-enrollment, you can select the following check boxes:

   "Renew expired certificates, update pending certificates, and remove revoked certificates enables auto-enrollment for certificate renewal, issuance of pending certificate requests, and the automatic removal of revoked certificates from a user's certificate store."

   "Update certificates that use certificate templates enables auto-enrollment for issuance of certificates that supersede issued certificates."

8. Click OK to accept your changes.

Key-Based Renewal for Non-Domain-Joined Computers

Windows Server 2012 R2 combines automatic certificate renewal with AD CS Certificate Enrollment Web Services to enable non-domain-joined computers to renew their certificates automatically before they expire like Internet-facing web servers.

Many organizations and service providers maintain servers that require SSL certificates. These servers are not typically joined to the same domain as an issuing certificate authority, and they do not have identity records or accounts in the organization's Active Directory. This means they cannot benefit from today's automatic certificate renewal, which is based on secured certificate templates in Active Directory. As a result, these organizations manage and renew SSL certificates manually, a time-intensive and error-prone process. Neglecting to renew a single SSL certificate can cause a massive and costly system outage.

Currently, Certificate Enrollment Web Services supports three types of server-side authentication modes:

- Windows integrated (Kerberos)
- Certificate-based
- Username and password

These authentication mode options, however, are not viable choices when the client is not joined to a domain and the enterprise certificate authority makes authorization decisions using templates that are based on the Active Directory group membership of the requestor.

Consider the following authentication options for automatic renewal:

Windows Integrated   This authentication option is not suitable for auto renewal because the two domains to which the certificate authority and the requesting server belong do not have a trust relationship between them or the requesting server is not joined to any domain.

Certificate-Based   The initially enrolled server certificate is not suitable for authentication because it contains no identity information within it that can be mapped to a directory account object.

Username And Password   Usernames and passwords can be cached within the system's identity vault and used for authentication to the enrollment server. However, passwords usually have shorter lifetimes than server SSL certificates. (Both default and recommended settings for passwords are shorter than the default and recommended certificate lifetime.) Thus, by the time renewal happens, the password will likely have changed.

Anonymous   This authentication option is not suitable since MS CEP and CES do not support this option, making automatic renewal impossible for these targeted server systems.

Enforcement of Certificate Renewal with Same Key

Windows 8/8.1 and Windows Server 2012 R2 provide an efficient mechanism to increase the security of renewing hardware-based certificates. This is accomplished by enforcing the certificate renewal to occur for the same key. This guarantees the same assurance level for the key throughout its life cycle. Additionally, Windows Server 2012 R2's Certificate

Template Management Console supports CSP/KSP ordering that clients may choose for generating a private/public key pair. This way, you can give a higher priority to hardware-based keys (Trusted Platform Module or smart card) over software-based keys.

Cryptographic Service Provider/Key Service Provider Ordering

Another problem addressed in Windows Server 2012 R2 is GUI support for CSP/KSP ordering. With increased interest in the deployment of Trusted Platform Module in enterprise scenarios, providing a mechanism for prioritizing TPM-based keys over other types of keys has become a "must-have" for certificate enrollment based on certificate templates. This is important from the client perspective when enrolling for a non-exportable key. You want to have assurance that the non-exportable keys are generated in the TPM and are not software-based (assuming that no malware is involved and the user is not malicious).

Currently this prioritization is captured as an attribute of a certificate template object in Active Directory; however, a user interface does not exist for modifying such properties, and Microsoft does not support it. Windows Server 2012 R2's Certificate Template Management Console fully supports CSP/KSP ordering.

Managing Certificate Authority: Certificate Templates Overview

Enterprise certificate authorities issue certificates from certificate templates, a preconfigured list of certificate settings. This allows administrators to enroll users and computers for certificates without the need to create complex certificate requests. Windows Server 2012 AD CS does include a minor user interface change and the Active Directory Certificate Services Administration module for Windows PowerShell. The new Compatibility tab in the Certificate Templates Management Console lets you identify incompatible certificate template settings between different versions of Windows-based certificate recipients and the certificate authority. The AD CS Administration module for Windows PowerShell lets you manage common AD CS management tasks using Windows PowerShell.

Certificate Template Compatibility

Multiple versions of certificate templates have been released for the family of Windows Server products. New certificate template versions include settings that control the features relevant to each new certificate authority. However, not all features are compatible with all certificate authorities and certificate requests. Therefore, it can be difficult to determine which certificate templates are compatible with different versions of certificate authorities and different Windows-based certificate requestors.

Version 2 certificate templates are customizable certificate templates that are supported with Windows Server 2008 Enterprise CAs or Windows Server 2003 Enterprise edition CAs. Version 2 certificate templates enable advanced CA features, such as key archiving and recovery and certificate auto-enrollment.

To use version 2 templates, Active Directory must be upgraded to support Windows Server 2008 or Windows Server 2003 schema changes. Standard editions of Windows Server 2008 and Windows Server 2003 support only version 1 certificate templates, which are not customizable and do not support key archival or automatic enrollment.

Version 3 certificate templates were new to Windows Server 2008. Version 3 certificate templates function similarly to version 2 templates, and they support new Active Directory Certificate Services features available in Windows Server 2008. These features include CNG, which introduces support for Suite B cryptographic algorithms such as elliptic curve cryptography (ECC).

The Windows Server 2012 R2 Certificate Template Management Console includes a new certificate template Compatibility tab that lets you select the Windows operating system of the certificate authority and the Windows operating system of the certificate recipient. The Certificate Template Management Console determines incompatible settings between the selections and shows a list of template settings that the management console adds or removes from template selection.

You view the compatibility table from the Certificate Template Management Console. You can launch the Certificate Template Management Console by typing **certtmpl.msc** in the Run dialog or on the Start screen and pressing Enter.

Creating Certificate Templates

When creating a new certificate template, you copy an existing template similar to the configuration defaults needed for your particular application. It is best to review the default list of certificate template and find the template that best matches your application's requirements.

The Request Handling tab (Figure 6.4) in the Certificate Templates Management console has the Renew With Same Key Certificate Template Configuration option. This certificate template option becomes visible in the user interface when you configure the Certification Authority and the Certificate Recipient options to Windows Server 2012 R2 and Windows 8/8.1, respectively.

You will create an example certificate template in Exercise 6.4.

EXERCISE 6.4

Creating a Certificate Template

1. Start the Certificate Templates snap-in, read through the certificate templates titles, and choose the Computer Template.

2. In the details pane, right-click an existing certificate and click Duplicate Template.

3. Choose to duplicate the template as a Windows Server 2008–based template.

4. On the General tab, enter the template display name and the template name and click OK.

5. Define any additional attributes for the newly created certificate template.

FIGURE 6.4   Request Handling tab of the Certificate Templates Management console

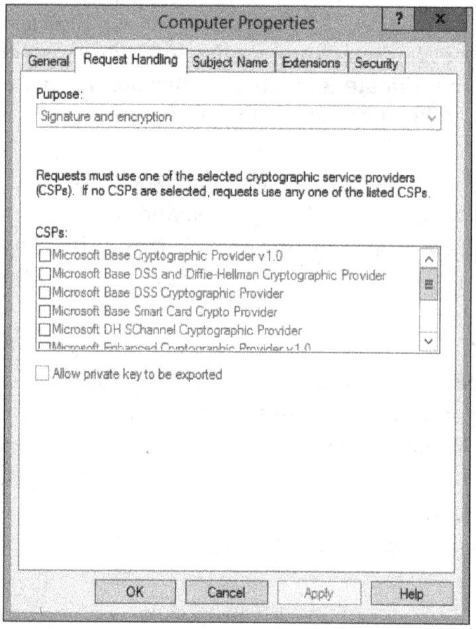

Publishing the Certificate Template

After creating a certificate template and applying the proper security permissions, you will want to deploy the new certificate template by publishing to the Active Directory where it can be shared with other Enterprise CAs. The following exercise will take us through the steps to perform the task.

In Exercise 6.5, you will deploy a certificate template.

EXERCISE 6.5

Publishing a Certificate Template

1. In Server manager, click Tools and then Certification Authority

2. In the Certification Authority MMC, expand the CA Server Name

3. Select the Certificate Templates container.

4. Right-click Certificate Templates container and then click New Certificate Template To Issue.

5. In the Enable Certificate Templates dialog box, select the certificate template or templates that you want the CA server to issue and click OK. The newly selected certificate template or templates should appear in the right side details pane.

If a certificate template is not displayed in the Enable Certificate Templates dialog box, the replication of the certificate template may not have finished on all domain controllers in the forest.

Certificate Revocation

Revocation renders a certificate invalid and lists the revoked certificate in the CRL. You can revoke a certificate in the Certificate Authority snap-in with the steps shown in Exercise 6.6.

EXERCISE 6.6

Revoking a Certificate

1. Start the Certification Authority snap-in.

2. In the console tree, click the Issuing certificate container.

3. In the right pane, select and right-click the target certificate.

4. Select All Tasks.

5. Select Revoke Certificate.

6. In Certificate Revocation dialog box, you must select one of the following reason codes:

   Unspecified: Default reason code. This lacks information during future audits.
   Key Compromise: Select this when you think the key has been compromised.
   CA Compromise: Select this when you suspect the issuing CA of being compromised.
   Change of Affiliation: Select this when the person has exited the organization or changed roles.
   Superseded: Select this when issuing a new certificate to replace an existing certificate.
   Cease of Operation: Select this when the issuing device or server has been decommissioned.
   Certificate Hold: Select this to suspend an existing certificate temporarily.

7. Click OK.

Display the Current Site Name for Certificate Authorities

Enter the following command to display current site names for one or more certificate authorities:

```
Certutil -ping caDnsName, [caDnsName, …]
```

The command utilizes the DsGetSiteName API on each named certificate authority. After determining the site for all the certificate authorities, certutil.exe uses the DsQuerySitesByCost API to obtain the client's site costs for all the name certificate authorities.

CA Policy Auditing

PKI auditing logging is not enabled on the Windows 2012 R2 CA server by default. After the auditing is enabled, all the events will be logged in the Security log.

Exercise 6.7 covers the steps that the CA administrator must complete to enable auditing.

EXERCISE 6.7

Configuring CA Policy Auditing

1. Enable Object Access/Success Auditing in the CA machine's local security policy.

   a. Start mmc.exe.

   b. Add the snap-in Group Policy Object Editor and select the Local Computer GPO.

   c. Under the path Computer Configuration\Windows Settings\Security Settings\Local Policies\Audit Policy, enable success auditing for Object Access.

2. Enable auditing on the CA.

   a. Start the CA Management snap-in.

   b. Open the CA Properties dialog.

   c. On the Auditing tab, check the Change CA Configuration and Change CA Security Settings options.

Backing Up the Certificate Authority Server

The AD CS certificate authority deployment creates a database. The CA records certificates issued by the CA, private keys archived by the CA, revoked certificates, and all certificate requests to the database regardless of issuance status.

Configure the database location on an NTFS partition on the server's disk drives to provide the best security possible for the database file. Specify the location for the database in the Certificate Database Location box. By default, the wizard configured the database location to systemroot\system32\certlog. The name of the database file uses the CA's name, with an .edb extension.

The certificate database uses a transaction log to ensure the integrity of the database. The CA records its transactions in its configured log files. The CA then commits each transaction from the log file into the database. The CA then updates the last committed transaction in the database, and the process continues.

The CA database logs are selected when restoring the CA from a backup. If a CA is restored from a backup that is one month old, then the CA database can be updated with more recent activity recorded in the log to restore the database to its most current state. When you back up a CA, the existing certificate database logs are truncated in size because they are no longer needed to restore the certificate database to its most current state.

The recommended method to back up a CA is to leverage the native Backup utility (included with the operating system) to back up the entire server, including the system state, which contains the CA's data. However, the Certificate Authority snap-in can be used to back up and restore the CA, but this backup method is intended only in cases where you want to migrate CA data to different server hardware. The public key and private key are backed up or restored using the PKCS #12 PFX format.

The Backup Or Restore Wizard will ask you to supply a password when backing up the public and private keys and CA certificates. This password will be needed to restore the CA.

Start the Certificate Authority snap-in for Exercise 6.8, which explains how to back up a CA.

EXERCISE 6.8

Backing Up the Certificate Authority Server

1. Start the Certification Authority MMC.

2. In the left pane, right-click the name of the server; then choose All Tasks > Back Up CA.

3. When the Certification Authority Backup Wizard appears, click Next.

4. At the Items To Back Up screen, click the Private Key And CA Certificate check box. Next to the Back Up To This Location field, click the Browse button. Choose a location for your backup and click OK. Click Next.

5. At the Select A Password screen, enter and confirm a password. For this exercise, enter **P@ssw0rd**. Click Next.

Configuring and Managing Key Archive and Recovery

The key archive stores a certificate's subject name, public key, private key, and supported cryptographic algorithms in its CA database. This procedure can be performed manually or automatically, depending on the configuration. If the certificate template requires key archiving, then the process requires no manual intervention. However, key archiving can also be performed manually if the private key is exported and then sent to an administrator for import into the CA database.

There is also a Key Recovery Agent template available in the standard templates within Active Directory Certificate Services. The Key Recovery Agent template enables Domain Admins and Enterprise Admins to export private keys. Additionally, you can add other accounts and groups to have the necessary permissions (Read and Enroll) through the Security tab of the template.

The Key Recovery Agent template also needs to be enabled, as with other certificate templates, through the Certification Authority tool by selecting Certificate Template To Issue. See "Publishing a Certificate Template" earlier in this chapter for more details on enabling a certificate template on a CA.

With the Key Recovery Agent template in place, the following process must take place for key archiving and recovery:

1. Request a key recovery agent certificate using the Certificates snap-in.

2. Issue the key recovery agent certificate using the Certification Authority tool.

3. Retrieve the enrolled certificate using the Certificates snap-in.

4. Configure the CA for key archiving and recovery.

The final step, configuring the CA for key archiving and recovery, takes place in the Properties dialog box of each CA that will need to archive and recover keys. Specifically, the Recovery Agents tab configures the behavior of the CA when a request includes key archiving.

Each Key Recovery Agent certificate should be added using the Add button on the Recovery Agents tab.

Implement Active Directory Federation Services

Active Directory Federation Services (AD FS) demands a great deal of preparation and planning to ensure a successful implementation. The type of certificate authority used to sign the AD FS server's certificate must be planned. The SSL encryption level must be negotiated with the partnering organization. For instance, how much Active Directory information should be shared with the partnering organization? What should the DNS structure look like to support federation communications? You must explore all of these questions before implementing AD FS. In this section, I will discuss how to deploy AD FS and the configurations used to set up a federated partnership between businesses.

What Is a Claim?

A *claim* is an identifiable element (email address, username, password, and so on) that a trusted source asserts about an identity, for example, the SID of a user or computer. An identity can contain more than one claim, and any combination of those claims can be used to authorize access to resources.

Windows Server 2012 R2 extends the authorization identity beyond using the SID for identity and enables administrators to configure authorization based on claims published in Active Directory.

Today, the claims-based identity model brings us to cloud-based authentication. One analogy to the claim-based model is the old airport check-in procedure.

1. You first check in at the ticket counter.

2. You present a suitable form of ID (driver's license, passport, credit card, and so on). After verifying that your picture ID matches your face (authentication), the agent pulls up your flight information and verifies that you've paid for a ticket (authorization).

3. You receive a boarding pass (token). The boarding pass lets the gate agents know your name and frequent flyer number (authentication and personalization), your flight number and seating priority (authorization), and more. The boarding pass has bar-code information (certificate) with a boarding serial number proving that the boarding pass was issued by the airline and not a (self-signed) forgery.

Active Directory Federation Service is Microsoft's claims-based identity solution providing browser-based clients (internal or external to your network) with transparent access to one or more protected Internet-facing applications.

When an application is hosted in a different network than the user accounts, users are occasionally prompted for secondary credentials when they attempt to access the application. These secondary credentials represent the identity of the users in the domain where the application is hosted. The web server hosting the application usually requires these credentials to make the most proper authorization decision.

AD FS makes secondary accounts and their credentials unnecessary by providing trust relationships that send a user's digital identity and access rights to trusted partners. In a federated environment, each organization continues to manage its own identities, but each organization can also securely send and accept identities from other organizations. This seamless process is referred to as *single sign-on (SSO)*.

Windows Server 2012 R2 AD FS federation servers can extract Windows authorization claims from a user's authorization token that is created when the user authenticates to the AD FS federation server. AD FS inserts these claims into its claim pipeline for processing. You can configure Windows authorization claims to pass through the pipeline as is, or you can configure AD FS to transform Windows authorization claims into a different or well-known claim type.

Claims Provider

A *claims provider* is a federation server that processes trusted identity claims requests. A federation server processes requests to issue, manage, and validate security tokens. Security tokens consist of a collection of identity claims, such as a user's name or role or an anonymous identifier. A federation server can issue tokens in several formats. In addition, a federation server can protect the contents of security tokens in transmission with an X.509 certificate.

For example, when a Stellacon Corporation user needs access to Fabrikam's web application, the Stellacon Corporation user must request claims from the Stellacon Corporation AD FS server claim provider. The claim is transformed into an encrypted security token, which is then sent to Fabrikam's AD FS server.

Relying Party

A *relying party* is a federation server that receives security tokens from a trusted federation partner claims provider. In turn, the relying party issues new security tokens that a local relying party application consumes. In the prior example, Fabrikam is the relying party that relies on the Stellacon's claim provider to validate the user's claim. By using a relying-party federation server in conjunction with a claims provider, organizations can offer web single sign-on to users from partner organizations. In this scenario, each organization manages its own identity stores.

Endpoints

Endpoints provide access to the federation server functionality of AD FS, such as token issuance, information card issuance, and the publishing of federation metadata. Based on the type of endpoint, you can enable or disable the endpoint or control whether the endpoint is published to AD FS proxies.

Table 6.3 describes the property fields that distinguish the various built-in endpoints that AD FS exposes. The table includes the types of endpoints and their methods of client authentication. Table 6.4 describes the AD FS security modes.

TABLE 6.3   AD FS Endpoints

Name	Description
WS-Trust 1.3	An endpoint built on a standard Simple Object Access Protocol (SOAP)–based protocol for issuing security tokens.
WS-Trust 2005	An endpoint built on a prestandard, SOAP-based protocol for issuing security tokens.
WS-Federation Passive/ SAML Web SSO	An endpoint published to support protocols that redirect web browser clients to issue security tokens.
Federation Metadata	A standard-formatted endpoint for exchanging metadata about a claims provider or a relying party.
SAML Artifact Resolution	An endpoint built on a subset of the Security Assertion Markup Language (SAML) version 2.0 protocol that describes how a relying party can access a token directly from a claims provider.
WS-Trust WSDL	An endpoint that publishes WS-Trust Web Services Definition Language (WSDL) containing the metadata that the federation service must be able to accept from other federation servers.
SAML Token (Asymmetric)	The client accepts a SAML token with an asymmetric key.

TABLE 6.4 AD FS Security Modes

Name	Description
Transport	The client credentials are included at the transport layer. Confidentiality is preserved at the transport layer (Secure Sockets Layer [SSL]).
Mixed	The client credentials are included in the header of a SOAP message. Confidentiality is preserved at the transport layer (SSL).
Message	The client credentials are included in the header of a SOAP message. Confidentiality is preserved by encryption inside the SOAP message.

Claim Descriptions

Claim descriptions are claim types based on an entity's or user's attribute like a user's email address, common name or UPN. AD FS publishes these claims types in the federation metadata and most common claim descriptions are pre-configured in the AD FS Management snap-in.

The claim descriptions are published to federation metadata which is stored in the AD FS configuration database. The claim descriptions include a claim type URI, name, publishing state, and description.

Claim Rules

Claim rules define how AD FS processes a claim. The most common rule is using a user's email address as a valid claim. The email address claim is validated through the partner's Active Directory email attribute for the user's account. If there is a match, the claim is accepted as valid.

Claim rules can quickly evolve into more complex rules with more attributes such as a user's employee ID or department. The key goal of claim rules is to process the claim in a manner that validates the user's claim and to assemble a user's profile information based on a sufficient number of attributes to place the user into a role or group.

The Attribute Store

Attribute stores are the repositories containing claim values. AD FS natively supports Active Directory by default as an attribute store. SQL Server, AD LDS, and custom attribute stores are also supported.

AD FS Role Services

The AD FS server role includes federation, proxy, and web agent services. These services enable the following:

- Web SSO
- Federated web-based resources

- Customizing the access experience
- Managing authorization to access applications

Based on your organization's requirements, you can deploy servers running any one of the following AD FS role services:

Active Directory Federation Service Microsoft federation solution for accepting and issuing claims based token for users to experience a single sign-on to a partnered web application.

Federation Service Proxy The Federation Service Proxy forwards user claims over the internet or DMZ using WS-Federation Passive Requestor Profile (WS-F PRP) protocols to the internal ADFS farm. Only the user credential data is forwarded to the Federation Service. All other datagram packets are dropped.

Claims-Aware Agent The claims-aware agent resides on a web server with a claims-aware application to enable the Microsoft ASP.NET application to accept AD FS security token claims.

Windows Token-Based Agent The Windows token-based agent resides on a web server with a Windows NT token-based application to translate an AD FS security token to an impersonation-level Windows NT token-based authentication.

What's New for AD FS in Windows Server 2012 R2?

The Active Directory Federation Services role in Windows Server 2012 R2 introduces the following new features:

- HTTP.SYS
- Server Manager integration
- AD FS deployment cmdlets in the AD FS module for Windows PowerShell
- Interoperability with Windows authorization claims
- Web proxy service

HTTP.SYS

Prior AD FS versions relied on IIS components for the AD FS claim functions. Microsoft has improved the overall claims handling performance and SSO customization by building the AD FS 3.0 code on top of the standard kernel mode driver—HTTP.SYS. This approach also avoids the huge security "no-no" of hosting IIS on a domain controller.

The classic netsh HTTP command can be entered to query and configure HTTP.SYS. AD FS proxy server introduces interesting deployment nuisances and "gotchas" with HTTP.SYS, which I will discuss in the "Web Proxy Service" section.

Improved Installation Experience

The installation experience for Active Directory Federation Services 3.0 was cumbersome, requiring multiple hotfixes, as well as .NET Framework 3.5, Windows PowerShell, and the

Windows Identity Foundation SDK. Windows Server 2012 R2's AD FS role includes all of the software you need to run AD FS for an improved installation experience.

Web Proxy Service

The kernel mode (HTTP.SYS) in Windows Server 2012 R2 includes server name indication (SNI) support configuration. I strongly recommend verifying that your current load balancer/reverse proxy firmware supports SNI. This prerequisite is a sore spot for most AD FS 3.0 upgrade projects in the field. Therefore, it's worthwhile checking the following:

- Your preferred load balancer/device needs to support SNI.
- Clients and user agents need to support SNI and should not become locked out of authentication.
- All SSL termination endpoints vulnerable to the recent heartbleed bug (http://heartbleed.com) need to be patched, exposing OpenSSL libraries and certificates.

AD FS Dependency Changes in Windows Server 2012 R2

Active Directory Federation Services was built on a claim-based identity framework called *Windows Identity Foundation (WIF)*. Prior to Windows Server 2012 R2, WIF was distributed in a software development kit and the .NET runtime. WIF is currently integrated into version 4.5 of the .NET Framework, which ships with Windows Server 2012 R2.

Windows Identity Foundation

WIF is a set of .NET Framework classes; it is a framework for implementing claims-based identity for applications. Any web application or web service that uses .NET Framework version 4.5 or newer can run WIF.

New Claims Model and Principal Object

Claims are at the core of .NET Framework 4.5. The base claim classes (Claim, ClaimsIdentity, ClaimsPrincipal, ClaimTypes, and ClaimValueTypes) all live directly in mscorlib. Interfaces are no longer necessary to plug claims in the .NET identity system. WindowsPrincipal, GenericPrincipal, and RolePrincipal now inherit from ClaimsPrincipal, WindowsIdentity, and GenericIdentity, and FormsIdentity now inherit from ClaimsIdentity. In short, every principal class will now serve claims. The integration classes and interfaces (WindowsClaimsIdentity, WindowsClaimsPrincipal, IClaimsPrincipal, and IClaimsIdentity) have thus been removed. The ClaimsIdentity object model also contains various improvements, which makes it easier to query the identity's claims collection.

As you climb further up "Mount Federation," you will realize that not all vendor SAML flavors are compatible, and configuration challenges can bring even the most seasoned system integrators to their knees. SAML deserves an entire book, so to avoid this chapter reaching encyclopedia size, I will touch on just a few pointers.

AD FS negotiates SAML authentication in order of security strength from the weakest to the strongest, as shown in Table 6.5. The default mode, Kerberos, is considered the strongest method. The authentication precedence can be tuned by executing the PowerShell command Set-AD FSProperties -AuthenticationContextOrder to select an order to meet your organization's security requirements.

TABLE 6.5 SAML-supported authentication methods

Authentication method	Authentication context class URI
Username/password	urn:oasis:names:tc:SAML:3.0:ac:classes:Password
Password-protected transport	urn:oasis:names:tc:SAML:3.0:ac:classes:PasswordProtectedTransport
Transport Layer Security (TLS) Client	urn:oasis:names:tc:SAML:3.0:ac:classes:TLSClient
X.509 certificate	urn:oasis:names:tc:SAML:3.0:ac:classes:X509
Integrated Windows authentication	urn:federation:authentication:windows
Kerberos	urn:oasis:names:tc:SAML:3.0:classes:Kerberos

Active Directory Federation Services Installation

This section describes how to install and deploy Active Directory Federation Services roles on computers running Windows Server 2012 R2 (see Exercise 6.9). You will learn about the following:

- Deploying AD FS role services using Windows PowerShell
- Supporting upgrade scenarios for AD FS

EXERCISE 6.9

Installing the AD FS Role on a Computer Using Server Manager

1. Start Server Manager.

2. Click Manage and click Add Roles And Features. Click Next.

3. The Add Roles And Features Wizard shows the Before You Begin screen. Click Next.

4. Click Role-Based Or Feature-Based Installation on the Select Installation Type screen. Click Next.

5. Click the server on which you want to install Active Directory Federation Services from the Server Pool list on the Select Destination Server screen. Click Next.

6. Select the Active Directory Federation Services check box on the Select Server Roles screen. Server Manager will prompt you to add other features associated with this role, such as management tools. Leave the default selections. Click Add Features to close the dialog.

7. Click Next on the Select Server Roles screen.

8. Click Next on the Select Features screen.

9. Server Manager shows the Active Directory Federation Services screen. This screen displays simple role introduction and important AD FS configuration information. Click Next.

10. From the Select Server Roles screen, select the check box next to the AD FS role services to install on the computer. Click Next.

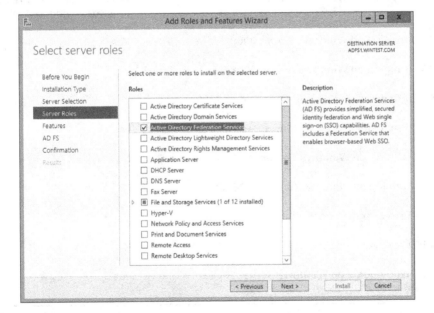

11. Server Manager prompts you to add other features associated with this role, such as management tools. Leave the default selections. Click Add Features to close the dialog.

12. Read the Confirm Installation Selections screen. This screen provides a list of roles, role services, and features that the current installation prepares on the computer. Click Install to begin the installation.

Role Installation Using Windows PowerShell

To view the installation state of AD FS using Windows PowerShell, open an elevated Windows PowerShell console, type the following command, and press Enter:

```
Get-WindowsFeature "adfs*","*fed*"
```

Upgrading to Windows AD FS 2012 R2

Windows Server 2012 R2's AD FS role supports upgrading version 3.0 of Active Directory Federation Services. You cannot upgrade versions of AD FS prior to version 3.0 using Windows Server 2012 R2.

Table 6.6 represents the support upgrade matrix for the AD FS role in Windows Server 2012 R2.

TABLE 6.6   Support upgrade matrix for the AD FS role in Windows Server 2012 R2

AD FS and operating system version	Windows Server 2012 R2 upgrade supported
AD FS 3.0 running on Windows Server 2008	Yes
AD FS 3.0 running on Windows Server 2008 R2	Yes
AD FS 3.0 Proxy running on Windows Server 2008	Yes
AD FS 3.0 Proxy running on Windows Server 2008 R2	Yes
AD FS 1.1 running on Windows Server 2008	No
AD FS 1.1 running on Windows Server 2008 R2	No
AD FS 1.1 Proxy running on Windows Server 2008	No
AD FS 1.1 Proxy running on Windows Server 2008 R2	No
AD FS 1.1 Web Agents on Windows Server 2008 or Windows Server 2008 R2	Yes

Configuring Active Directory Federation Services

Windows Server 2012 R2 delineates role installation and role deployment. Role installations make staged role services and features available for deployment. Role deployment enables you to configure the role service, which enables the role service in your environment. AD FS in Windows Server 2012 R2 uses the same deployment tools as AD FS 3.0. However, an entry point to start these tools is included in Server Manager. Server Manager indicates that one or more role services are eligible for deployment by showing an exclamation point inside a yellow triangle on the Action Flag notification. Click the action flag to show the role services you can deploy (see Figure 6.5).

FIGURE 6.5   Alert for role services eligible for deployment in Server Manager

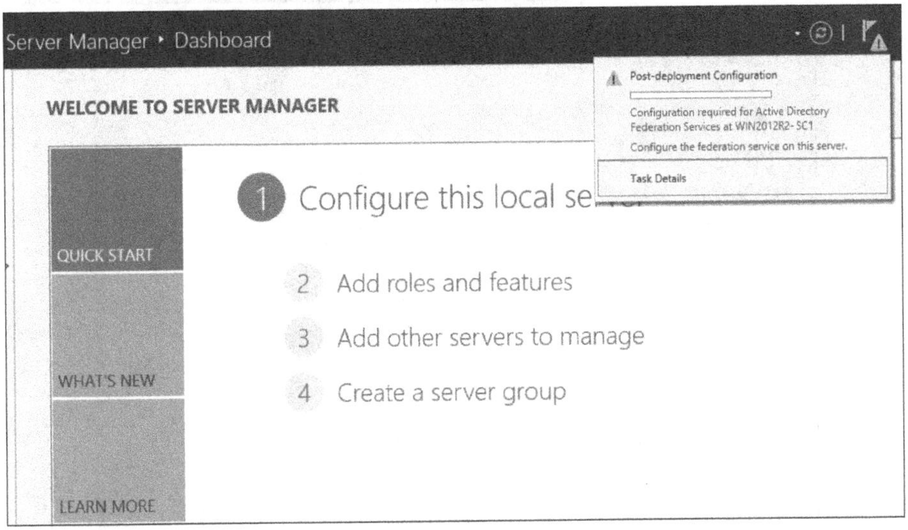

AD FS Graphical Deployment

The Run The AD FS Management snap-in link in Windows Server 2012 R2 Server Manager is how you perform the initial configuration for the AD FS roles using the graphical interface. Alternatively, you can start the AD FS management console using the AD FS Management tile on the Start screen. The Start screen tile points to the Microsoft. IdentityServer.msc file located in the c:\windows\adfs folder.

To configure AD FS, select Start ➤ Run and type **FsConfigWizard.exe**; alternatively, click the FsConfigWizard.exe file located in the c:\windows\adfs folder.

Exercise 6.10 uses the AD FS Federation Server Configuration Wizard. To complete this exercise, you'll need an active SSL certificate assigned to the server and a managed service account for AD FS service.

EXERCISE 6.10

Configuring the AD FS Role on the Computer Using Server Manager

1. Select Create The First Federation Server In The Federation Server Farm.

2. Select the administrative account with permissions to configure the AD FS server and click Next.

3. Select the server certificate from the SSL certificate drop-down list.

4. Select the AD FS service name from the drop-down list.

5. Type **ADFS-Test** in the federation service's Display Name field and click Next.

EXERCISE 6.10 *(continued)*

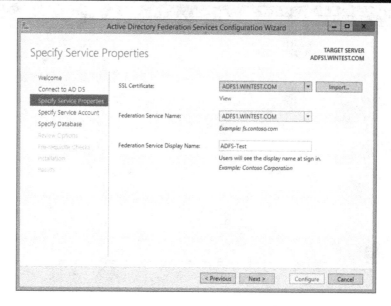

6.   Select Create A Database On This Server Using Windows Internal Database and click Next.

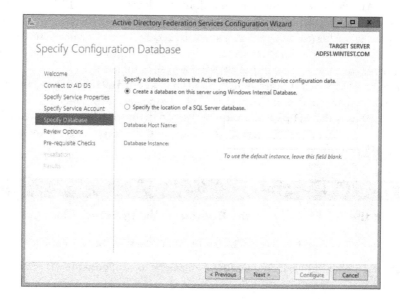

7.   Click Next on the Review Options screen.

8.   If the prerequisites check is successful, click Configure on the Prerequisite Check screen.

9.   If the Result screen displays "This Server was successfully configured," you can click Close.

Deployment Using Windows PowerShell

Windows Server 2012 R2 includes the Active Directory Federation Services module for Windows PowerShell when you install the AD FS role using Server Manager. The AD FS module for Windows PowerShell includes five new cmdlets to deploy the AD FS role.

- `Add-AdfsProxy`
- `Add-AdfsFarmNode`
- `Export-AdfsDeploymentSQLScript`
- `Install-AdfsStand-alone`
- `Install-AdfsFarm`

> These AD FS cmdlets provide the same functionality as the command-line version of the AD FS Federation Server Configuration Wizard, `fsconfig.exe`. The AD FS role in Windows Server 2012 R2 includes `fsconfig.exe` to remain compatible with previously authored deployment scripts. New deployments should take advantage of the deployment cmdlets included in the AD FS module for Windows PowerShell.

Add-AdfsProxy   Configures a server as a federation server proxy.

FederationServiceName   Specifies the name of the federation service for which a server proxies requests.

FederationServiceTrustCredentials   Specifies the credentials of the Active Directory identity that is authorized to register new federation server proxies. By default, this is the account under which the federation service runs or an account that is a member of the Administrators group on the federation server.

ForwardProxy   Specifies the DNS name and port of an HTTP proxy that this federation server proxy uses to obtain access to the federation service.

Add-AdfsFarmNode   Adds this computer to an existing federation server farm.

CertificateThumbprint   Specifies the value of the certificate thumbprint of the certificate that should be used in the SSL binding of the default website in IIS. This value should match the thumbprint of a valid certificate in the Local Computer certificate store.

OverwriteConfiguration   Must be used to remove an existing AD FS configuration database and overwrite it with a new database.

SQLConnectionString   Specifies the SQL Server database that will store the AD FS configuration settings. If not specified, AD FS uses Windows Internal Database to store configuration settings.

ServiceAccountCredential   Specifies the Active Directory account under which the AD FS service runs. All nodes in the farm must have the same service account.

PrimaryComputerName   Specifies the name of the primary federation server in the farm that this computer will join.

PrimaryComputerPort   Specifies the value of the HTTP port that this computer uses to connect with the primary computer in order to synchronize configuration settings. Specify a value for this parameter only if the HTTP port on the primary computer is not 80.

Active Directory Federation Services Certificates

There are three types of certificates used by an AD FS implementation:

- Service communications
- Token decrypting
- Token signing

The service communications certificate is required for communication with web clients over SSL and with web application proxy services using Windows Communication Foundation (WCF) components. This certificate is specified at configuration time for AD FS.

The token decrypting certificate is required to decrypt claims and tokens received by the federation service. The public key for the decrypting certificate is usually shared with relying parties and others to encrypt the claims and tokens using the certificate.

The token signing certificate is required to sign all claims and tokens created by the server. You can have multiple token encrypting and signing certificates for an implementation, and new ones can be added within the AD FS management tool, shown in Figure 6.6.

FIGURE 6.6   Active Directory Federation Certificate Console screen

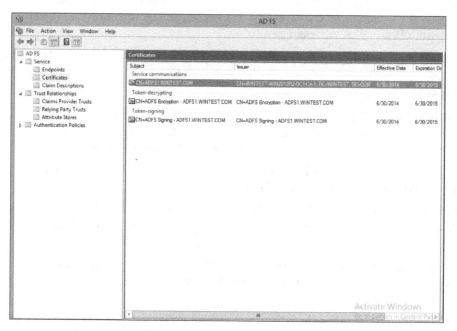

Relying-Party Trust

The federation service name originates from the SSL certificate used for AD FS. The SSL certificate can be template-based and needs to be enrolled and used by IIS.

The next step in setting up AD FS is to configure a relying-party trust. A relying-party trust can be configured with a URL acquired from the relying party. The URL contains the federation metadata used to complete the federation trust configuration. The federation metadata may also be exported to a file that can then be imported into the relying-party trust. There is also a manual option for configuring a relying-party trust.

See Table 6.7 for the Federation Metadata fields.

TABLE 6.7 Federation Metadata Fields

Field	Description
Display Name	This is the friendly display name given to this relying party trust.
Profile	Select AD FS Profile for the standard Windows Server 2012 AD FS, or select AD FS 1.0 And 1.1 Profile for AD FS configurations that need to work with older versions of AD FS.
Certificate	This is the optional certificate file from the relying party for token encryption.
URL	This is the URL for the relying party. WS-Federation Passive Protocol URL or SAML 2.0 WebSSO protocols are supported.
Identifiers	This is the unique identifier used for this trust.
Authorization Rules	Selecting this permits all users to access the relying party or denies all users access to the relying party, depending on the needs of this trust.

Configuring Claims Provider and Transform Claims Rules

Claims provider trust rules are configured within the AD FS management console and are configured on a per-trust basis. Planning claims rules involves determining what claims are needed by the relying party to complete the authentication and authorization process and which users will need access to the relying-party trust. The relying party determines what claims need to be received and trusted from the claims provider.

Trust rules start with templates as the basis for the rule. There are different types of claims templates depending on the type of rule being used. The claims rule templates for transforms are described in Table 6.8.

TABLE 6.8   Transform claims rule templates

Template	Description
Send LDAP Attributes as Claims	Attributes found in an LDAP directory (such as Active Directory) can be used as part of the claim.
Send Group Membership as Claim	The group memberships of the logged-in user are sent as part of the claim.
Transform an Incoming Claim	This is used for configuring a rule to change an incoming claim. Changes include both the type and the value of an incoming claim.
Pass Through or Filter an Incoming Claim	This performs an action such as pass-through or filter on an incoming claim based on certain criteria, as defined in the rule.
Send Claims Using a Custom Rule	This creates a rule that's not covered by a predefined template, such as an LDAP attribute generated with a custom LDAP filter.

Defining Windows Authorization Claims in AD FS

Windows Server 2012 R2 stores information that describes Windows authorization claims in the configuration partition of Active Directory. Windows refers to this information as *claim types*; however, Active Directory Federation Services typically refers to this information as claim descriptions (see Figure 6.7). There are more than 40 new claims descriptions available in the AD FS Windows Server 2012 R2 release.

The Active Directory Federation Services role included in Windows Server 2012 R2 lets you configure AD FS to include Windows authorization claims in the AD FS claim pipeline. To simplify this configuration, you can create *claim descriptions* in AD FS. Claim types in Windows authorization claims are analogous to claim descriptions in AD FS. The Windows authorization claim ID maps to the AD FS claim description's claim identifier (see Figure 6.8).

To simplify AD FS configuration using Windows authorization claims, create a claim description in AD FS for each Windows authorization claim you intend to deploy in AD FS.

Create Claim Pass-Through and Transformation Rules

You need to configure a claim rule with the Active Directory Claims Provider Trusts Wizard to insert Windows authorization claims into the AD FS claims pipeline.

Creating a claim description makes it easier to select the incoming claim type. Alternatively, you can type the claim type ID directly in the Incoming Claim Type list. A *pass-through claim rule* enables the Windows authorization claim to enter the AD FS claim

FIGURE 6.7   AD FS claim descriptions

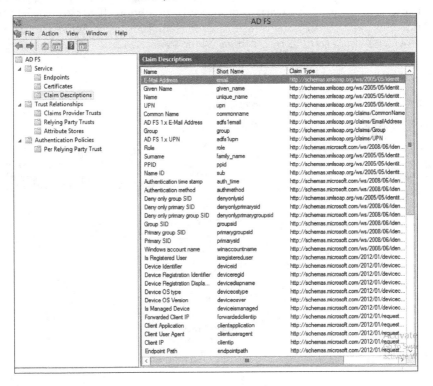

FIGURE 6.8   Adding a claim description

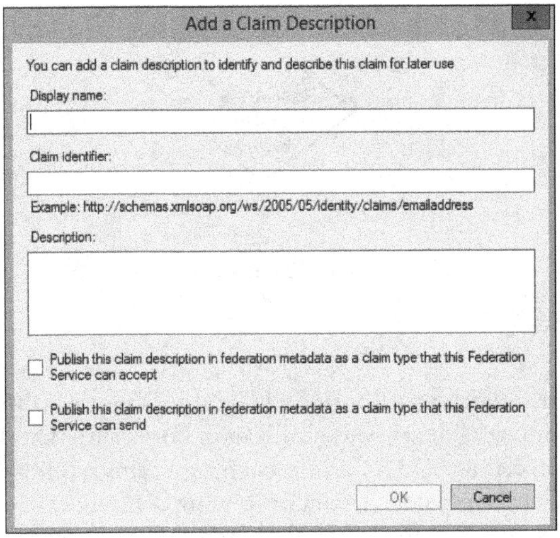

pipeline. A pass-through claim leaves the claim type ID intact. Therefore, the pass-through claim ID begins with ad://ext, whereas most claim description URIs begin with http://. In addition, you can create a claim transformation claim rule on the Active Directory Claim Provider Trust Wizard to transform a Windows authorization claim into a well-known claim description (see Figure 6.9).

FIGURE 6.9 Claim transformation claim rule

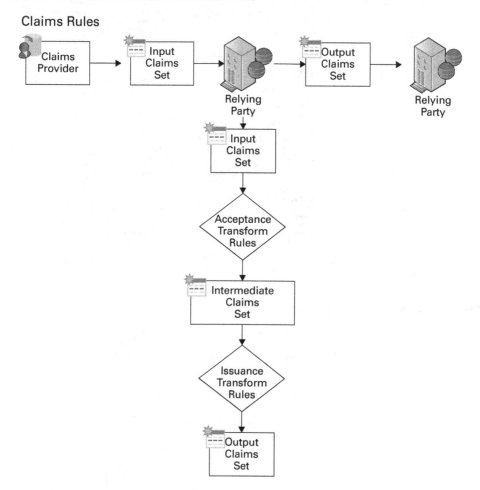

Creating a claim provider trust claim rule enables the Windows authorization claim to enter the AD FS claim pipeline. However, this does not ensure that AD FS sends the Windows authorization claim. AD FS claim processing begins with the claim provider. This allows the claim to enter the pipeline. Claim processing continues for the targeted relying party—first with the issuance authorization rules and then with the issuance transform rules.

You can configure Windows authorization claims in claims rules configured on a relying party. By default, a relying party does not have any issuance transform rules. Therefore, AD FS drops all claims in the pipeline destined for a relying party when the relying party does not have any rules that pass incoming claims. Additionally, issuance authorization rules determine whether a user can receive claims for a relying party and, therefore, access the relying party.

Choose the claims types from the list of inbound rules created in the Active Directory claim provider trust that you want to send to the designated relying party. Then create rules that continue to pass the selected claim types through the pipeline to the relying party. Alternatively, you can create a rule that passes all the inbound claims to the relying party (see Figure 6.10).

FIGURE 6.10   Editing the claims rules

 The AD FS role in Windows Server 2012 R2 cannot provide claim information when the incoming authentication is not Kerberos. Clients must authenticate to AD FS using Kerberos authentication. If Windows authorization claims are not entering the AD FS claim pipeline, then make sure the client authenticates to AD FS using Kerberos and the correct service principal name is registered on the computer/service account.

Enabling AD FS to Use Compound Authentication for Device Claims: Compound Authentication

Windows Server 2012 R2 enhances Kerberos authentication by introducing compound authentication. Compound authentication enables a Kerberos TGS request to include two identities: the identity of the user and the identity of the user's device. Windows accomplishes compound authentication by extending Kerberos Flexible Authentication Secure Tunneling (FAST) or Kerberos armoring.

During normal Kerberos authentication, the Kerberos client requesting authentication for a service sends the ticket-granting service (TGS) a request for that service. Using Kerberos armoring, the TGS exchange is armored using the user's ticket-granting ticket (TGT). Prior to sending the ticket-granting service reply (TGS-REP) to the client, the KDC checks the 0x00020000 bit in the value of the msDS-SupportedEncryptionTypes attribute of the security principal's object running the service. An enabled bit means that the service can accept compound authentication. The KDC sends the TGS-REP, which includes the service's ability to support compound authentication.

The Kerberos client receives the ticket-granting service TGS-REP that includes compound authentication information. The Kerberos client then sends another ticket-granting service request (TGS-REQ), with the difference being that this TGS-REQ is armored with the device's TGT rather than the user. This allows the KDC to retrieve authentication information about the principal and the device.

The Active Directory Federation Services role included in Windows Server 2012 R2 automatically enables compound authentication when creating an AD FS web farm. During the creation of the first node in the farm, the AD FS configuration wizard enables the compound authentication bit on the msDS-SupportedEncryptionTypes attribute on the account that you designate to run the AD FS service. If you change the service account, then you must manually enable compound authentication by running the Set-ADUser -compoundIdentitySupported:$true Windows PowerShell cmdlet.

In Exercise 6.11, you will learn how to configure multifactor authentication.

EXERCISE 6.11

Configuring Multifactor Authentication

1. In the AD FS Management Console, traverse to Trust Relationships And Relying Party Trusts.

2. Select the relying party trust that represents your sample application (claimapp) and then either by using the Actions pane or by right-clicking this relying party trust, select Edit Claim Rules.

3. In the Edit Claim Rules For Claimapp window, select the Issuance Authorization Rules tab and click Add Rule.

4. In the Add Issuance Authorization Claim Rule Wizard, on the Select Rule Template screen, select Permit Or Deny Users Based On An Incoming Claim Rule Template and click Next.

5. On the Configure Rule screen, complete all of the following tasks and click Finish.

   a. Enter a name for the claim rule, for example **TestRule**.

   b. Select Group SID As Incoming Claim Type.

   c. Click Browse, type in **Finance** for the name of your AD test group, and resolve it for the Incoming Claim Value field.

   d. Select the Deny Access To Users With This Incoming Claim option.

   e. In the Edit Claim Rules For Claimapp window, make sure to delete the Permit Access To All Users rule that was created by default when you created this relying party trust.

Verify Multifactor Access Control Mechanism

In this phase, you will verify the multifactor access control policy that you set up in the previous phase. You can use the following procedure to verify that a test AD user can access your sample application because the test account belongs to the Finance group. Conversely, you will use the procedure to verify that AD users who do not belong to the Finance group cannot access the sample application.

1. On your client computer, open a browser window and navigate to your sample application: `https://webserv1.contoso.com/claimapp`. This action automatically redirects the request to the federation server, and you are prompted to sign in with a username and password.

2. Type in the credentials of a test AD account to be granted access to the application.

3. Type in the credentials of another test AD account that does not belong to the Finance group.

At this point, because of the access control policy that you set up in the previous steps, an access denied message is displayed for an AD account that does not belong to the Finance group. The default message text is "You are not authorized to access this site. Click here to sign out, and sign in again or contact your administrator for permissions." However, this text is fully customizable.

Workplace Join

Today's employees are mobile and remote, working across a plethora of consumer platforms. The age of bring your own device (BYOD) is here to stay. CIOs, IT security workers, and administrators cringe at the idea of storing company data on unmanaged devices. The Workplace Join feature adds a safety measure to ensure that only registered devices have access to company data.

For Workplace Join to work, a certificate is placed on the mobile device. AD FS challenges the device as a claims-based authentication to applications or other resources without requiring administrative control of the device.

Device Registration Service

Workplace Join is supported by the Device Registration Service (DRS) included with the Active Directory Federation Services role in Windows Server 2012 R2. When a device is set up with Workplace Join, the DRS registers a device as an object in Active Directory and sets a certificate on the consumer device that is used to represent the device identity. The DRS is meant to be both internal and external facing.

DRS requires at least one global catalog server in the forest root domain. The global catalog server is needed to run the PowerShell cmdlet -Initialize-ADDeviceRegistration during AD FS authentication.

Workplace Join Your Device

For Workplace Join to succeed, the client computer must trust the AD FS SSL certificate. It must also be able to access and validate revocation information for the certificate from the CRL.

In Exercise 6.12, you will configure the DRS.

EXERCISE 6.12

Workplace Joining a Device

1. Start a Windows PowerShell command window and type **Initialize-ADDevice Registration**.

2. When prompted for a service account, type **contoso\fsgmsa$**. Now run the Windows PowerShell cmdlet.

   Enable-AdfsDeviceRegistration

3. On the AD FS server, in the AD FS Management console, navigate to the Authentica-tion Policies tab. Select Edit Global Primary Authentication. Select the Enable Device Authentication check box and click OK.

   Finally, you will need to make sure you have the following DNS records for the DRS.

Entry	Type	Address
adfs1	A	IP address of the AD FS server
enterpriseregistration	Alias (CNAME)	adfs1.contoso.com

4. Log on to the client with your Microsoft account.

5. On the Start screen, start the Charms bar and then select the Settings charm. Select Change PC Settings.

6. On the PC Settings screen, select Network and click Workplace.

7. In the Enter Your UserID To Get Workplace Access Or Turn On Device Management box, type the user's UPN or email address—for example, **RobertM@contoso.com**—and click Join.

8. When prompted for credentials, type the user's UPN or email address—for example, **roberth@contoso.com**—and a password such as **P@ssword**. Click OK.

9. You should now see the message "This device has joined your workplace network."

Active Directory Rights Management Services

Active Directory Rights Management Services (AD RMS), included with Microsoft Windows Server 2012 R2, helps safeguard sensitive information created and distributed using AD RMS–enabled applications such as Word, Outlook, or InfoPath, similar to Adobe Acrobat's permissions for print, save, fill-form, and copy functions. Unlike traditional file permission methods, RMS rights stay with the content and ensure exclusive access to the intended recipient.

Application developers may enable their applications to work with RMS extensions. AD RMS uses policies managed from the RMS server to provide a consistent experience for users across the enterprise.

You can enforce AD RMS usage policy templates directly to protect confidential information. You can install AD RMS easily using Server Manager, and you can administer it through the MMC snap-in. These three new administrative roles allow you to delegate AD RMS responsibilities:

- AD RMS Enterprise Administrators

- AD RMS Template Administrators

- AD RMS Auditors

AD RMS integrates with AD FS, which allows two organizations to share information without requiring AD RMS in both organizations.

Self-enrollment AD RMS server enrollment allows for the creation and signing of a server licensor certificate (SLC). This SLC enables the AD RMS server to issue certificates and licenses whenever required.

Considerations and Requirements for AD RMS

Before installing Active Directory Rights Management Services on Windows Server 2012 R2 for the first time, you must meet several requirements:

AD RMS Server   Install the AD RMS server as a member server in the same Active Directory domain as the user accounts that will be using rights-protected content.

AD RMS Service Account Create a domain user account that has no additional permissions that can be used as the AD RMS service account. I recommend using a group-managed service account to ensure that the account password is managed by Active Directory and that it does not require a manual password change by an administrator.

If you are registering the AD RMS service connection point during installation, the user account installing AD RMS must be a member of the AD DS Enterprise Admins group or equivalent.

Which database AD RMS Will Store Configuration Data Microsoft SQL Server 2008 or newer and WID are supported databases for the AD RMS configuration data. Windows Internal Database is more suitable for small and/or test environments. If you are using an external SQL database server for the AD RMS databases, the user account installing AD RMS must have the right to create new databases.

AD RMS URL Reserve a URL for the AD RMS cluster that will be available throughout the lifetime of the AD RMS installation. Make sure the reserved URL differs from the computer name.

Cryptographic Mode Mode 1 is composed of RSA 1024-bit keys and SHA-1 hashes. Mode 2 includes RSA 2048-bit keys and SHA-256 hashes for a more secure and recommended option.

Location for Cluster Key Storage By default, the cluster key is stored within AD RMS. You may also deploy a cryptographic service provider to store the cluster key. However, you will have to distribute the key manually when installing additional AD RMS servers.

Cluster Key Password The Cluster Key password helps to encrypt the cluster key, and it must be provided when adding AD RMS servers to the cluster. The Cluster Key password must also be provided when recovering an AD RMS cluster from backup.

Cluster Name Choose the fully qualified domain name to be hosted on the AD RMS server. An SSL certificate should be configured with the FQDN of the AD RMS server. The cluster address and port cannot be changed after AD RMS is deployed. A non-SSL address can be configured, but you will lose the AD RMS with Identity Federation functionality.

AD RMS Add-on for Internet Explorer

The Windows Rights Management Add-on (RMA) for Internet Explorer enables rights-protected content to be viewed only. Because you can only view and not alter these restricted files, this prevents sensitive documents, web-based information, and email messages from being forwarded, edited, or copied by unauthorized individuals. For you to run RMA for Internet Explorer successfully, you must first install the Windows Rights Management (RM) client. The Extensible Rights Markup Language (XrML) is the XML verbiage used by AD RMS to express usage rights for rights-protected content.

AD RMS Requirements

AD RMS requires an AD RMS–enabled client. Windows Vista, Windows 7, and Windows 8/8.1 include the AD RMS client by default. If you are not using Windows Vista, Windows 7, Windows 8/8.1, Windows Server 2008, Windows Server 2008 R2, or Windows Server 2012 R2, you can download the AD RMS client for previous versions of Windows from Microsoft's Download Center.

File System: The NTFS file system is recommended.

Messaging: Message Queuing.

Web Services: Internet Information Services (IIS). ASP.NET must be enabled.

Active Directory Domain Services

AD RMS must be installed in an Active Directory domain in which the domain controllers are running Windows Server 2008, Windows Server 2008 R2, or Windows Server 2008 R2. All users and groups that use AD RMS to acquire licenses and publish content require an email address configured in Active Directory.

Database Server: AD RMS requires a SQL database server. Microsoft SQL Server 2005, 2008, and 2012 are supported SQL versions.

The new AD RMS administrative roles are as follows:

AD RMS Service Group When the AD RMS role is installed onto a server, a local AD RMS service account is created and added to the local AD RMS service group. The server uses the service account to start services at system startup and cannot be the same account used to install the service.

AD RMS Enterprise Administrators The AD RMS policies and settings are managed by members of the local AD RMS Enterprise Administrators group. When AD RMS is installed onto the server, the user account installing the role is added to the AD RMS Enterprise Administrators group. Only administrators who manage RMS should be added to this group.

AD RMS Template Administrators Users who belong to the local AD RMS Templates Administrators group are allowed to manage rights policy templates. AD RMS template administrators have the rights to read cluster data, list rights policy templates, create new rights policy templates, modify existing rights policy templates, and export rights policy templates.

AD RMS Auditors The local AD RMS Auditors role allows administrators who have this right to manage logs and reports. The AD RMS Auditors role is a read-only role that is restricted to running reports available on the AD RMS cluster, reading cluster information, and reading logging settings.

Installing AD RMS

AD RMS deployment is described as a root cluster, which is not used in terms of failover or network balancing clustering. An AD RMS root cluster manages all of the AD RMS licensing and certificate provisions for the forest. There can be only one AD RMS root cluster per AD forest. After a root cluster is deployed, there is the option of installing additional licensing-only clusters, which issue licenses to clients for publishing their content.

Now that you have a basic understanding of AD RMS, let's take the next step and install it. In Exercise 6.13, you will install AD RMS using the Server Manager MMC.

EXERCISE 6.13

Installing an AD RMS Role on the Local Computer Using Server Manager

1. Start Server Manager. Click Manage and then click Add Roles And Features.

2. The Add Roles And Features Wizard shows the Before You Begin screen. Click Next.

3. Select the Active Directory Rights Management Services Role and click Next.

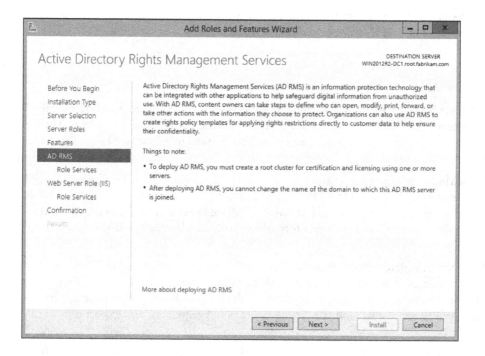

4. Add the required Active Directory Rights Management Services by default and click Add Features.

5. Click Next.

6. On the screen that explains ADRMS, click Next.

7. On the Select Role Services screen, by default Active Directory Rights Management Server is selected. Identity Federation Support uses AD FS federated trust between organizations to establish user identities and provide access to the RMS-protected content across the federation. Click Next.

8. Click Next on the Web Server (IIS) screen.

9. At the confirmation screen, click Install.

10. Once the installation is complete, click Close.

11. While still in Server Manager, click the AD RMS link on the left side.

12. Click the More About The AD RMS Service Account link next to Configuration Required For Active Directory Rights Management Service.

13. Under Action, click the Perform Additional Configuration link.

14. At the AD RMS introduction screen, click Next.

15. On the Create Or Join An AD RMS Cluster screen, choose Create A New AD RMS Cluster. (The other choice will not be available because you are installing the first AD RMS server and must start the cluster.) Click Next.

16. AD RMS uses a database to store configuration and policy information. At the Select Configuration Database screen, choose Use Windows Internal Database on this server. (The other option is to use a third-party database engine or MSSQL.) Click Next.

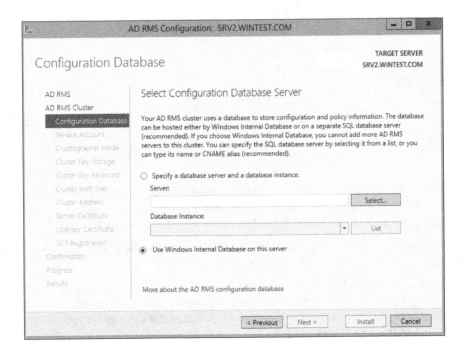

17. On the Specify Service Account screen, choose the service account that AD RMS will use. Click the Specify button and type in an administrator account and password other than the ones with which you are currently logged in. Click Next.

18. At the Cryptographic Mode screen, choose Cryptographic Mode 2 (RSA 2048-bit keys/ SHA-256 hashes) and click Next.

19. At the Configure AD RMS Cluster Key Storage screen, choose Use AD RMS Centrally Managed Key Storage and click Next.

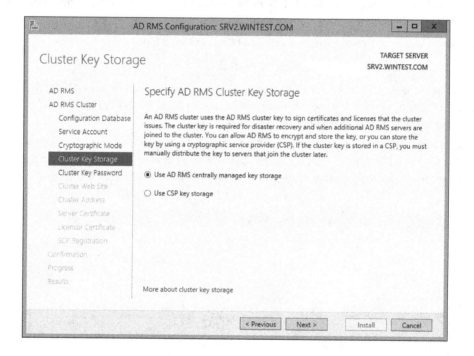

20. Next you will be asked to enter a password in the AD RMS Cluster Key Password field. The AD RMS cluster key password is used to encrypt the AD RMS cluster key that is stored in the AD RMS database. Type **P@ssw0rd**, confirm it, and click Next.

21. On the Select Website screen, click default website and click Next. AD RMS needs to be hosted in IIS. This will set up a default website for AD RMS.

22. On the Specify Cluster Address screen, choose whether to use a secure or a nonsecure website. Choose the Use An SSL-Encrypted Connection (https://) check box. In the Internal Address box, type in the server name and click the Validate button. After the address is verified, click Next.

23. The Choose A Server Authentication Certificate For SSL Encryption screen appears. If you receive a message stating the certificate for this server is already created, just click Next. If the message doesn't appear, choose one of your certificates and click Next.

24. The Name The Server Licensor Certificate screen appears. Accept the default server and click Next.

25. You have the option to register AD RMS now or later. If you register the server now, AD RMS will take effect immediately. If you register the server later, AD RMS will not work until you register. You will not register during this exercise. Choose Register Later and click Next.

26. At the Configure Identity Federation Support screen, specify the name of the web server that Identity Federation will use and click the Validate button. The Next button will become available once the server is validated. If an error appears during validation, it will not affect this exercise. Click Next.

27. At the Confirm Installation Selections screen, verify all of your settings and click Install.

28. The install progress screen appears. When the install is complete, click Close.

29. Close the Server Manager MMC.

Managing AD RMS: AD RMS Service Connection Point

The *service connection point (SCP)* is used to store the URL of the AD RMS cluster. The SCP is stored as an object in Active Directory. The SCP can be configured when AD RMS is being installed or later through the Active Directory Rights Management Services console. Only one SCP can exist in an Active Directory forest.

The AD RMS SCP can be registered automatically during AD RMS installation, or it can be registered after installation has finished. To register the SCP, you must be a member of the local AD RMS Enterprise Administrators group and the Active Directory Domain Services (AD DS) Enterprise Admins group, or you must have been given the appropriate authority.

Managing the SCP is accomplished on the SCP tab of the AD RMS cluster's Properties dialog box.

If a client computer is not located within the Active Directory forest, you must use registry keys to point the AD RMS client to the AD RMS cluster. These registry keys are created in HKEY_Local_Machine\Software\ Microsoft\MSDRM\ServiceLocation. Create a key called Activation with the value of http(s)://<your_cluster>/_wmcs/certification, where <your_cluster> is the URL of the root cluster used for certification.

AD RMS Templates

As you know, a template is a mold that you can use over and over again. AD RMS templates are no different. Before you start creating AD RMS templates, you must first create a shared directory where the templates can be stored. An administrator can then create AD RMS rights policy templates on the AD RMS cluster and export those templates to the shared directory. If your users are connected to the company intranet and they are using AD RMS–enabled applications, they can access the AD RMS templates right from the shared directory as long as they have read access to the shared folder. If your users are not connected to the company intranet, just copy the template to their computers, and this will allow AD RMS–enabled applications to continue to function properly.

When publishing protected content, the author selects the rights policy template to apply from the templates that are available on the local computer. Visibility of the templates is controlled via NTFS permissions. If the user does not have NTFS read access, the respective template will not be visible in an RMS-aware application.

When a user attempts to use protected content, the RMS-enabled application obtains the latest version of the rights policy template that was used to publish the content from the configuration database. The RMS-enabled application then applies its settings to the content. When the rights policy template is modified on the RMS server, RMS updates the template accordingly, in both the configuration database and the shared folder.

If a rights policy template is deleted, it is removed from the configuration database and also from the shared folder (that is specified as the file location for storing copies of templates) location when the template is deleted.

When working with rights policy templates, perform the following tasks:

1. Create and edit rights policy templates.

2. When creating a rights policy template, define the users and rights that apply. Also define how the rights policy template is to be applied to content.

3. Edit the rights policy templates later when they need to be updated.

4. Create as many rights policy templates as are required to manage rights in the organization, but consider that some applications are limited in the number of templates that can be displayed in the application's user interface. If more than a few templates are created in a cluster, you might want to scope the different templates to different groups of users by modifying NTFS permissions.

5. When a template is no longer appropriate, archive the rights policy template and update the distribution of the rights policy templates to the clients so that users do not try to protect content with the retired template. Users attempting to use content protected with the template will still be able to do so because the archived template is still accessible to the RMS servers issuing licenses.

6. If usage of all documents protected with a template is no longer desired, you can delete the template instead of archiving it. If users attempt to use content that was published by using the deleted rights policy template, they will not be issued licenses to do so.

See Table 6.9 for a description of the RMS template rights.

TABLE 6.9 Description of rights in RMS templates

Right	Description
Full control	If established, this right enables a user to exercise all rights in the license, whether or not the rights are specifically established to that user.
View	If this right is established, the AD RMS client enables protected content to be decrypted. Usually, when this right is established, the RMS-aware application will allow the user to view protected content.
Edit	If this right is established, the AD RMS client enables protected content to be decrypted and re-encrypted by using the same content key. Usually, when this right is established, the RMS-aware application will allow the user to change protected content and then save it to the same file. This right is effectively identical to the Save right.
Save	If this right is established, the AD RMS client enables protected content to be decrypted and then re-encrypted by using the same content key. Usually, when this right is established, the RMS-aware application will allow the user to change protected content and then save it to the same file. This right is effectively identical to the Edit right.
Export (Save As)	If this right is established, the AD RMS client enables protected content to be decrypted and then re-encrypted by using the same content key. Usually, when this right is established, the RMS-aware application will allow the user to use the Save As feature to save protected content to a new file.
Print	Usually when this right is established, the RMS-aware application will allow the user to print protected content.
Forward	Usually when this right is established, the RMS-aware application will allow an email recipient to forward a protected message.
Reply	Usually when this right is established, the RMS-aware application will allow an email recipient to reply to a protected message and include a copy of the original message.
Reply All	Usually when this right is established, the RMS-aware application will allow an email recipient to reply to all recipients of a protected message and include a copy of the original message.
Extract	Usually when this right is established, the RMS-aware application will allow the user to copy and paste information from protected content.
Allow Macros	Usually when this right is established, the RMS-aware application will allow the user to run macros in the document or use an editor to modify macros in the document.
View Rights	If this right is established, the AD RMS client enables a user to view the user rights that are assigned by the license.
Edit Rights	If this right is established, the AD RMS client enables a user to edit the user rights that are assigned by the license.

Backing Up AD RMS

Follow these steps to allow you to recover from any AD rights management server failure:

1. Record your cluster key password and store it in a safe manner.

2. Export the trusted publishing domain (see Exercise 6.18).

3. Create database backups.

Record and Store Your Cluster Key Password

During installation, take note of the cluster key password and securely store it. If you inherited the AD RMS server and the cluster key password hasn't been documented, you should change it before backup. To accomplish this, start the Active Directory Rights Management Services console under ServerName ➤ Security Policies ➤ Cluster Key Password. Click Change Cluster Key Password.

Create a Backup of the AD RMS Database

AD RMS uses three databases in the database server:

Configuration Database   This is a critical component of an AD RMS installation. The database stores, shares, and retrieves all configuration data and other data that the service requires to manage account certification, licensing, and publishing services for a whole cluster.

Directory Services Database   This contains information about users, identifiers (such as email addresses), security IDs, group membership, and alternate identifiers. This information is a cache of directory services data.

Logging Database   This is all of the historical data about client activity and license acquisition. For each root or licensing-only cluster, by default AD RMS installs a logging database in the same database server instance hosting the configuration database.

In Exercise 6.14, we will perform a backup of the RMS database.

EXERCISE 6.14

Backing Up an AD RMS Database

1. Log on to the SQL server.

2. Click Start ➤ All Programs ➤ Microsoft SQL Server 2008 or 2012 and select SQL Server Management Studio. The Connect To Server dialog box will appear. Verify the server name is correct and that authentication is set for Windows Authentication.

3. Click Connect.

4. Expand the Databases node.

5. Right-click DRMS_Config_rms_domain_com_443, select Tasks, and then select Back Up.

6. Click Add in the Destination section and select the location.

7. Click OK to finish the backup.

8. Repeat these steps to back up the logging and directory services cache database.

 If you cannot restore the configuration database, you can recover your AD RMS infrastructure with the exported TPD and the cluster key password.

AD RMS Trust Policies

Trust policies are implemented to define how content licensing requests are processed throughout the enterprise, including rights-protected content from other AD RMS clusters. Trust policies are defined as follows:

Trusted User Domains   A trusted user domain (TUD) is the boundary mechanism for the AD RMS root cluster to process client licensor certificates or use licenses from users whose rights account certificates (RACs) were issued by another AD RMS root cluster. You must import the server licensor certificate of the AD RMS cluster to be trusted, to define your TUD.

Trusted Publishing Domains   A trusted publishing domain (TPD) is another boundary type for one AD RMS cluster to issue licenses against publishing licenses issued by another AD RMS cluster. You must also import the server licensor certificate and private key of the server to be trusted, to define the TPD.

Windows Live ID   Microsoft offers an online RMS service for an AD RMS user to send rights-protected content to another user with their Windows Live ID. The Windows Live ID recipient is then able to read rights-protected content from the originating AD RMS cluster registered through Microsoft's online RMS service. This extended AD RMS implantation does not allow the Windows Live ID user to create rights-protected content from the on-premise AD RMS cluster.

Federated Trust   With a federated trust established between AD forests, users from one organization can share rights-protected content with another organization without requiring AD RMS implementation on both sides of the trust.

Microsoft Federation Gateway   Microsoft also offers federated trust through the Microsoft Federation Gateway, which is essentially a trusted broker between organizations. Microsoft Federation Gateway handles all of the identity verifications with all participating Microsoft federated organizations. Microsoft federated organizations can take advantage of this gateway by filtering lists to select which domains can receive certificates or licenses from the on-premise AD RMS cluster.

Managing Trusted User Domains   Trusted user domains enable trust between domains running AD RMS, and they are often used to connect users between forests. TUD management is accomplished in the AD RMS Management console. TUD information is exported to a .bin file and then subsequently imported using the Import Trusted User Domain dialog box.

Adding a Trusted User Domain   By default, Active Directory Rights Management Services (AD RMS) will not process requests from users whose rights account certificate was issued by a different AD RMS installation. However, you can add user domains to the list of trusted user domains, which allows AD RMS to process such requests.

For each TUD, you can also add and remove specific users or groups of users. In addition, you can remove a TUD; however, you cannot remove the root cluster for this Active Directory forest from the list of TUDs. Every AD RMS server trusts the root cluster in its own forest. In Exercise 6.15 we'll add a TUD into the test domain.

EXERCISE 6.15

Adding a Trusted User Domain

Before getting started, the TUD of the AD RMS installation should already be exported and available.

1. Start the Active Directory Rights Management Services console and expand the AD RMS cluster.

2. In the console tree, expand Trust Policies and click Trusted User Domains.

3. In the Actions pane, click Import Trusted User Domain.

4. In the Trusted User Domain File dialog box, type the path to the exported server licensor certificate of the user domain to trust or click Browse to locate it.

5. In Display Name, type a name to identify this trusted user domain. If you would like to extend this trust to federated users, select Extend Trust To Federated Users Of The Imported Server.

7. Click Finish.

Exporting the Trusted User Domain

TUDs allow an AD RMS cluster to issue licenses to users whose rights account certificate was established by another server in an AD RMS cluster. Exporting a TUD's key and importing it into another AD RMS cluster allows the cluster to process requests for use licenses from users whose rights account certificates are in a different cluster.

Membership in the local **AD RMS Enterprise Admins group,** or equivalent, is the minimum required to complete this procedure. In Exercise 6.16, we will export the TUD and store the data in a location you provide.

EXERCISE 6.16

Exporting the Trusted User Domain

1. Start the Active Directory Rights Management Services console and expand the AD RMS cluster.

2. In the console tree, expand Trust Policies and click Trusted User Domains.

3. In the Actions pane, click Export Trusted User Domain.

4. The Save As dialog box appears. I recommend you modify the .bin file name to include the name of your server, such as ADRMS_Cluster1_LicensorCert.bin.

5. Click Save to save the file with the name and location you specified.

Exporting the Trusted Publishing Domain

Unlike a trusted user domain, a trusted publishing domain enables an AD RMS cluster to issue licenses as if it was a different AD RMS cluster. To accomplish this, both the certificate and the private key need to be imported. This is different from a TUD scenario, where only the certificate is imported.

Importing a TPD is accomplished within the AD RMS Management console using the Import Trusted Publishing Domain dialog box. Saving a copy of the trusted publishing domain can be done from within the AD RMS administration console. In the Exercise 6.17, we will export the TPD.

EXERCISE 6.17

Exporting the Trusted Publishing Domain

1. Start the AD RMS administration console.

2. In the console tree view, select Trusted Publishing Domains node.

3. In the details pane on the right, select Export Trusted Publishing Domain. The Export Trusted Publishing Domain dialog box will appear.

4. From the Export Trusted Publishing Domain dialog box, click Save As. The Export Trusted Publishing Domain File Save As dialog box will appear. On the left pane, select the folder you want to save the trusted publishing domain.

5. In File Name enter a filename; then verify the XML File (*.xml) type is selected for Save As Type.

6. Click Save. This will close the Export Trusted Publishing Domain As dialog box.

7. In the Export Trusted Publishing Domain dialog box, enter a password in the Password box.

8. Enter a password again in the Confirm Password dialog box.

9. Click Finish.

Adding a Trusted Publishing Domain

Exercise 6.18 assumes you have exported the trusted publishing domain of another AD RMS cluster (as described in the preceding section). Membership in the local AD RMS Enterprise Admins group, or equivalent, is the minimum required to complete this procedure.

EXERCISE 6.18

Adding the Trusted Publishing Domain

1. Start the Active Directory Rights Management Services console and expand the AD RMS cluster.

2. In the console tree, expand Trust Policies and click Trusted Publishing Domains.

3. In the Actions pane, click Import Trusted Publishing Domain.

4. In the Trusted Publishing Domain File dialog box, type the path to the trusted publishing domain file or click Browse to locate it. This file contains the licensor certificate, private key (if the key is stored in software), and rights policy templates. This file is encrypted.

5. In Password, type the password required to decrypt this file.

6. In Display Name, type a name to identify this trusted user domain.

7. Click Finish.

Managing Distributed and Archived Rights Policy Templates

Rights policy templates are managed in the AD RMS Management console. Planning and overviews of rights policies are available here:

    http://technet.microsoft.com/en-us/library/ee221094

    http://technet.microsoft.com/en-us/library/dd996658

You can designate the location for the templates as well as set whether the templates can be exported by using the properties of the Rights Policy Template tab.

Summary

In this chapter, I discussed the certificate authority role and some of the new features in Microsoft Windows Server 2012 R2, including additional management options, new certificate templates, and better support for globalized organizations with limited IDN support. I also covered the details of the same-key certificate renewal requirement and the effects of the new increased default security settings on the CA role service.

I also discussed Active Directory Federation Services, which provides Internet-based clients with a secure identity access solution that works on both Windows and non-Windows operating systems.

Finally, I talked about Active Directory Rights Management Services. I explained that AD RMS is included with Microsoft Windows Server 2012 R2 and discussed how it allows administrators or users to determine what access to give other users in an organization.

Exam Essentials

Understand the concepts behind certificate authority.   Certificate authority servers manage certificates. Make sure you understand why companies use certificate servers and how they work.

Understand certificate enrollment.   You need to understand the many different ways to issue certificates to users and computers. You also need to understand the differences between installing certificates using GPOs, auto-enrollment, and web enrollment.

Understand Active Directory Federation Service.   Active Directory Federation Service gives users the ability to do a single sign-on and access applications on other networks without needing a secondary password. Organizations can set up trust relationships with other trusted organizations so that a user's digital identity and access rights can be accepted without a secondary password.

Know how to install Active Directory Rights Management Services.   Active Directory Rights Management Services, included with Microsoft Windows Server 2012 R2, allows administrators and users to determine what access (open, read, modify, and so on) they give to other users in an organization. This access can be used to secure email messages, internal websites, and documents.

Review Questions

1. Channel Fishing Company wants to configure a CA server in the DMZ to issue certificates to remote users. How would you accomplish this? (Choose all that apply.)

   A. You should consider having the Certificate Enrollment Policy Web Server role included in the solution.

   B. You should consider having the online responder included in the solution.

   C. You should consider having the Network Device Enrollment Service included in the solution.

   D. You should consider having the web service included in the solution.

   E. You should consider having the Certificate Enrollment Web Service included in the solution.

   F. You should consider having the Web Enrollment service included in the solution.

2. The certificate revocation list (CRL) polling begins to consume bandwidth. What steps should you consider to reduce network traffic?

   A. You should consider implementing the Certificate Enrollment Policy Web Server role and Certificate Enrollment Web Services role.

   B. You should consider implementing an online responder.

   C. You should consider implementing an online issuing CA and a root CA.

   D. You consider publishing more CRLs.

3. ABC Industries wants configuration modifications of the Certification Authority role service to be logged. How would you implement this? (Choose all that apply.)

   A. You should consider enabling auditing of system events.

   B. You should consider enabling logging.

   C. You should consider enabling auditing of object access.

   D. You should consider enabling auditing of privilege use.

   E. You should consider enabling auditing of process tracking.

4. Federation proxy services are installed through which of the following?

   A. Separate Active Directory Federation Proxy install download

   B. Server Manager ➤ Remote Access ➤ Web Proxy

   C. Server Manager ➤ Active Directory Federation Services ➤ Active Directory Proxy services

   D. Windows PowerShell ➤ Install-Windows-Feature Web Proxy

5. The new Workplace Join feature supports which of following? (Choose all that apply.)

    A. Federates an iPhone to the corporate intranet

    B. Allows Windows 8 clients to process claim-based trusts

    C. Allows Windows 8 clients to form claim-based trusts automatically with the home domain

    D. None of the above

6. You install and configure four Windows Server 2012 R2 servers as an AD FS server farm. The AD FS configuration database is stored in a Microsoft SQL Server 2012 database. You need to ensure that AD FS will continue to function in the event of an AD FS server failure. You also need to ensure that all four servers in the AD FS farm will actively perform AD FS functions. What should you include in your solution?

    A. Windows Failover Clustering

    B. Windows Identity Foundation 3.5

    C. Network Load Balancing

    D. Web Proxy Server

7. Your network contains an Active Directory domain named contoso.com. You plan to deploy a Windows 2012 R2 Active Directory Federation Services (AD FS) farm that will contain eight federation servers. You need to identify which technology or technologies must be deployed on the network before you install the federation servers. Which technology or technologies should you identify? (Choose all that apply.)

    A. Network Load Balancing

    B. Microsoft Forefront Identity Manager 2010

    C. Windows Internal Database feature

    D. Microsoft SQL Server 2012 R2

    E. The Windows Identity Foundation 3.5 feature

8. You are the system administrator at JavaCup, which hosts a web RMS-aware application that the JavaCup forest and Boston Tea Company forest users need to access. You deploy a single AD FS server in the JavaCup forest. Which of the following is a true statement about your AD FS implementation? (Choose all that apply.)

    A. You will configure a relying-party server on the JavaCup AD FS server.

    B. The AD FS server in the Boston Tea Company forest functions as the claims provider.

    C. The AD FS server in the Boston Tea Company forest functions as the relying-party server.

    D. You will configure a claims provider trust on the JavaCup AD FS server.

9. You store AD FS servers in an OU named Federation Servers. You want to auto-enroll the certificates used for AD FS. Which certificates should you add to the GPO?

   A. The CA certificate of the forest

   B. The third-party (VeriSign, Entrust) CA certificate

   C. The SSL certificate assigned to the AD FS servers

   D. The Token Signing certificate assigned to the AD FS Servers

10. You plan to implement Active Directory Rights Management Services (AD RMS) across the enterprise. You need to plan the AD RMS cluster installations for the forest. Users in all domains will access AD RMS–protected documents. You need to minimize the number of AD RMS clusters. Which of the following will help you determine how many AD RMS root clusters you require?

   A. You need at least one AD RMS root cluster for the enterprise.

   B. You need at least one AD RMS root cluster per forest.

   C. You need at least one AD RMS root cluster per domain.

   D. You need at least one AD RMS root cluster per Active Directory site.

   E. An AD RMS root cluster is not required.

Appendix A

Answers to Review Questions

Chapter 1: Configure and Manage High Availability

1. A, B and D. Only the Standard, Datacenter, and Hyper-V editions of Windows Server 2012 R2 can participate in a failover cluster.

2. A, B and D. All versions of Windows Server 2012 R2 can participate in an NLB cluster except for the Windows Server 2012 R2 Hyper-V edition.

3. D. A Windows Server 2012 R2 cluster can contain up to 64 nodes.

4. B. Drainstop is the function that allows the current session to end before stopping the cluster on the node. Evict is used to remove a node completely from a failover cluster. Pause is used to keep resources from failing over to a failover cluster node. Stop will immediately end the cluster service on the NLB cluster node, not allowing the current sessions to complete.

5. D. A Windows Server 2012 R2 NLB cluster can contain up to 32 nodes.

6. A and C. SQL Server and Exchange Server are supported only on failover clusters. Websites and VPN services are network-based services, so they are better suited for NLB clusters.

7. B and D. Websites and Terminal Services are all designed to work with NLB clusters. Database servers such as SQL Server do not work on NLB clusters.

8. B. To use unicast communication between NLB cluster nodes, each node must have a minimum of two network adapters.

9. B. Up to two votes can be lost before quorum can no longer be achieved. These votes can come from the file share witness or a cluster node.

10. B. In a three-node cluster, only one node can be offline before quorum is lost; a majority of the votes must be available to achieve quorum.

Chapter 2: Configure File and Storage Solutions

1. B, E, G and H. The Group Policy Management Console allows system administrators to change auditing options and to choose which actions are audited. At the file system level, LaDonna can specify exactly which actions are recorded in the audit log. She can then use Event Viewer to view the recorded information and provide it to the appropriate managers.

2. A. The iSCSI default port is TCP 3260. Port 3389 is used for RDP, port 1433 is used for Microsoft SQL, and port 21 is used for FTP.

3. C. Account logon events are created for domain account activity. For example, you have a user who logs onto a server so that they can access files; the act of logging onto the server creates this audit event.

4. A. File servers are used for storage of data, especially for users' home folders. Home folders are folder locations for your users to store data that is important and that needs to be backed up.

5. A, B, C and D. Improved security, quotas, compression, and encryption are all advantages of using NTFS over FAT32. These features are not available in FAT32. The only security you have in FAT32 is shared folder permissions.

6. D. The `iscsicli addisnsserver server_name` command manually registers the host server to an iSNS server. `refreshisnsserver` refreshes the list of available servers. `removeisnsserver` removes the host from the iSNS server. `listisnsservers` lists the available iSNS servers.

7. A. Windows Server 2012 R2 Features On Demand allows an administrator not only to disable a role or feature but also to remove the role or feature's files completely from the hard disk.

8. D. The iSNS feature is used to provide for the automatic discovery of iSCSI targets that are available on the network. This is a useful feature within a larger environment. Note that without iSNS DHCP configured, iSNS clients must be registered manually with the `iscsicli` command.

9. A. After generating hashes on the Colorado Springs file server that will be preloading Tampa's file server cache with file share data, the next logical step is to run Export-BCCachePackage to get the data to FS02 from FS01.

10. B. Since there is a classification rule that is currently configured and applied to company resources, you will be unable to delete the Contains Personal Information classification property manually because the Classification Rule controls the property. In this case, you have to delete the Classification Rule in order to be able to delete the classification property.

Chapter 3: Implement Business Continuity and Disaster Recovery

1. A. Using images allows you to back up and restore your entire Windows Server 2012 R2 machine instead of just certain parts of data.

2. C. If you need to get a stalled computer up and running as quickly as possible, you should start with the Last Known Good Configuration option. This option is used when you've made changes to your computer's hardware configuration and are having problems restarting but have not logged into the machine. Last Known Good Configuration will revert to the configuration used the last time the computer was successfully booted.

3. D. Daily backups back up all of the files that have changed during a single day. This operation uses the file time/date stamps to determine which files should be backed up and does not mark the files as having been backed up.

4. B. To create a restore point manually or to restore your computer to a previous restore point, you use the Shadow Copies tab of the System Properties dialog box. Although System Restore uses restore points, you do not use the System Restore utility to create a restore point.

5. B. You should start with the Last Known Good Configuration option. This option is used when you've made changes to your computer's hardware configuration and are having problems restarting. The Last Known Good Configuration will revert to the configuration used the last time the computer was successfully booted. Although this option helps overcome configuration errors, it will not help when there are hardware errors.

6. C. When you enable boot logging, the file created is \Windows\ntbtlog.txt. This log file is used to troubleshoot the boot process.

7. C. To repair the system files quickly, you can use the Startup Repair tool. You can restore an image by using the Backup and Repair Center, but it is faster to use the Startup Repair tool. Additionally, you will not lose any personal files by using the Startup Repair tool. Alternatively, you could try to use System Restore to go back to a previous checkpoint.

8. B. When you run your computer in Safe Mode, you simplify your Windows Server 2012 R2 configuration. Only the drivers that are needed to get the computer up and running are loaded.

9. C. The Backup Once link allows you to start a backup on the Windows Server 2012 R2 system.

10. D. If you need to back up and restore your Windows Server 2012 R2 machine, you need to use the Windows Server Backup MMC.

Chapter 4: Configure Advanced Network Services

1. C. Out of the possible answers provided, the only DHCP configuration option that would be both fault-tolerant and redundant is DHCP failover.

2. B, C and D. DNS registration is an advanced DHCP configuration. All three other options provide additional security for DNS on your network.

3. D. DNS netmask ordering is the only way to ensure that clients will get the closest DNS server to their subnet when performing DNS queries on your network. If DNS netmask ordering were not enabled, requests would go through a round-robin approach from all of the DNS servers available to provide lookup services. You could end up with a poor connection depending on which DNS server responds to your client's requests.

4. D. The DNSAdmins security group is the best fit for this administrator's responsibilities. If you were to place this administrator in either the Domain Admins or Enterprise Admins security group, that individual would have too many unnecessary permissions granted within the environment, making their Active Directory account a security vulnerability. The Schema Admins group does not pertain to this question.

5. B. DHCP name protection ensures that DNS host A records are never overwritten during DNS dynamic updates. The other three possible answers would not fulfill this question's requirements.

6. C. The IPAM ASM Administrators group is specifically designed for the delegation of IPAM Address Space Management. The IPAM Administrators group would give her domain account way to much access within the environment, and the other two possible answers would not provide her with enough permissions to perform her required responsibilities.

7. B. Out of the three real possible deployment methods—Distributed, Centralized, and Hybrid—only the Centralized deployment method allows one primary IPAM server to manage the entire enterprise. The Distributed method places an IPAM server at each site location, and the Hybrid method uses a primary server with an additional IPAM server at each site location within the enterprise.

8. D. The only way to accommodate the use of short, single-labeled host names within your DNS infrastructure is to implement a GlobalNames zone.

9. C. After you have successfully installed and provisioned your IPAM server, the next logical step in the IPAM deployment configuration is to configure and run server discovery. Be sure to follow the step-by-step configuration guide found on the IPAM Overview page in Server Manager when going through your IPAM test deployment.

10. A. The proper PowerShell syntax to display current IPAM database configuration settings is `Get-IpamDatabase`. The other possible answers are not valid PowerShell cmdlets.

Chapter 5: Configure the Active Directory Infrastructure

1. B. The NTDS settings for the site level are where you would activate and deactivate UGMC.

2. A. By decreasing the Replication interval for the DEFAULTIPSITELINK object, you will decrease the replication latency for all sites using the DEFAULTIPSITELINK.

3. D. In the Active Directory Sites and Services console, the Server NTDS settings are where you would activate and deactivate global catalogs.

4. D. Preferred bridgehead servers receive replication information for a site and transmit this information to other domain controllers within the site. By configuring one server at each site to act as a preferred bridgehead server, Daniel can ensure that all replication traffic between the two sites is routed through the bridgehead servers and that replication traffic will flow properly between the domain controllers.

5. C. By default, connection objects are automatically created by the Active Directory replication engine. You can choose to override the default behavior of Active Directory replication topology by manually creating connection objects, but this step is not required.

6. B. The Knowledge Consistency Checker (KCC) is responsible for establishing the replication topology and ensuring that all domain controllers are kept up-to-date.

7. D. Site link bridges are designed to allow site links to be transitive. That is, they allow site links to use other site links to transfer replication information between sites. By default, all site links are bridged. However, you can turn off transitivity if you want to override this behavior.

8. B. Simple Mail Transfer Protocol was designed for environments in which persistent connections may not always be available. SMTP uses the store-and-forward method to ensure that information is not lost if a connection cannot be made.

9. D. The Directory Service event log contains error messages and information related to replication. These details can be useful when you are troubleshooting replication problems.

10. A and D. By creating new sites, Christina can help define settings for Active Directory replication based on the environment's network connections. She can use connection objects to define further the details of how and when replication traffic will be transmitted between the domain controllers.

Chapter 6: Configure Access and Information Protection Solutions

1. A and E. Certificate Enrollment Web Service with the Certificate Enrollment Policy Web Server role is the preferred Microsoft solution for issuing certificates through the internet.

2. B. The online responder uses a lightweight HTTP protocol that responds faster and more efficiently than downloading a traditional CRL.

3. B and C. To enable AD FS 3.0 auditing, you must check the boxes for Success Audits and Failure Audits on the Events tab of the Federation Service Properties dialog box. You must also enable Object Access Auditing in Local Policy or Group Policy.

4. B. Federation Proxy Services are installed under Remote Access as a web application proxy server in Windows Server 2012.

5. A, B and C. By using Workplace Join, information workers can join their personal devices with their company's workplace computers to access company resources and services. When you join your personal device to your workplace, it becomes a known device and provides seamless second-factor authentication and single sign-on to workplace resources and applications. Windows Server 2012 R2, Windows 8.1, and iOS devices can be joined by using Workplace Join.

6. C. Network Load Balancing (NLB) is the only support Microsoft solution for providing high availability across an ADFS server farm. Windows Failover Clustering does not currently support ADFS as one master server is allowed to write to the configuration database per farm.

7. D. The AD FS configuration database stores all of the configuration data. It contains information that a federation service requires to identify partners, certificates, attribute stores, claims, and so forth. You can store this configuration data in either a Microsoft SQL Server 2005 or newer database or the Windows Internal Database feature that is included with Windows Server 2008, Windows Server 2008 R2, and Windows Server 2012 R2. The Windows Internal Database supports only up to five federation servers in a farm.

8. A and B. The relying-party server is a member of the Active Directory forest that hosts resources that a user in the partner organization wants to access. In this case, the relying party server should be the JavaCup AD FS server. A claims provider provides users with claims. These claims are stored within digitally encrypted and signed tokens. In this case, Boston Tea Party is the claims provider.

9. A. The Forest CA certificate is the only certificate that is automatically trusted, does not require user interaction and digital signature does not change in this scenario

10. B. Licensing Server/Cluster is the component in charge of delivering publishing and use licenses. Several clusters can be installed per forest depending on the technical needs (servers' workload and bandwidth constraints).

Appendix B

About the Additional Study Tools

IN THIS APPENDIX:

- Additional Study Tools
- System requirements
- Using the Study Tools
- Troubleshooting

Additional Study Tools

The following sections are arranged by category and summarize the software and other goodies you'll find from the companion website. If you need help with installing the items, refer to the installation instructions in the "Using the Study Tools" section of this appendix.

The additional study tools can be found at www.sybex.com/go/mcsawin2012r2config. Here, you will get instructions on how to download the files to your hard drive.

Sybex Test Engine

The files contain the Sybex test engine, which includes two bonus practice exams, as well as the Assessment Test and the Chapter Review Questions, which are also included in the book itself.

Electronic Flashcards

These handy electronic flashcards are just what they sound like. One side contains a question, and the other side shows the answer.

PDF of Glossary of Terms

We have included an electronic version of the Glossary in .pdf format. You can view the electronic version of the Glossary with Adobe Reader.

Adobe Reader

We've also included a copy of Adobe Reader so you can view PDF files that accompany the book's content. For more information on Adobe Reader or to check for a newer version, visit Adobe's website at www.adobe.com/products/reader/

System Requirements

Make sure your computer meets the minimum system requirements shown in the following list. If your computer doesn't match up to most of these requirements, you may have problems using the software and files. For the latest and greatest information, please refer to the ReadMe file located in the downloads.

- A PC running Microsoft Windows 98, Windows 2000, Windows NT4 (with SP4 or later), Windows Me, Windows XP, Windows Vista, or Windows 7
- An Internet connection

Using the Study Tools

To install the items, follow these steps:

1. Download the .ZIP file to your hard drive, and unzip to an appropriate location. Instructions on where to download this file can be found here: www.sybex.com/go/mcsawin2012r2config
2. Click the Start.EXE file to open up the study tools file.
3. Read the license agreement, and then click the Accept button if you want to use the study tools.

The main interface appears. The interface allows you to access the content with just one or two clicks.

Troubleshooting

Wiley has attempted to provide programs that work on most computers with the minimum system requirements. Alas, your computer may differ, and some programs may not work properly for some reason.

The two likeliest problems are that you don't have enough memory (RAM) for the programs you want to use or you have other programs running that are affecting installation or running of a program. If you get an error message such as "Not enough memory" or "Setup cannot continue," try one or more of the following suggestions and then try using the software again:

Turn off any antivirus software running on your computer. Installation programs sometimes mimic virus activity and may make your computer incorrectly believe that it's being infected by a virus.

Close all running programs. The more programs you have running, the less memory is available to other programs. Installation programs typically update files and programs; so if you keep other programs running, installation may not work properly.

Have your local computer store add more RAM to your computer. This is, admittedly, a drastic and somewhat expensive step. However, adding more memory can really help the speed of your computer and allow more programs to run at the same time.

Customer Care

If you have trouble with the book's companion study tools, please call the Wiley Product Technical Support phone number at (800) 762-2974. 74, or email them at http://sybex .custhelp.com/

Index

Note to the Reader: Throughout this index **boldfaced** page numbers indicate primary discussions of a topic. *Italicized* page numbers indicate illustrations.

M

N

Free Interactive Online Study Environment